FIFTH
UPDATEI

MW00678943

1994·1995

DIRECTORY OF
AMERICAN
YOUTH
ORGANIZATIONS

A Guide to
500 Clubs,
Groups, Troops,
Teams, Societies,
Lodges, and More
for Young People

JUDITH B. ERICKSON, Ph.D.

Free Spirit
PUBLISHING

ISBN 0-915793-63-6

ISSN 1044-4440

Inclusion of a youth organization in this directory does not imply an endorsement of it or its programs by the author, the Indiana Youth Institute, or Free Spirit Publishing Inc.

Printed in the United States of America

5   4   3   2   1

Cover and text design: MacLean & Tuminelly
Edited by M. Elizabeth Salzmann
Index compiled by Eileen Quam and Theresa Wolner

FREE SPIRIT PUBLISHING INC.
400 First Avenue North, Suite 616
Minneapolis, MN 55401
612/338-2068
FAX: 612/337-5050

Dedication

To the thousands of individuals—mostly unknown, and often unappreciated—who continue to keep these organizations going from generation to generation.

Table of Contents

Acknowledgments

This Directory was developed through the American Youth Organizations Project, supported from 1980–1982 by the Visiting Fellows program of the Boys Town Center at Father Flanagan's Boys' Home. The first edition was published under their auspices in 1983.

In 1983, the project was transferred to the Center for Youth Development and Research at the University of Minnesota, St. Paul, and continued there until 1989, when it was moved to Indianapolis.

I continue to be grateful to the many organization executives and staff members who have provided information for this project, and to colleagues and friends who have kept making suggestions for improvements and have helped discover organizations that have been overlooked. A special thank you goes to Karen Sheridan, whose turn it was this time around to learn more about youth organizations than she wanted to know.

I wish to thank colleagues, especially Richard Swan, at the Indiana Youth Institute for their patience and help. The Indiana Youth Institute Resource Center has made the process of adding information a great deal easier. Thanks go also to Judy Galbraith and Liz Salzmann of Free Spirit Publishing Inc. for their usual patience and fortitude!

Introduction

"I don't have anything to do!"

"I want to try something new!"

"I wish I knew someone who liked the same things I like."

"I'd like to help someone, but I don't know where to start."

Do any of these sound like you? If so, you've come to the right place. This Directory will point you towards *hundreds* of organizations that will give you plenty to do and lots of new things to try, introduce you to many people who share your interests, and make boredom a thing of the past.

There are organizations based on hobbies and special interests, organizations that focus on sports and school subjects, and organizations that celebrate your ethnic heritage. There are patriotic organizations, religious organizations, and organizations that can help you prepare for a career. For those of you who want to play a bigger part in the world, there are political organizations, social service organizations, conservation groups, and more.

Some groups can be joined by individuals (meaning you, all by yourself). Others require that a certain number of people (it varies) form a group or a chapter and join together. Still others share programs that can be adopted by clubs, troops, and other groups already in existence. Many of these groups offer opportunities for service that will make your school, your neighborhood, your community—maybe even the world—better places, now and in the future.

So, where to start? First, think of a topic or activity that interests you. Is there something you're fascinated by? Concerned about? Or simply curious about? Next, scan the Contents, skim the Index, or flip through the pages to see if anything catches your eye. Then look over the list of organization types and read the descriptions. The rest is up to you!

When you find a group you want to know more about, then *find out more about it*. It's easy. Just write or call for more information. Most organizations have prepared brochures or other printed materials they'll be happy to send you, if you ask. (Some may request that you send a self-addressed, stamped envelope (SASE). Since all organizations listed here are nonprofit, meaning they're not in it for the money, that's fair.) Some have 800 telephone numbers so you can call them toll-free. (For those that don't, we recommend that you check with your parents before placing the call. That's fair, too.)

Once you get the information you ask for, there's a way to learn even more about a particular organization. Get the name of a member who lives in your area, then arrange to meet with him or her. You may want to prepare some questions ahead

1

of time. Here are a few suggestions to start with:

- Why did you join this organization? What first got you interested in it?

- How long have you been a member?

- What are some of the things you do as a member?

- What do you like best about this organization?

- Is there anything you don't like about it?

- Does this organization hold regular meetings? When and where?

- What usually goes on at a meeting?

- Has belonging to this organization made a difference in your life? How?

- Have you made new friends by joining this organization?

- What are some other advantages of being a member?

- Why do you think people should join this organization?

Come up with more questions of your own. Or just let the person tell you about the organization. Joiners and belongers usually enjoy talking about their experiences, and listening can help you make up your mind.

Get your parents involved, too. Share what you learn with them, and ask for their advice and opinions. In fact, if you want to do a really thorough job of researching an organization on your way to deciding whether to join it (or not), have your parents work with you to develop a checklist of what you want from the organization and what you want to give to it in return. One way to do this is by reading

the section called Differences among Organizations Today on pages 126–132. That will give you a good start on organizing your thoughts and questions.

Here's another reason to get your parents involved in your decision making process: Most of the organizations listed here encourage adults to participate as volunteers or leaders. Who knows—you may end up joining together!

Somewhere on these pages is an organization that's right for you. As you start your search, good luck—and have fun.

Judith Erickson

January 1994

About This Directory

Americans have been known as a nation of joiners since the early days of the Republic. Yet we think you'll be surprised at the great number of choices available to young people today.

In preparing this Directory, we found more than 500 adult-sponsored organizations enrolling millions of American children and youth in groups, troops, teams, and clubs. These young people are led by a veritable army of volunteers, and the programs are administered by some 50,000 staff members.

Together these organizations represent a vast, nonformal system of education through which members may learn a broad spectrum of skills, attitudes, and values. They offer a wide range of options for children and adolescents looking for something to do; for children, older youths and adults looking for avenues for volunteer service; and for those seeking career opportunities in the youth work field.

Each organization here is in some ways similar to many others, but in other ways is quite different—the product of its unique history and development. But all share these characteristics:

- They serve children and youths of high school age and under.

- They foster groups, troops, or teams of young peers that are conducted under adult supervision.

- They are nonprofit (although a few are associated with profit-making corporations).

- They are national in scope—members are drawn from more than one state, and there is a central coordinating office.

This Directory is designed as a tool for young people, their parents, educators, librarians, youth workers (and those thinking about becoming youth workers), volunteers of all ages, and youth policymakers. We have made every effort to make it as complete as possible.

We have also tried to make this Directory easy to use. We decided that the best way to do this was to group the organizations within the categories described on the following pages. When an organization could have been placed in more than one category, we consulted with a member of its staff before making our final decision.

We welcome your comments.

Hobby and Special Interest Groups, School Subject Matter Clubs, and Honor Societies

(pages 11–16)

Groups in this category are generally devoted to the pursuit of a single interest, although a few, such as the general honor societies, have broader programs.

Career Education and Vocational Student Groups

(pages 16–21)

The primary activity of these organizations is to provide introductions to various occupations. Many also stress the development of good work habits and attitudes, and of effective public speaking, parliamentary skills, and service to the community.

Science, Math, and Technology Organizations

(pages 21–27)

These groups encourage activities related to science, mathematics, engineering, and/or technology. Some foster career exploration and offer opportunities for concentrated study. **See also** Conservation and Humane Education Groups (pages 91–96), Character-Building Organizations (pages 62–67), and Career Education and Vocational Student Groups (pages 16–21) for additional opportunities.

Sports Organizations

(pages 27–49)

The various organizations have been classified by sport: baseball/softball, biking, bowling, boxing, and so on. In this edition, we have added several organizations that provide sports programs for young people with disabilities. **See also** Character-Building Organizations (pages 62–67) and Ethnic Heritage Groups (pages 106–114) for other organizations that have sports programs.

Civic Education and Political Organizations

(pages 50–55)

These groups have as their primary aim the socialization of youth to political responsibility. Some are associated with a particular party; others are nonpartisan.

Peace and Global Understanding Groups

(pages 55–62)

Groups included here have as their focus resolving conflict in nonviolent ways, concern about the nuclear arms race and world peace, and understanding other peoples and cultures. Several offer opportunities for service overseas and for international student exchanges.

Character-Building Organizations

(pages 62–67)

These groups provide comprehensive, primarily secular programs aimed at the development of the "whole person." They are usually open to all members of the community.

4

Social Welfare and Community Betterment Groups

(pages 67–69)

These organizations provide services to youth. In some cases, these services are general; in others, they are related to a particular problem. Several groups provide avenues for young people to help themselves and others.

Religious Organizations

(pages 69–91)

Protestant

(pages 69–82)

Catholic

(pages 82–84)

Jewish

(pages 84–89)

Other Religious Organizations

(pages 89–90)

Some are comprehensive programs, offering a wide range of activities; some are associated with a particular denomination, and some are nondenominational.

Conservation and Humane Education Groups

(pages 91–96)

These groups are dedicated to the preservation and wise use of the natural environment and/or to promoting the humane treatment of animals. **See also** Science, Math, and Technology Organizations (pages 21–27) and Character-Building Organizations (pages 62–67) for additional related groups.

Service Organization Youth Programs

(pages 96–99)

Like the adult organizations that sponsor them, these programs stress service to school and community.

Self-Help Organizations

(pages 99–101)

These national groups are dedicated to helping youth cope with particular problems.

Substance Abuse Prevention and Temperance Organizations

(pages 101–104)

These groups promote abstinence from alcohol, tobacco, and other drugs. Most provide education against all forms of substance abuse.

Hereditary, Veterans, Military, and Patriotic Groups

(pages 104–106)

Nearly all of these are associated with adult organizations. Some have restrictions on membership that apply to the sponsoring organization.

Ethnic Heritage Groups

(pages 106–114)

Most of these exist to preserve and promote the material culture and traditions of a specific ethnic heritage. Some may be restricted to individuals of a particular ethnic heritage; others are open to all interested youth.

Youth Lodges and Orders
(pages 114–117)

These include the junior divisions of adult fraternal and sororal organizations. Membership in some of them is restricted to relatives of adult group members.

Agriculture and Livestock Associations
(pages 117–119)

These organizations are youth branches of adult groups seeking to ensure the future quality of agricultural breeding stock. Most members are actively engaged in breeding and raising the livestock that are the focus of each group.

If You Can't Find What You're Looking For Under a Particular Heading...

See the Index on pages 177–189, which includes an alphabetical listing of all of the organizations and sponsoring bodies listed in this Directory.

Resources

We have also included a number of organizations that provide materials, services, and/or information of potential interest and usefulness to youth groups seeking to enrich their programs. When these resources relate to specific types of groups, they are found at the ends of those sections within the Directory. Other groups that provide more general services of potential interest to all youth-serving organizations are listed and described on pages 140–163. We have also cross-referenced several organizations.

How to Read the Entries

Each individual entry contains several types of information. The sample entry on page 7 shows you what you can expect to find and where.

You'll notice that a few organization names are followed by an asterisk (*). In compiling this updated and expanded 1994–1995 edition, we attempted to contact every group listed to make sure that our information was both current and accurate. An asterisk indicates a group we were unable to contact directly, but have reason to believe is still active. We have presented the latest available information about such groups and have left them in the body of the Directory accompanied by the note, *Unable to obtain current information*. Groups for which no verification was possible have been removed.

Changed Status Organizations

Some organizations that were listed in the fourth edition of this Directory have changed their names. Others are now defunct or inactive, or could not be located. These changes are listed on pages 120–123.

Finally...

To remain vital, a youth organization requires the continuing dedication of adults; a steady flow of well-managed resources, both human and capital; and the development and support of creative programs regularly adjusted to meet the changing needs and interests of young members. This Directory is a tribute to the survivors and a welcome to new groups not included in the first four editions.

Within these many organizations lies great potential perhaps not fully recognized, and surely not fully realized. It is our hope that organization members and staffs will seek one another out to explore their mutual concerns and develop new avenues of collaboration and advocacy.

Sample Entry

National Forensic League (1925)........Name of organization and year of founding

104 W. Jackson Street ....Address or P.O. Box number

Ripon, WI 54971 ....City, state, ZIP code

James Copeland, Executive Secretary ....Name and title of contact person

414/748-6206..Area code and telephone number (when available, the toll-free 800 number and the FAX number are also listed)

A high school honor society ....Description
promoting debate, public speaking, and oral interpretation.

A Special Note to Parents

Joining some youth organizations represents a potential commitment for most of childhood and adolescence; membership in others may be of relatively short duration. Because there are so many organizations and the differences between them may be too subtle for a younger child to appreciate, your child may well need your help in deciding what to do.

Before you encourage your son or daughter to join a particular program, make sure that you understand the values it promotes. Then help your youngster consider the program in light of his or her overall schedule of activities, including needed time for study and practice. Research has shown that parental involvement and support are important factors in a young person's tenure and success in an organization.

If your child seems reluctant to become involved in any organized activity, try to learn why. Is it because of lack of time or interest or is it due to shyness or low self-esteem? You shouldn't force a shy or insecure child to join a group, no matter how attractive it may seem to you. But if you look hard enough, you should be able to find one to fit his or her interest and personality. Offer gentle encouragement. If appropriate, accompany him or her to the first few meetings. Show your loving support; it's worth it. While many children who are not "joiners" become successful and effective adults, evidence suggests that, in our organization-oriented society, group experience in childhood and adolescence is beneficial.

Younger children are motivated to join organizations mainly because they expect them to be "fun." Their concept of fun, however, encompasses more than entertainment; it extends to general feelings of comfort, satisfaction, and well-being. The initial push to join a group may come from the assurances of you or a friend, but if expectations are not met, the young person will not want to remain in the group. If this happens, you should take an active part in the dropout process as well, encouraging or discouraging according to his or her understanding of the circumstances.

Older children and adolescents may have many more in-school and out-of-school options available, and their motivations are likely to be more complex. Teenagers may join a group that focuses on a skill, career, or hobby interest or because it offers opportunity for growth in other ways. They may be attracted to some groups because membership will "look good" on college application forms.

Youths may drop out of one group because of peer pressure and join another for the same reason. When children reach junior high school, it becomes almost a rite of passage into the adolescent world to quit the youth programs they enjoyed in earlier years. In some schools, there is a great deal of pressure felt by youth who continue in groups dubbed "baby stuff" by their peers. Decisions about group membership—staying in an unpopular group, or refusing to join one that is popular—may be among the first important acts of independent judgment a young person makes. The process of choosing can contribute to overall growth and a sense of maturity.

At the high school level, in-school activities begin to take precedence over non-school choices. A recent poll of Minnesota youth suggests that this is so because in-school activities have the advantages of ease of access and familiarity and offer "highly desirable and visible benefits, such as prestige, status, and recognition." These teens identified two very different groups of peers who were most involved in out-of-school groups: those who were not successful in school organizations, and those who had outgrown the school activities and were looking for greater challenges. Non-school organizations were felt to offer intangible and private benefits, such as meeting new people, learning new skills, and using time effectively.

This poll and other studies have pointed out that high school youth know little about the senior level programs of non-school organizations; many have never been invited to join them. You may want to help your teenager find out more about these. Several are listed in this Directory.

Finally: If you really want to get involved, see Volunteers: The Vital Ingredient on pages 132–133.

DIRECTORY OF AMERICAN YOUTH ORGANIZATIONS

Hobby and Special Interest Groups, School Subject Matter Clubs, and Honor Societies

Most of these organizations are devoted to the pursuit of a single interest. Many of them meet in school; others are organized outside of school. A number of the groups—for example, the honor societies—may have programs that incorporate a broad range of activities.

American Checker Federation (1948)

P.O. Box 365
Petal, MS 39465
Charles Walker, Secretary
601/582-7090
FAX: 601/583-9761

ACF is the governing group for the mind sport of checkers in the U.S. Young people ages 7–20 may play as Juniors, or may enter the adult division of any tourney as Associates. ACF publishes rules, trains referees, sanctions tournaments, and provides bylaws for ratings in world championships. ACF offers guidelines for starting school-based checker programs; teams of American youth have played in Russia, Barbados, and England as guests of the host countries

American Numismatic Association (1891)

818 N. Cascade Avenue
Colorado Springs, CO 80903
James Taylor, Education Director
Robert Hoge, Museum Curator
800/367-9723
FAX: 719/634-4085

The ANA has a junior membership category available to young people up to age 18 who are interested in coins, paper money, medals, and tokens. Publishes *First Strike* for junior members. Provides courses, scholarships, and other educational materials; a new correspondence course for high school students is now available.

Bands of America, Inc. (1975)

P.O. Box 665
Arlington Heights, IL 60006
Chuck Henson, Promotions Coordinator
800/USA-BAND (800/872-2263)
708/956-8282
FAX: 708/956-8370

Bands of America is a non-profit educational organization that produces events for high-school band programs. The annual calendar of events includes six regional marching band competitions, the Grand National Championship, and the Summer Band Symposium—the nation's largest high school summer music camp. A new event is the National Concert Band

Festival, a noncompetitive showcase event for high school symphonic band programs.

Children's Express (1975)
Children's Express Foundation, Inc.

1440 New York Avenue, N.W., Suite 510
Washington, DC 20005
Robert Clampitt, President
202/737-7377
FAX: 202/737-0193

A news service reported by children ages 13 and under who are trained and led by teen assistant editors (ages 14–18). Children's Express has six news bureaus in the U.S. and overseas. Its weekly child-reported column is syndicated to newspapers around the country. CE has just published its third book, *Voices from the Future: Our Children Tell Us About Violence in America*. Their print column was nominated for a Pulitzer Prize in 1982 and the TV series won Peabody and Emmy awards for coverage of the 1988 political campaign.

Clowns of America (1968)

P.O. Box 570
Lake Jackson, TX 77566-0570
Jack Anderson, President

A coeducational organization for individuals who are interested in the art of clowning; 235 local alleys. Publishes *The New Calliope* (bimonthly).

Drum Corps, International (1971)

P.O. Box 548
Lombard, IL 60148
Donald Pesceone, Director
708/495-9866
FAX: 708/495-3792

A federation of community youth drum and bugle corps; seeks to preserve operational and artistic standards, and to successfully operate musical events and competitions.

Friends Forever PenPals (1989)

Friends Communications
P.O. Box 20103
Park West Post Office
New York, NY 10025

Pen pal organization for young people ages 7–17; provides each member with five or more pen pals rather than just one; pen pals are of the same age and have similar interests. Sport PenPals is a special group for young people who love sports.

Also conducts Friends Forever School PenPal Network for teachers; other adult networks include those for youth group leaders and children's librarians. Enclose self-addressed, stamped envelope when requesting information about current dues.

Gavel Club Program, Toastmasters International (1957)

P.O. Box 9052
Mission Viejo, CA 92690-7052
Greg Giesen, Manager, Membership and Club Extension
714/858-8255
FAX: 714/858-1207

Fosters self-improvement through study and practice of public speaking and parliamentary procedure.

International Thespian Society (1929)

3368 Central Parkway
Cincinnati, OH 45225
Ronald L. Longstreth
Executive Director
513/559-1996

An organization serving high school theater students and teachers. The Society seeks to increase the students' personal skills and knowledge of the theater arts by recognizing their achievements and by offering educational resources. Sponsors state conferences and the annual International Thespian Festival. Publishes *Dramatics* (monthly) for drama students and teachers.

The Theater Education Association provides resources and opportunities for professional development for theater teachers (for grades K–12); publishes *Teaching Theater.*

International Wizard of Oz Club, Inc. (1957)

220 N. 11th Street
Escanaba, MI 49829
Fred Meyer, Secretary

Not primarily a youth organization, but invites young enthusiasts of the world created by L. Frank Baum as members. Sponsors annual convention with special youth activities.

Junior Fire Marshal Program (1947)

Herman Marketing, Inc.
1400 N. Price Road
St. Louis, MO 63132-2308
800/325-1965

Fire prevention and fire safety program sponsored by The Hartford Insurance Group; it is the oldest public education program under corporate sponsorship. Conducted mainly in grades K–3, generally in cooperation with local fire departments.

Junior Great Books (1947)

Great Books Foundation
35 E. Wacker Drive
Chicago, IL 60601
Denise Ahlquist
National Training Director
800/222-5870
312/332-5870
FAX: 312/407-0334

Fosters the education of kindergarten through high school students through the reading and discussion of books dealing with issues basic to humankind.

Junior Philatelists of America (1963)

P.O. Box 850
Boalsburg, PA 16827
Sally Horn, Executive Secretary

Organized to help young stamp collectors (ages 18 and younger) learn about the hobby and maintain a solid background in and knowledge about postage stamps. Please include a long (#10) self-addressed, stamped envelope with requests.

Magical Youths International (1955)

61551 Bremen Highway
Mishawaka, IN 46544
Steve Kelley, Advisor
219/255-4747
FAX: 219/255-6817

This is primarily a correspondence organization for teens and young adults interested in magic, but there are chapters in major cities. Publishes *Top Hat* (quarterly). In 1994, MYI will initiate an Amateur Press Association application to facilitate sharing information.

Mensa (1960)

2626 E. 14th Street
Brooklyn, NY 11235
Sheila Skolnik, Executive Director
718/934-3700

An international high IQ membership organization with 143 local groups throughout the U.S. Not primarily a youth organization, but local affiliates are encouraged to develop special activities for young members. Members must have achieved scores in the upper two percent on a standard intelligence test.

National Beta Club (1934)

151 W. Lee Street
P.O. Box 730
Spartanburg, SC 29304
George W. Lockamy
Executive Director (CEO)
800/845-8281
FAX: 803/542-9300

An academic, leadership, service organization for students (grades 5–12) who exemplify outstanding character. Members are chosen by local chapters.

National Forensic League (1925)

104 W. Jackson Street
Ripon, WI 54971
James Copeland, Executive Secretary
414/748-6206

A high school honor society promoting debate, public speaking, and oral interpretation.

National Gardening Association (1972)

180 Flynn Avenue
Burlington, VT 05401
Tim Parsons
Education Programs Director
David Els, Executive Director
802/863-1308
FAX: 802/863-5962

Dedicated to helping people become successful gardeners; publishes NGA's *Guide to Kids' Gardening* and other resources for K–8 teachers to assist students in learning about scientific inquiry and interdisciplinary investigations with plants. A grant from the National Science Foundation provides ongoing support to classroom gardening efforts.

National Honor Society (1921)
National Junior Honor Society (1929)

National Association of Secondary
School Principals
1904 Association Drive
Reston, VA 22091
Dale D. Hawley, Director
Rocco M. Marano, Deputy Director,
Division of Student Activities
David Cordts, Associate Director
Mary Jo Patterson
Assistant Programs Administrator
703/860-0200
FAX: 703/476-5432

For students who excel in scholarship, leadership, character, and service; members are chosen by local chapters. Societies provide service to their schools and communities, conduct peer tutoring programs, volunteer at homeless shelters, etc., and raise funds for charitable causes.

National Junior Classical League (1936)

Miami University
Oxford, OH 45056
Geri Dutra, Administrative Secretary
513/529-7741
FAX: 513/529-7742

For high school students studying Latin; promotes interest in classical cultures of Greece and Rome.

National Junior Horticultural Association (1935)

401 N. 4th Street
Durant, OK 74701
Joe Maxson, Executive Secretary
405/924-0771

An educational program for young people interested in horticulture; sponsors projects and contests; there are no membership dues.

North American Association of Ventriloquists (1940)

800 W. Littleton Boulevard
P.O. Box 420
Littleton, CO 80160
Clinton Detweiler, President
303/798-6830
FAX: 303/798-3160

Seeks to assist and encourage individuals interested in the art of ventriloquism; serves as a clearinghouse for conference and product information; helps solve technical problems; publishes *Newsy*

Vents newsletter. Not primarily a youth organization, but welcomes young people as members.

Omega Gamma Delta (1902)

89 Longview Road
Port Washington, NY 11050
Robert S. Tarleton, Secretary
516/883-2897

A high-school social fraternity for young men; encourages leadership qualities among members.

Quill and Scroll Society (1926)

School of Journalism
and Mass Communication
University of Iowa
Iowa City, IA 52242
Richard P. Johns, Executive Secretary
319/335-5795

An international honorary society of high school journalism students; members are selected by their schools.

Teen Association of Model Railroaders (1962)

c/o John Reichel
1800 E. 38th Street
Oakland, CA 94602-1720
Brent Johnson, President
530 W. Alex Bell Road
Centerville, OH 45459

Promotes building and operating model railroads; for ages 10–21.

Tri-M Music Honor Society (1936)

1806 Robert Fulton Drive
Reston, VA 22091-1597
Sandra V. Fridy, Program Manager
703/860-4000
FAX: 703/860-1531

A program of the Music Educators National Conference, Tri-M is the international music honor society for junior and senior high school students. Emphasizes service through music. Founded by Alexander M. and Frances M. Harley as the Modern Music Masters.

Career Education and Vocational Student Groups

American Cadet Alliance, Inc. (1960)
c/o Thomas W. Nouza, Sr.
8706 252nd Street
Jamaica, NY 11426
718/343-8491

Begun as the Maritime Brigade in 1909, this is a navy-oriented youth program conducted by veterans and reservists. Seeks to teach vocational skills and to promote and instill a sense of discipline, respect for authority, and patriotism.

Business Professionals of America (1966)
5454 Cleveland Avenue
Columbus, OH 43231
614/895-7277
FAX: 614/895-1165

Promotes personal, professional, and leadership growth for secondary and post-secondary students enrolled in business and/or office education programs.

Civil Air Patrol (1941)
Building 714
105 S. Hansell Street
Maxwell Air Force Base, AL 36112-6332
205/953-5463
FAX: 205/953-5296

The civilian auxiliary of the U.S. Air Force. Cadets (grade school through college) receive training in air search and rescue work and aerospace education and aviation. If the Billy Mitchell Award is earned, a cadet may join the military at an E-2 rank.

Distributive Education Clubs of America (1946)
1908 Association Drive
Reston, VA 22091
Dr. Ed Davis, Executive Director
703/860-5000
FAX: 703/860-4013

A vocational organization of students in high schools and junior colleges interested in marketing, retail, and wholesale distribution.

DPMA Club Program (1951)
DPMA, The Association of Information Systems Professionals
505 Busse Highway
Park Ridge, IL 60068
Barbara Meade, Membership Services
708/825-8124
FAX: 708/825-1693

A program for students interested in data processing careers. Student memberships in the parent organization are available. Parent organization formerly known as Data Processing Management Association.

Exploring Division
Boy Scouts of America (1910)

1325 W. Walnut Hill Lane
P.O. Box 152079
Irving, TX 75015-2079
Donald E. Winston
National Exploring Director
214/580-2000
414/580-2433

A career-oriented program for young men and women ages 14 (or who have completed grade 8) through 20. Posts are organized around a career or possible lifetime avocational interest. Members get hands-on experience with the "tools of the trade" under the guidance of professionals. Career Awareness Exploring is an in-school program for junior high and high-school students. Local business and professional people come to the schools to share information about their fields of work.

Future Business Leaders of America (1942)

1912 Association Drive
Reston, VA 22091
Edward D. Miller, President and CEO
703/860-3334
FAX: 703/758-0749

A vocational organization for high school and college students preparing for business or office careers. In colleges, this organization is known as Phi Beta Lambda.

Future Homemakers of America (1945)

1910 Association Drive
Reston, VA 22091
Alan T. Rains, Jr., Executive Director
703/476-4900
FAX: 703/860-2713

For young men and women in high school who are interested in careers related to home economics, family life, and consumer education. HERO chapters stress career preparation.

Future Secretaries Association®

Professional Secretaries International®
10502 N.W. Ambassador Drive
P.O. Box 20404
Kansas City, MO 64195-0404
Susan Fenner, Ph.D., Education and Professional Development
816/891-6600

Promotes preparation for office careers through student organizations with school chapters, newsletter, annual conference, and other professional activities. Also conducts Collegiate Secretaries International.

Jobs for America's Graduates (1970)

1729 King Street, Suite 200
Alexandria, VA 22314
Judith Boylson
Director of National Programs
703/684-9479
FAX: 703/684-9489

A school-to-work transition program that includes a dropout prevention component for non-seniors and a senior school-to-work component. Currently more than 30,000 at-risk and disadvantaged youth are participating in 550 high schools in 21 states. There is also a program in the United Kingdom servicing 1,200 students. Sponsors Career Association, a student-run organization for young people in affiliated school districts.

Junior Achievement (1919)

One Education Way
Colorado Springs, CO 80906
Karl Flemke, President
719/540-8000

Junior Achievement brings business executives into classrooms across America to help professional educators teach economics to students in kindergarten through grade 12. By providing the basics of the private enterprise system, these role models help prepare young people for entry into the work force of the twenty-first century. More than 1.5 million students are involved in these economic-education programs annually.

Junior Deputy Sheriffs' Program (1946)

National Sheriffs' Association
1450 Duke Street
Alexandria, VA 22314
JoAnn B. Kline
Coordinator, Junior Deputy Program
703/836-7827
FAX: 703/683-6541

Aspires to lower the rates of juvenile delinquency through a program aimed at reducing accidents, acquainting youth with local government, providing training in emergency preparedness, enlisting youth in keeping peers out of trouble, and stimulating interest in law enforcement careers.

National FFA Organization (1928)

National FFA Center
5632 Mount Vernon Highway
P.O. Box 15160
Alexandria, VA 22309
Larry D. Case, National Advisor
703/360-3600
FAX: 703/360-5524

For secondary and post-secondary school students (up to age 20) of vocational agriculture and agribusiness.

National Student Nurses Association (1952)

555 W. 57th Street, Suite 1327
New York, NY 10019
Dr. Robert V. Piemonte
Executive Director
212/581-2211
FAX: 212/581-2368

Promotes interest in nursing careers. The membership is drawn from among students already enrolled in nursing and pre-nursing programs in state-approved schools.

Naval Sea Cadet Corps (1962)

Naval Sea Cadet Corps Headquarters
2300 Wilson Boulevard
Arlington, VA 22201
Captain Alfred J. Kreiser
Executive Director
703/243-6910

A nautically oriented youth training program providing instruction and practical experience in seamanship; instilling the attributes of leadership and good citizenship. For boys and girls ages 11–18. Sponsored by the Navy League of the United States, supported by the U.S. Navy and the U.S. Coast Guard.

Safe Sitter (1980)

1500 N. Ritter Avenue
Indianapolis, IN 46219
Jan Petty, Executive Director
800/255-4089
317/355-4888

Safe Sitter is a medically-oriented instructional program designed for young people ages 11–13. The program seeks to provide teens with improved child care skills for their babysitting charges in order to reduce the number of accidental and preventable deaths among children, particularly while under a babysitter's care. The curriculum covers medical emergencies including rescue breathing, responsibilities and ethics of safe babysitting, age-appropriate entertainment, and the basics of starting a business.

Adult instructors for the program must be trained and certified. Young people must go through a 13-hour training course and pass a rigorous written exam proving mastery of key concepts. Students must demonstrate rescue breathing and care of a choking child. Begun in Indiana, the Safe Sitter program is being made available through hospitals and other organizations nationwide.

Technology Student Association (1978)

1914 Association Drive
Reston, VA 22091
Rosanne White, Executive Director
703/860-9000
FAX: 703/620-4483

For high school, intermediate, and elementary school students who are or have been enrolled in technology education courses. Fosters exploration of problem solving and critical thinking.

Vocational Industrial Clubs of America (1965)

P.O. Box 3000
Leesburg, VA 22075
Stephen Denby, Executive Director
703/777-8810

For high school and junior college students interested in trade, industrial, technical, and health occupations.

WAVE, Inc. (1969)

501 School Street, S.W., Suite 600
Washington, DC 20024
Larry Brown, President
202/484-0103
FAX: 202/488-7595

WAVE—Work, Achievement, Values and Education—was created to provide educational opportunities, training services and motivational activities for young people facing barriers to success. WAVE operates in more than 150 locations in communities, schools, and workplaces.

Young Actors Guild (1975)

125 S. 4th Street
Connellsville, PA 15425
Aaron White, President
412/628-3939
FAX: 412/628-0682

A membership organization that protects the interests of young performing artists (most of them professionals) ages 2–16. Provides training and education in singing, dancing, and acting.

Young Marines of the Marine Corps League, Inc. (1964)

Young Marine Headquarters
P.O. Box 70735
Southwest Station
Washington, DC 20024
Jim Parker, National Director
202/889-8745
FAX: 202/889-0502

A character-building and physical fitness program for boys and girls ages 8–18. Stresses honesty, fairness, courage, respect, loyalty, dependability, attention to duty, love of God, and fidelity to our country and its institutions. Sponsors outdoor encampments. Youth must complete Recruit Training before acceptance in a regular platoon.

See also:

The Student Conservation Association, Inc., page 95.

Resources

National Federation of Business and Professional Women's Clubs

2012 Massachusetts Avenue, N.W.
Washington, DC 20036
Audrey T. Haynes, Executive Director
202/293-1100

BPW/USA created the Young Careerist Program in 1964 to recognize the accomplishments of young successful working people while introducing them to the ideals and mission of BPW. BPW members have the opportunity to meet and network with young women (and men), who are in the early stages of their careers, to learn about the changing roles, the problems, and rewards for young people in today's business and professional world.

National Youth Employment Coalition (1979)

1001 Connecticut Avenue, N.W.
Suite 719
Washington, DC 20036
Alan Zuckerman, Executive Director
202/659-1064
FAX: 202/775-9733

A coalition of agencies sharing a common interest in increasing employment, education, and training opportunities for America's youth, especially those who are disadvantaged. Seeks to improve public understanding and support for youth employment programs and initiatives; monitors and analyzes the impact of current and planned policy on the development of a comprehensive approach to youth employment. Serves as a clearinghouse of information and as a catalyst for cooperative ventures among Coalition members, voluntary organizations, the education system, and the private sector. Monthly newsletter distributed to members and subscribers.

Navy Recruiting Command

Educational Liaison and Youth
Programs Division (Code 82)
801 N. Randolph Street
Arlington, VA 22203
Head, Youth Programs Branch
703/696-4889
FAX: 703/696-6430

The U.S. Navy provides a range of services and types of program assistance to youth groups. For information, contact the Youth Program Petty Officer at your local Navy Recruiting District.

NEA Student Program

National Education Association (1857)
1201 16th Street, N.W., Suite 320
Washington, DC 20036
Garfield Bright
Student Program Manager
202/822-7132
FAX: 202/822-7624

The NEA no longer directly sponsors Future Teachers of America programs for high school students, but provides materials on organizing such groups to state and local education associations and interested student groups. The NEA Student Program is active on college and university campuses across the country. NEA offers a wide range of publications, primarily for educators; many would be of interest to youth groups, including those that encourage minorities to enter the teaching profession.

See also:

Science, Math, and Technology Organizations, pages 21–27; **Youth Communication**, page 162.

Science, Math, and Technology Organizations

Academy of Model Aeronautics (1936)

5151 E. Memorial Drive
Muncie, IN 47302
Jay Mealy, Public Relations
317/287-1256
FAX: 317/289-4248

The Academy promotes aviation education through model aviation activities; provides insurance and a magazine for members. Sponsors contests, a National Convention, and a scholarship program. Clubs are organized at the local level; most are not exclusively youth. Those under age 19 join as youth members. The Delta Dart materials published by the academy teach basic aeronautic principles and are used widely by schools and organizations. They are available at low cost.

American Junior Academy of Science (1930s)

c/o Southern California Academy of Sciences
900 Exposition Boulevard
Los Angeles, CA 90007
Gloria Takahashi, Director
213/744-3384
818/333-2173

Encourages students to conduct scientific investigations and prepare written and oral presentations of their findings. Junior Academies must be organized through state-level affiliates of the National Association of Academies of Science, which sponsors the American

Junior Academy at the national annual meeting of the American Association for the Advancement of Science.

Invent America! (1987)

United States Patent Model Foundation
1505 Powhatan Street
Alexandria, VA 22314
703/684-1836

A national, nonprofit elementary school education program and student invention contest designed to "bring bright ideas out of young minds." Children learn math, science, literacy and analytical thinking skills through creating their own inventions to solve everyday problems. More than 30,000 elementary schools have participated in the program and invention contests held at state, regional, and national levels.

JETS, Inc. (1950)

1420 King Street, Suite 405
Alexandria, VA 22314-2794
Dr. Daniel W. Kunz, Executive Director
703/548-5387
FAX: 703/548-0769 or 703/836-4875

JETS—the Junior Engineering Technical Society—is a national educational society emphasizing the understanding of engineering and technology, and competence in mathematics and science for high school students. JETS coordinates pre-college engineering career guidance efforts for the profession. Initiatives include the National Engineering Aptitude Search (NEAS); the annual Tests of Engineering Aptitude, Mathematics and Science (TEAMS) competition; and the annual National Engineering Design Challenge (NEDC) competition. Publishes *JETS Report* newsletter.

Mu Alpha Theta (1957)

Department of Mathematics
University of Oklahoma
601 Elm Avenue, Room 423
Norman, OK 73109
Stanley B. Eliason, Secretary-Treasurer
405/325-4489

A high school and junior college honorary society sponsored by the Mathematical Association of America. To be eligible, students must have completed two years of college preparatory mathematics and be enrolled in a third-year program, with no grade lower than a B.

North American Simulation & Gaming Association (1967)

c/o Workshops by Thiagi
4423 East Trailridge Road
Bloomington, IN 47408-9633
Sivasailam Thiagarajan, President
812/332-1478
FAX: 812/332-5701

NASAGA is an international, interdisciplinary organization committed to supporting the development and use of simulation and gaming for a wide variety of issues and activities. Good simulation games are slices of life that often help demonstrate the complex web of actions and consequences that interact in real systems. NASAGA brings together individuals interested in applying simulation and gaming technology in their own fields of professional activity or research; members are interested not only in understanding how and why simulations and games are effective, but also in how they can be useful for trainers and educators.

Games have been used in corporations, nonprofit organizations, government agencies, and schools for a myriad of purposes such as developing empathic thinking skills in adults and children, addressing problem behaviors such as underage drinking, fostering intercultural understanding and communication, etc.

NASAGA membership is mainly adult, but includes students as young as 12. Programs exist for all age levels: K–12 in-school and non-school educational settings, college and professional education. A number of games address the issues of disability directly in the simulations.

Odyssey of the Mind

OM Association
P.O. Box 547
Glassboro, NJ 08028
Carole Micklus, Executive Director
Janet Vincz, Assistant Director
609/881-1603
FAX: 609/881-3596

An educational program that fosters the development of creative thinking and problem-solving skills among participating students in grades kindergarten through high school. Under the guidance of a coach, five to seven students work together to solve an OM "long-term problem" and practice solving "spontaneous problems" in preparation for competition. Regional, state, and international competitions allow students to showcase their solutions. OM program uses these activities to develop cooperation, self-respect and the appreciation and understanding of others.

The Planetary Society (1980)

65 N. Catalina Avenue
Pasadena, CA 91106
Carl Sagan, President
818/793-5100
FAX: 818/793-5528

Formed to focus the energies and resources of people everywhere who want the age of planetary exploration to continue and who want their voices and opinions heard; programs seek to foster excellence in science among students and to involve them in a deeper understanding of the ramifications of planetary exploration; sponsors student contests and offers scholarships for students interested in planetary-related science.

Society of Physics Students (1968)

1825 Connecticut Avenue, N.W.,
Suite 213
Washington, DC 20009
Donald Kirwan, Director
202/232-6688
FAX: 202/234-7053

Promotes the study of physics. There are no high school chapters at present, but membership is open to high school students individually, or through one of the college chapters. Sponsors Sigma Pi Sigma, an honor society for those who excel in physics.

SPACE CAMP
Space Academy (1982)

The Space and Rocket Center
One Tranquility Base
Huntsville, AL 35807
Reservations/General Information
800/63-SPACE (800/637-7223)
FAX: 205/837-6137

SPACE CAMP provides youth in grades 4–7 (Florida camp) or grades 4–6 (Alabama camp) with hands-on activities in rocket propulsion, early manned flights, space suits, microgravity, computers, and two simulated shuttle missions. Space Academy Level I, for trainees in grades 7–9, focuses on preparations for a pair of simulated missions. Space Academy Level II is a college-accredited program for high school students (grades 10, 11, and 12) which emphasizes the academic foundations required for space-related careers in technology, engineering, and aerospace.

Students for the Exploration and Development of Space (1980)

77 Massachusetts Avenue
Room W20-445
Cambridge, MA 02139
David J. Kalman, Chair
617/253-8897
FAX: 617/253-8897

An international organization of high school and university students interested in promoting the exploration and development of space. Several university chapters are currently working on building their own satellites. High school students are invited to participate through these local chapters. Chapters also sponsor speakers, conduct astronomy demonstrations, and give presentations to groups and schools in their local areas.

Students Watching Over Our Planet Earth

Los Alamos National Laboratory
MS J447
Los Alamos, NM 87545
Dianne Hyer, Project Director
Roger Eckhardt, Science Director
505/667-8950
FAX: 505/665-5759

SWOOPE is an innovative environmental science education program for grades K–12. Teachers and students do real, hands-on science; they gather data on an item of concern in the environment, send these data to a database, and have their results sent back to them. The data are available to scientists, agencies, and the community at large. SWOOPE provides training and background materials, instruments, protocols for taking measurements, and other supports. Current units include water quality, radiation, and radon; additional units are under development.

Young Astronaut Program (1984)

1308 19th Street, N.W.
Washington, DC 20036
Jennifer Rae, Director of Membership
202/682-1984

This organization is designed to ignite enthusiasm for scientific inquiry among pre-school, elementary, and junior high school students and their teachers, and to promote the study of mathematics, science, and technology. Four program levels: Youngest Astronauts (ages 3–5); Trainee (grades K–3); Pilot (grades 4–6); Commander (grades 7–9). Students, teachers, schools, youth groups, and community organizations can form chapters. Space School is a live, interactive cable television course for grades 4–6, available to school districts throughout the U.S. Activity guides available.

Young Entomologists Society, Inc. (1965)

International Headquarters
1915 Peggy Place
Lansing, MI 48910-2553
Gary Dunn, M.S., F.R.E.S.
Director of Education
517/887-0499

Promotes interest in the science of entomology (the study of insects) among youth and adult amateurs. Publishes *Y.E.S. Quarterly* (a member-written journal), *Insect World, Flea Market, Insect Study Sourcebook, Six-legged Science, Insect Identification Study Guide*, and *Caring for Insect Livestock*. Catalog of educational materials available.

Resources

American Association for the Advancement of Science (1848)

1333 H Street, N.W.
Washington, DC 20005
Dr. Shirley Malcolm, Head
Directorate for Education
and Human Resources Programs
202/326-6680
Fax: 202/371-9849

AAAS has almost 300 societies and academies as affiliates, including the Junior Academy of Science; offers extensive materials and programs for school-based science and technology education. Project 2061: Education for a Changing Future is a long-range effort to improve science education at all levels.

The Directorate for Education and Human Resources Programs offers a variety of programs and publications to enhance the status and accelerate the advancement of women, minorities, and persons with disabilities in science and engineering professions. The Linkages program joins community-based advocacy and youth-serving organizations with scientists and engineers, as individuals and through their associations, to create and implement improved mathematics, science, and technology education, through both in-school and out-of-school programs.

AAAS publications of particular interest to youth organizations include *Science Education News, Source Book*, and *Science Books and Films*. Publication list available.

American Indian Science and Engineering Society (1977)

1630 30th Street, Suite 301
Boulder, CO 80301-1041
Norbert S. Hill, Jr. (Oneida)
Executive Director
303/492-8658
FAX: 303/492-3400

This society provides Native American youth with the opportunity to enter the world of science while preserving their rich cultural heritage. It seeks to help them meet the challenge of technological change, to enable them to pursue careers outside of traditional Native American life, and to return to share that education with their people. Scholarship aid available.

Lawrence Hall of Science (1969)

University of California at Berkeley
Centennial Drive
Berkeley, CA 94720
Barbara Ando
Director of Public Programs
510/642-2858
FAX: 510/642-1055

The Lawrence Hall of Science is a public science center offering public programs on-site and publications of activities for distribution nationally and internationally. It is a center for teacher education and curriculum development in science and mathematics education. Its curricula and activities are used in schools, youth recreation groups, Scout groups, and camps all over the world. Catalogs of materials available on request.

National Geographic Society

Educational Services
1145 17th Street, N.W.
Washington, DC 20036
202/857-7378

National Geographic carries extensive youth-oriented print and audiovisual materials, created primarily for classroom use, reflecting the diversity of the Society's interests. Catalog available (800/368-2728).

National Science Teachers Association (1895)

1840 Wilson Boulevard
Arlington, VA 22201-3000
Marilyn DeWall, Associate Executive Director, Student Award Programs (including Toshiba ExploraVision, Duracell Competition)
Lyn Moritt, Space Science Student Improvement Program
703/243-7100
FAX: 703/243-7177

Navy Recruiting Command

(Code 82)
801 N. Randolph Street
Arlington, VA 22203-1991
LCDR Bob Lawson, Youth Programs
703/696-4889
FAX: 703/696-6430

The Math and Science: START NOW! program shows students the relevance of mathematics and science courses to a variety of challenging fields such as computers, photography, electronics, medicine, engineering, and robotics. Encourages students to enroll in mathematics and science courses to prepare for higher education and careers in today's technology-oriented society. You may arrange for a Navy representative to visit a school or youth organization by calling your nearest Naval Recruiting office; if you need more help, contact the youth programs headquarters at the above address.

Science Service

1719 N Street, N.W.
Washington, DC 20036
Alfred S. McLaren, President
202/785-2255

Science Service administers the Westinghouse Science Talent Search (STS) and the International Science and Engineering Fair (ISEF), and publishes the *Directory of Student Science Training Programs for Precollege Students* and *Science News* magazine.

The STS is an annual scholarship competition for high school seniors, conducted in partnership with Westinghouse Electric Corporation. Students must submit a report of an independent research project in science, mathematics, or engineering, along with available standardized test scores, transcript, and entry form. Early December entry deadline. Call or write to Science Service Inc. for the Official Rules and Entry Form Booklet.

The ISEF is a competition for students in grades 9–12. To participate, students must be named individual or Team Project Finalists at an ISEF-affiliated fair. Write or call for details about the fair in your area.

The annual *Directory*, which lists more than 500 programs and internships in mathematics, science, and engineering, is available for $3. *Science News* is a weekly newsmagazine of science. Write or call for subscription information.

See also:

World Future Society, page 161; **National Energy Foundation**, page 94; **National Wildlife Federation**, page 94; **Girls Incorporated**, pages 64–65.

Sports Organizations

Following the Civil War, interest in playing sports and in watching them being played developed rapidly among Americans of all ages. Professional and college leagues developed around the turn of the century, followed closely by organized play in high school and community-based recreation programs. Much of the play among youngsters was very informal, with equipment, rules, and playing conditions varying according to team resources.

The earliest youth tournaments tended to be disorganized affairs, with frequent conflicts over rules of play. Safeguards were generally inadequate, and injuries often resulted. Yet interest in sports among young people continued to grow, and by the 1920s, out-of-school youth sports organizations began to appear.

Most of these groups were founded with similar aims: to promote playing the sport under a uniform set of rules and conditions: to teach related skills to young players and other participants; and to organize fair competitive events. Today most sports organizations also pay close attention to safety and have developed protective gear and playing rules to reduce risks to young players. Even so, contact sports are often played by younger and younger children, competition has become more marked, and injuries have continued to mount.

Frequently, excesses in youth sports programs are a consequence of local zeal subverting national guidelines for operation and play. National organizations try to counter such problems by providing training courses for coaches, referees, and other officials.

Most youth sports organizations also profess objectives that reach beyond skill development and the playing of the game. In addition to stressing fair play and good sportsmanship, they seek to promote the development of character and citizenship. Several also encourage good academic performance and offer college scholarships for players.

Note: Most of the organizations listed in the Character-Building Organizations section (pages 62–67) include sports among their activities. Many of the Ethnic Heritage Groups (pages 106–114) also sponsor youth athletic programs. (For example, some Olympic gymnasts got their earliest training through Sokols.) A small number of sports organizations are associated with for-profit corporations.

AAU/USA Youth Sports Program (1948)

Amateur Athletic Union of the U.S., Inc.
3400 W. 86th Street
P.O. Box 68207
Indianapolis, IN 46268
Jerry Duhamell
Director, AAU/USA Youth Programs
317/872-2900
FAX: 317/875-0548

The Amateur Athletic Union of the U.S., Inc. is the nation's largest amateur multi-sport program, offering 21 sports for athletes ages 8–19. Conducts competitions at the local, regional, and national levels; holds national AAU Junior Olympic Games each summer in a selected U.S. city.

American Youth Hostels (1934)

733 15th Street, N.W., Suite 840
Washington, DC 20005
Richard Martyr, Executive Director
202/783-6161
FAX: 202/783-6171

Sponsors low-cost recreational and educational travel for all ages (biking, hiking, skiing, canoe and automobile trips); maintains inexpensive overnight accommodations in the U.S. Affiliated with international network of hostels. Has 38 regional offices, several of which have programs for disadvantaged youth. Directory available.

Direction Sports (1968)

600 Wilshire Boulevard, Suite 320
Los Angeles, CA 90017-3215
Tulley N. Brown, Executive Director
213/627-9861
FAX: 213/627-7704

Programs are based on the recognition that destructive behaviors often result from a sense of failure to gain the affirmation that leads to self-esteem. Direction Sports teams (which involve stimulating interest in academic work as well) demonstrate how all youth can be affirmed through meaningful involvement from the earliest ages in teaching, coaching, and counseling their peers. The program has proved to be effective in raising self-confidence, learning skills, and improving motivation to learn even in the high-risk environments of Los Angeles public housing projects. Direction Sports operates in or after school and in recreation centers, YMCAs, housing projects, settlements, and youth detention camps in the U.S. and in ten other countries around the world. For information on starting Direction Sports peer-run academic/athletic program and a video of clips from network television shows, send $20 to the above address.

The IronKids Health and Fitness Program (1985)

P.O. Box 660217
Dallas, TX 75266-0217

A physical fitness program for youth ages 7–14, operated through schools and in other youth-serving settings in regions where Rainbo, Colonial, and Kilpatrick bakery products are sold. IronKids Triathlon combines short-distance swimming, biking and running sports; holds mini-triathlons in selected U.S. cities; IronKids Path to Health and Fitness is a school-based curriculum provided free to elementary schools; promotes good nutrition, fitness and a positive attitude. The Iron Kids Club seeks to inspire young people ages 7–14 to pursue personal excellence and a physically-healthy way of life.

National Association of Police Athletic Leagues (1944)

200 Castlewood Drive
North Palm Beach, FL 33408
Joseph F. Johnson, Executive Director
407/844-1823
FAX: 407/863-6120

An association of local leagues dedicated to preventing juvenile crime through building positive relationships between youth and police. Local programs will vary; most are coeducational, and altogether they include over 100 athletic and related activities. Sponsors national tournaments in boxing, basketball, baseball, and softball.

National Council of Youth Sports

200 Castlewood Drive
North Palm Beach, FL 33408
Joe Johnson, President
407/844-1823
FAX: 407/863-6120

An organization of staff executives of youth sports programs; seeks to foster the growth of youth through organized youth sports.

National Youth Sports Program (1968)

National Collegiate Athletic Association
6201 College Boulevard
Overland Park, KS 66211
Rochelle Collins, Program Coordinator
913/339-1906
FAX: 913/339-0028

NYSP is a unique partnership of selected institutions of higher education, the National Collegiate Athletic Association (NCAA) and the U.S. Department of Health and Human Services Office of Community Services. This 5-week summer program brings young people from low-income families to college and university campuses where they receive sports-skill, fitness, and health instruction. The educational program also helps youths develop personal and social skills, provides instruction in alcohol and other drug abuse prevention, and makes them aware of career and educational opportunities. NYSP gives NCAA member institutions and their personnel the opportunity to participate more fully in community life and the solution of community problems. In 1993, 175 campuses in 44 states and the District of Columbia hosted National Youth Sports Programs.

The President's Council on Physical Fitness and Sports (1956)

701 Pennsylvania Avenue, N.W.,
Suite 250
Washington, DC 20004
Phillip F. Wiethorn
Director of Information
202/272-3421
FAX: 202/504-2064

Formed during the Eisenhower Presidency, the Council encourages regular participation in sports and physical fitness activities for people of all ages. It sponsors a Physical Fitness Awards program to recognize outstanding and basic levels of fitness among youth ages 6–17. For information about the Awards program, write: President's Challenge, Poplars Research Center, 400 E. 7th Street, Bloomington, IN 47405.

YMCA Youth Sports (1851)

YMCA of the USA
37 W. Broad Street, Suite 600
Columbus, OH 43215
Dick Jones, Director, Youth Sports
614/621-1231
FAX: 614/224-5611

A youth sports program open to all elementary and secondary school students. The most popular programs are soccer, basketball, gymnastics, baseball, and softball. The program stresses the value of teamwork and cooperation, fair play, and leadership development; all participants play in every game. Many local YMCAs have developed adaptive sports programs for young people with disabilities.

See also:

Athletes in Action, page 70; **Fellowship of Christian Athletes**, pages 71–72.

Angling

American Bass Association (1985)

2810 Trotters Trail
Wetumpka, AL 36092
Bob Barker, President
205/567-6035
FAX: 205/567-8632

An organization of adult anglers who also provide fishing opportunities for children in their own communities. Provides grants to state ABA affiliates and member clubs for youth outings, demonstrations, and fishing activities. Uses the Aquatic Resource Council curriculum to promote good conservation practices. Competitive events include parent/child teams.

Brotherhood of the Junglecock (1939)

c/o Bosley Wright
Glen Burnie, MD 21061
Bosley Wright, Executive Vice President
410/761-7727

Anglers (now involving a third generation) dedicated to teaching youth angling techniques (including fly-tying), good sportsmanship, and the preservation of American game fish. Full certification program takes several years to complete. Program involves youth from ages 7 1/2 to 16. Organization is named for the junglecock, a bird whose neck feathers were prized by fly-tyers.

Archery

Junior Bowhunter Program (1986)

National Field Archery Association
31407 Outer Interstate 10
Redlands, CA 92373
Pam Shilling, Executive Secretary
909/794-2133
FAX: 909/794-8512

The NFAA Junior Bowhunter Program introduces the sport of shooting with compound bows under adult supervision; provides guidance for the young recreational archer or bow-hunter; also provides an award system and competitions for youths under age 18. If junior archers wish to go beyond the local level to compete in NFAA state, sectional or national tournaments, they must join NFAA as junior members.

Junior Olympic Archery Development (ca. 1970)

National Archery Association
One Olympic Plaza
Colorado Springs, CO 80909-5778
Christine McCartney, Executive Director
719/578-4576
FAX: 719/632-4733

NAA is the national governing body for archery in the U.S. More than 250 JOAD clubs around the nation offer instruction and tournament participation for recurve and compound bow archers under age 18. The program furnishes standards for rank certification from qualified archer level to Olympian level, as well as provides guidance for those interested in recreational archery.

Baseball/Softball

All American Amateur Baseball Association (1944)

340 Walker Drive
Zanesville, OH 43701
Tom J. Checkush, Executive Director
614/453-7349
FAX: 614/453-7349

Organized to foster, develop, and regulate amateur baseball. Limited Division play is restricted to players under age 21.

Amateur Softball Association (1933)

2801 N.E. 50th Street
Oklahoma City, OK 73111
Don E. Porter, Executive Director
405/424-5266
FAX: 405/424-3855

The national governing body for the sport of softball in the U.S.; runs a Junior Olympic youth program for girls and boys in Slow Pitch and Fast Pitch. Four age groups: 18 and under, 16 and under, 14 and under, 12 and under. Also offers a complete Softball Coaches' Education Program for all volunteer coaches.

American Amateur Baseball Congress, Inc. (1935)

118 Redfield Plaza
P.O. Box 467
Marshall, MI 49068
Joseph R. Cooper, President
616/781-2002
FAX: 616/751-2060

American Legion Baseball (1925)

American Legion National Headquarters
P.O. Box 1055
Indianapolis, IN 46206
Jim Quinlan, Program Coordinator
317/635-8411
FAX: 317/638-1801

Offers supervised play for teens; teams are formed locally, and are financed by service clubs, businesses, and individuals.

Babe Ruth League, Inc. (1951)

1770 Brunswick Pike
P.O. Box 5000
Trenton, NJ 08638
Ronald Tellefson, President/CEO
609/695-1434

Offers supervised baseball and softball league play for youth ages 5–18. Baseball leagues are organized in four divisions: Bambino (ages 5–12); Prep (age 13); 13–15 Division; Prep (age 16); and 16–18 Division. Softball designed for girls is organized in three levels: ages 5–12, 13–15, and 16–18. Also known as Babe Ruth Baseball and Babe Ruth Softball.

Cinderella Softball Leagues (1958)

P.O. Box 1411
Corning, NY 14830
Peter Ekenstiema, President
607/937-5469

Conducts leagues for girls ages 18 and under. Levels of play include: Sweetpeas (9 and under); 10 and under; 12 and under; 14 and under; 16 and under; and 19 and under. Program is open to all girls, stresses fair play and fun over winning. Operates mainly in New York state.

Dixie Baseball, Inc. (1956)

P.O. Box 222
Lookout Mountain, TN 37350
Nick F. Senter, Executive Director
615/821-6811

The umbrella organization for three separate programs: Dixie Youth Baseball, Inc. (T-ball, ages 6 and under; Minors, 10 and under; Majors, 12 and under); Dixie Boys Baseball, Inc. (Boys, 13–14; Pre-Majors, 15–16; Majors, 15–18); Dixie Softball, Inc. (Sweetees, 6 and under; Angels, 9 and under; Ponytails, 12 and under; Belles, 15 and under; Debs, 18 and under).

George Khoury Association of Baseball Leagues (1936)

5400 Meramec Bottom Road
St. Louis, MO 63128
George G. Khoury, Executive Director
314/849-8900

For boys and girls ages 7 and older; organized in leagues sponsored by local churches and community organizations.

Little League Baseball, Inc. (1939)

P.O. Box 3485
Williamsport, PA 17701
Dr. Creighton J. Hale
President and CEO
717/326-1921
FAX: 717/326-1074

For youth ages 6–18; organized in all U.S. states and territories and 75 foreign countries; conducts annual International World Series in August. The Challenge Division offers non-competitive play for physically and mentally disabled young people ages 6–18.

National Amateur Baseball Federation (1914)

P.O. Box 705
Bowie, MD 20718
Charles M. Blackburn
Executive Director
301/262-5005

Promotes non-commercialized baseball tournaments at the national level for seven age groups: Freshman Division (12 and under); Sophomore Division (14 and under); Junior Division (16 and under); High School Division (high school eligible); Senior Division (18 and under); College Division (22 and under); and Major Division (unlimited age).

Pony Baseball, Inc. (1951)

P.O. Box 225
Washington, PA 15301
Roy Gillespie, President
412/225-1060
FAX: 412/225-9852

Leagues organized in seven divisions: Shetland (ages 5–6); Pinto (ages 7–8); Mustang (ages 9–10); Bronco (ages 11–12); Pony (ages 13–14); Colt (ages 15–16); and Palomino (ages 17–18). Also sponsors softball leagues that are currently restricted to female participants.

USA Baseball (1965)

2160 Greenwood Avenue
Trenton, NJ 08609
Mike Lantz
Program Development Director
Pam Case, Operations Director
609/586-2381
FAX: 609/587-1818

Selects Olympic Festival Team of 64 players, primarily ages 17–18, during years when Olympic Games are not held. From Olympic Festival participants, USA Baseball selects the USA Junior National Team of 18 players to compete internationally at the Junior World Championships.

Basketball

Gus Macker 3-on-3 Charity Basketball Tournament (1974)

Gus Macker Enterprises
121 E. Main Street
Belding, MI 48809
616/794-1500
FAX: 616/794-3750

A tournament system for teams of three players (with one alternate) ages 3 and up. Teams are matched by age, height, and experience. Macker Enterprises organizes tournaments as fund-raisers in local communities. Tournaments involved 190,000 hoopsters of all ages in 60 U.S. cities in 1993.

Hoop-It-Up (1989)

3-on-3 Street Basketball Tournament
4006 Beltline Road. Suite 230
Dallas, TX 75244
214/991-1110
FAX: 214/991-1135

Tournament play for teams of three starters and an alternate; players ages 10 and up are arranged in divisions according to age, height, and ability. Program operated in 50 U.S. and 13 European cities in 1993.

USA Basketball (1974)
5465 Mark Dabling Boulevard
Colorado Springs, CO 80918-3842
Warren S. Brown, Executive Director
719/590-4800

Does not sponsor youth league play; high school seniors, college students, and professional athletes may play on national teams. National governing body for basketball in the U.S.

Youth Basketball of America, Inc. (1989)
P.O. Box 3067
Orlando, FL 32802
Don Ruedlinger, President
407/363-YBOA (363-9262)
FAX: 407/363-0599

Basketball leagues and tournaments for children and teens that stress court safety and enjoyment of the game. Offers training courses for coaches and referees; content includes modification of rules to make the game safer and more fun for young players; offers referee training for youth ages 14–15.

BMX Bicycling

American Bicycle Association (1977)
P.O. Box 718
Chandler, AZ 85244
Clayton John, President
602/961-1903
FAX: 602/961-1842

Promotes the sport of BMX bicycle racing; sanctions local and national competitions; organized as a for-profit corporation.

National Bicycle League (1975)
211 Bradenton Avenue, Suite 100
P.O. Box 729
Dublin, OH 43017
Bob Tedesco, Chief Executive Officer
614/766-1625
FAX: 614/766-5302

Promotes the sport of bicycle motocross racing throughout the U.S. and Canada, for boys and girls as young as age 3, to adults age 60; sanctions and supervises age-graded races at local, state, and national levels. Affiliated with the International Bicycle Motocross Federation active in 24 countries, and the United States Cycling Federation.

Bowling

Young American Bowling Alliance (1946)
5301 S. 76th Street
Greendale, WI 53129
Joseph A. Wilson, Executive Director
414/421-4700

Bowling program for young people up to age 21. Pee Wee Division for beginners; Youth Division (to age 21); and Collegiate Division for young men and women who are enrolled in an institution of higher learning. Upper age limit waived for mentally disabled bowlers.

Boxing

Knights Boxing Team— International (1976)
2350 Ventura Road, S.E.
Smyrna, GA 30080-1327
Don Wade, Executive Director
404/432-3632

A nonprofit youth charity with the primary goal of providing young people with an alternative to drugs through amateur boxing. Emphasis is placed on clean living, health, and conditioning. Team membership is open to all youth ages 12 and over; operates Knights Training Camp; affiliated with USA Boxing.

National Golden Gloves Association of America, Inc. (1964)

8801 Princess Jeanne, N.E.
Albuquerque, NM 87112
Stan Gallup, Executive Director
505/298-8042

Through 32 franchises throughout the U.S., organizes tournaments for amateur boxers ages 8–30, grouped according to weight, age, and experience. Youths ages 16 and over with 20 prior fights may compete as open boxers, grouped according to weight class only.

USA Boxing (1980)

United States Amateur Boxing, Inc.
One Olympic Plaza
Colorado Springs, CO 80909
Bruce Mathis, Interim Executive Director
719/578-4506
FAX: 719/632-3426

Sponsors age-specific tournaments for youth ages 8–15 that begin at the local level. Youths ages 10–15 move through regional and national levels of competition; culminates in Junior Olympics. Separate program for youth ages 16 and over. Prior to 1980, USA Boxing was known as the Amateur Athletic Union Men's Senior Boxing Committee, with roots going back to 1888.

Canoeing

American Canoe Association

7432 Alban Station Boulevard, Suite B-226
Springfield, VA 22150
Jeffrey Yeager, Executive Director
703/451-0141
FAX: 703/451-2245

Provides canoeing and kayaking programs and instruction for people of all ages.

Cycling

League of American Wheelmen (1880)

190 W. Ostend Street, Suite 120
Baltimore, MD 21230
Gilbert Clark, Executive Director
410/539-3399
FAX: 410-539-3496

Promotes safe bicycling as a form of recreation and as transportation. Government Relations Division works at federal, state, and local levels to promote safe cycling policies and legislation.

U.S. Junior National Cycling Program

U.S. Cycling Federation (1920)
One Olympic Plaza
Colorado Springs, CO 80909
Susie Barton, Coordinator of Athlete and Coaching Programs
719/578-4845
FAX: 719/578-4764

The national governing body for cycling for the U.S. Olympic Committee; offers age-graded programs and races for junior cyclists ages 10–18. Organized at the local club level, young people can learn the fine points of competitive cycling from specially trained coaches, at local and regional clinics. Races start at the local club levels and progress through national and international competitions.

Drag Racing

National Hot Rod Association (1951)

2035 Financial Way
Glendora, CA 91741-4602
Dallas Gardner, President
818/914-4761
FAX: 818/914-8963

NHRA promotes interest in construction and racing of modified and specially-built automobiles, trucks, and motorcycles. NHRA Youth and Education Services develop and promote Career Opportunities Fairs and Youth Achievement Programs for elementary, secondary, and community college students at selected race sites; production of classroom supplementary curriculum materials in progress. NHRA Jr. Drag Racing League is a membership organization for youth ages 8–17 who build and race half-scale dragsters powered by 5 hp engines. A Jr. Dragster publication is available to league members.

Equestrian Sports

American Horse Shows Association (1917)

220 E. 42nd Street, Suite 409
New York, NY 10017-5876
Bonnie B. Jenkins, Executive Director
212/972-2472
FAX: 212/983-7286

Governing body for equestrian sports in the U.S.; sponsors junior and adult competitions.

Pony of the Americas Club, Inc. (1954)

5240 Elmwood Avenue
Indianapolis, IN 46203
Clyde Goff, Executive Secretary
317/788-0107

Forty member clubs conduct 300 horse shows annually. There are also state, regional, and international shows; annual world show rotates between the east and west coasts. Educational foundation provides schools at all levels with information and materials relating to the breed; organization encourages breeders to donate ponies to facilities serving persons with disabilities.

United States Pony Clubs, Inc. (1954)

The Kentucky Horse Park
4071 Iron Works Pike
Lexington, KY 40511
Michael C. Kromer, Executive Director
606/254-7669
FAX: 606/233-4652

Seeks to develop in youth the characteristics of responsibility, moral judgment, leadership, and self-confidence through education in equestrian activities. Competitions for members up to age 21, based on Standards of Proficiency; offers exchange program with members of Pony Clubs overseas.

U.S. Dressage Federation, Inc. (1973)

P.O. Box 80668
Lincoln, NE 68501
402/434-8550
FAX: 402/434-8545

Junior Young Rider program for youths under age 16; Advanced Young Rider Programs for youths ages 16–21 who ride at 4th level or above.

Fencing

U.S. Fencing Association (1891)

One Olympic Plaza
Colorado Springs, CO 80909
Carla-Mae Richards, Executive Director
719/578-4511
FAX: 719/632-5737

Three levels of youth participation include: Youth (ages 15 and under), Cadet (under 17), and Junior (under 20). Governing body for sport of fencing in the U.S. Selects U.S. team for international competitions.

Field Hockey

U.S.A. Youth Field Hockey
U.S.A. Field Hockey Association

One Olympic Plaza
Colorado Springs, CO 80909-5773
Tammy Neel
U.S.A. Youth Hockey Director
719/578-4567
FAX: 719/632-0979

Seeks to introduce and promote the sport of field hockey among youth ages 5–13. Youth Field Hockey Program offers safe, fun activity that can be introduced inexpensively through schools, parks and recreation groups, and other youth organizations. Game may be adapted for play indoors or outdoors. The U.S.A. Field Hockey Association is the U.S. Olympic governing body.

Football

Pop Warner Football (1929)

920 Town Center Drive, Suite I-25
Langhorne, PA 19047-1748
Jon Butler, Executive Director
215/752-2691
FAX: 215/752-2879

Tackle and flag football, and cheerleading leagues open to youth ages 5–16. Teams organized in eight levels of play according to age/weight criteria. Levels include Mitey-Mite, Junior Peewee, Peewee, Junior Midget, Midget, Senior Midget, Junior Bantam, and Bantam. Organization promotes scholarship through academic team ranking and individual scholar awards for participants. Tackle programs may participate in regional and national championships.

NFL Punt, Pass & Kick Program
National Football League Properties
410 Park Avenue
New York, NY 10022
212/838-0660
FAX: 212/750-2432

Competitive events based on distance and accuracy for boys and girls ages 8–15. Program runs from August to February annually, beginning with local competitions. Team championships take place during half-times at NFL games; final competition is held at the Pro-Ball game in Hawaii each February.

Golf

American Junior Golf Association (1977)
2415 Steeplechase Lane
Roswell, GA 30076
Stephen A. Hamblin, Executive Director
404/998-4653

Dedicated to the development of young men and women ages 18 and under through competitive junior golf.

Gymnastics

USA Gymnastics (1963)
Pan American Plaza, Suite 300
201 S. Capitol Avenue
Indianapolis, IN 46225
Mike Jacki, President
317/237-5050
FAX: 317/237-5069

U.S. governing body for the sport of gymnastics; operates competitive program at five levels, based on proficiency in the sport. Selects U.S. national team for international competitions. Also promotes sport among recreational gymnasts not engaged in competition.

Handball

U.S. Team Handball Federation (1957)
1750 E. Boulder Street
Colorado Springs, CO 80909-5768
Mike Cavanaugh, Executive Director
719/578-4582
FAX: 719/475-1240

Competitive program; most participants are in junior and senior high school; As U.S. governing body for the sport, forms Senior and Junior National Teams (men and women) that represent the U.S. in international competition. Youth Program is also used across the U.S. by Boys and Girls Clubs of America, Police Athletic Leagues, and the Catholic Youth Organization.

Ice Hockey

American Hearing Impaired Hockey Association (1973)
1143 W. Lake Street
Chicago, IL 60607
Stan Mikita, President
312/829-2250
FAX: 312/829-2098

Promotes sport of amateur hockey among hearing-impaired young men ages 6–26; conducts annual hockey school.

American Sledge Hockey Association (1989)

Sister Kenny Institute
800 E. 28th Street
Minneapolis, MN 55407
John Schatzlein, President
612/863-4184
612/881-2129
FAX: 612/863-2591

Open to individuals with impaired physical mobility, sledge hockey is played on sleds mounted on skate blades and propelled across the ice with hockey sticks; game is played with a regular puck and requires full gear. Rules allow able-bodied players to fill up to three slots on a team, seated on sleds. Game has been adopted by adaptive physical education programs for boys and girls, ages 12–18 in schools and parks and recreation programs; mixed teams are formed on the basis of ability.

USA Hockey, Inc. (1937)

4965 N. 30th Street
Colorado Springs, CO 80919-4102
Dave Ogrean, Executive Director
719/599-5500
FAX: 719/599-5994

National governing body for the sport of ice hockey; selects U.S. national team for international competitions. Youth programs seek to promote and expand involvement in amateur ice hockey. Teams for boys organized at six levels: ages 8 or under, 10 or under, 12 or under, 14 or under, 17 or under, and 19 or under. Program for girls has five levels of play: Novice, High School/Prep, 12 or under, 15 or under, and 19 or under.

Ice Skating

Amateur Speedskating Union of the United States (1927)

1033 Shady Lane
Glen Ellyn, IL 60137
Shirley Yates, Executive Secretary
708/790-3230

For individuals ages 6 and up who are interested in speed skating.

Ice Skating Institute of America (1960)

355 W. Dundee Road
Buffalo Grove, IL 60089-3500
Justine Townsend Smith
CAE, Executive Director
708/808-7528
FAX: 708/808-8329

ISIA, an international organization of ice rink operators, managers, coaches, industry builders and suppliers, and ice skaters, is dedicated to providing quality ice skating programs for the community and the recreational skater. ISIA promotes recreational ice skating among people of all ages and ability levels; ISIA offers group figure skating and hockey/goalie "Learn to Skate" programs to both community and privately-owned ice rinks; conducts figure skating and hockey/goalie proficiency tests; hosts educational seminars; and, sponsors two national championship competitions annually (winter and summer) for member of all ages and ability levels.

United States Figure Skating Association (1921)

20 First Street
Colorado Springs, CO 80906
Jerry Lace, Executive Director
719/635-5200
FAX: 719/635-9548

The national governing body for the sport of figure skating; selects U.S. teams for international competition. Supervises graded competitive events, based on proficiency, at regional, sectional, and national levels. Member clubs are eligible to hold amateur figure skating carnivals in the U.S. The USFSA also provides a beginning/recreational curriculum to skating rinks, instructors, and parks and recreation departments. The program, Skate with U.S., introduces the fundamentals of the sport to people of all ages.

U.S. International Speedskating Association (1966)

P.O. Box 16157
Rocky River, OH 44116
216/899-0128
FAX: 216/899-0109

Governing body for the sport of speedskating in the U.S.

Judo

United States Judo Federation (1952)

1535 E. Tudor Road
Anchorage, AK 99507
Bob Brink, President
907/563-2114

Graded program for boys and girls ages 4 and over.

United States Judo, Inc. (1979)

P.O. Box 10013
El Paso, TX 79991
Frank Fullerton, President
915/565-8754
FAX: 915/566-1668

Governing body for amateur judo in the U.S. Supervises competitive events for boys and girls ages 6–20, as well as adults. Affiliated with the International Judo Federation and the U.S. Olympic Committee.

Karate

USA Karate Federation All American Youth

The USA Karate Federation
1300 Kenmore Boulevard
Akron, OH 44314
George Anderson, President
Jeff Ellis, Director, Junior Programs
216/753-3114
FAX: 216/753-6967

Member U.S. Olympic Committee. Organizes graded competitive program for youth in elementary through high school.

Luge

U.S. Luge Association (1979)

P.O. Box 651
Lake Placid, NY 12946
Fred Zimny, Manager of Recruitment and Development
518/523-2071
FAX: 518/523-4106

Junior program for youth ages 12–17; competitive program for selecting national junior team. Conducts NYNEX Junior

Luge Series, a multi-city summer and fall wheeled sled program to introduce the sport of luge to interested youth (boys and girls).

Orienteering

U.S. Orienteering Federation
P.O. Box 1444
Forest Park, GA 30051
404/363-2110

Orienteering is an outdoor sport using map and compass to move from point to point to a destination. The Federation offers programs at all skill levels and encourages family participation. Many camps and organizations include orienteering among their outdoor activities. Youngest children can progress through the four levels of the Little Troll program from following string courses (not requiring a compass) to courses of 2–3 kilometers. Competitive events are arranged according to skill level; courses progress in the difficulty of navigational skills and physical endurance required. ROGAINE (Rugged Outdoor Group Activity Involving Navigation and Endurance) is a new variant of the sport that takes place over large areas and usually lasts for 12 or 24 hours.

Pentathlon

U.S. Modern Pentathlon Association (1912)
530 McCullough, Suite 1010
San Antonio, TX 78215
210/246-3000
FAX: 210/246-2646

Junior development program for youths ages 8–17.

Riflery

National Rifle Association of America Junior Clubs (1926)
1600 Rhode Island Avenue, N.W.
Washington, DC 20036
Rosemary Herr
Youth Development Programs
202/828-6021
FAX: 202/223-2691

In addition to the Junior Club program, NRA has the Eddie Eagle™ Gun Safety Program that teaches a four-part safety message to very young children: Stop, Don't Touch, Leave the Area, Tell an Adult. Self-paced qualification courses (with awards) are available for older youth interested in developing marksmanship skills in rifle, pistol, shotgun, pellet, or BB gun. NRA Junior Olympic Shooting Camps provide training in the Olympic shooting disciplines at beginner, intermediate, or advanced skill levels. NRA also publishes materials (many at no charge) on safety, hunting, and conservation.

Rodeo

National High School Rodeo Association (1949)
11178 N. Huron, Suite 7
Denver, CO 80234
303/452-0820
FAX: 303/452-0912
Membership Hotline: 800/46-NHSRA
(800/466-4772)

Aims to develop sportsmanship, horsemanship, and character in youth; promotes rodeo on a national scale for youth under 20 in grades 9–12. Participants must also meet academic and conduct standards set by the association.

National Little Britches Rodeo Association (1952)

1045 W. Rio Grande
Colorado Springs, CO 80906
Jim Chamley, General Manager
719/389-0333
FAX: 719/578-1367

Promotes good character, sportsmanship, and citizenship through the sport of rodeo; sponsors competitive events for youth ages 8–18. Awards college scholarships.

Women's Professional Rodeo Association (1948)

Route 5, Box 698
Blanchard, OK 73010
Lydia Moore, Secretary-Treasurer
405/485-2277
FAX: 405/485-3177

A service organization for women in barrel racing. Not a youth organization, but about ten percent of the membership is between the ages of 14 and 18.

Roller Skating

United States Amateur Confederation of Roller Skating (1973)

4730 South Street
P.O. Box 6579
Lincoln, NE 68506
Kirk Spellman
Public Information Director
402/483-7551
FAX: 402/483-1465

Governing body for the sport of roller skating in the U.S.; sponsors competitive events at state, regional, and national levels; selects U.S. teams to participate in international competitions. Additional programs include Roller Hockey, Artistic Roller Skating, and Roller Speed Skating.

Rope Jumping

National Double Dutch League (1975)

P.O. Box 776
Bronx, NY 10451
David Walker, Founder
212/865-9606

Has organized local leagues for thousands of rope jumpers. Sanctions local and regional events; sponsors annual national championships.

Rowing

Scholastic Rowing Association of America (1933)

P.O. Box 528
Berlin, NJ 08009
Matthew J. Ledwith, President
609/767-5656
FAX: 609/767-9230

Program for young men and women organized through high schools in the U.S. and Canada; holds annual Regatta on Memorial Day weekend.

USRowing (1872)

Pan American Plaza, Suite 400
201 S. Capitol Avenue
Indianapolis, IN 46225
317/237-5656
FAX: 317/237-5646

Most Juniors (ages 18 and under) row through a school- or club-sponsored program; USRowing is the U.S. governing body for the sport.

Skiing

U S Skiing (1904)
1500 Kearns Boulevard
P.O. Box 100
Park City, UT 84060
Mike Jacki, Chief Executive Officer
801/649-9090
FAX: 801/649-3613

The governing body for amateur skiing in the U.S.; sponsors competitions in Alpine, Jumping, Nordic Combined, Cross-country, Freestyle, Snow-boarding, etc. Selects U.S. national teams to participate in international competitions. Also sponsors events for recreational skiers. Administers Bill Koch Youth Ski League, a cross-country program for youth of all ages, and Alpine Youth Ski League. Sponsors Cross-country and Alpine programs for disabled skiers.

Soap Box Derby

International Soap Box Derby (1933)
Derby Downs
P.O. Box 7233
Akron, OH 44306
Jeff Iula, General Manager
216/733-8723
FAX:216/733-1370

A youth racing program for boys and girls with three divisions: Stock Car Division (ages 9–16) cars can be constructed in about six hours; Kit Car Division (ages 9–16) cars require more complex skills and may be constructed in about 40 hours; Masters Division (ages 11–16) cars are even more complex and require 100–200 hours to construct.

Soccer

American Youth Soccer Organization (1964)
5403 W. 138th Street
Hawthorne, CA 90250
Dick Wilson
National Executive Director
800/USA-AYSO (800/872-2976)
310/643-6455
FAX: 310/643-5310

Youth compete in seven divisions based on age: under 6, under 8, under 10, under 12, under 14, under 16, and under 19.

Soccer Association for Youth (1966)
4903 Vine Street, Suite 1
Cincinnati, OH 45217
Rene A. Durand, Jr.
Executive Vice-President
800/233-7291
513/351-7291
FAX: 513/242-1178

Organizes and supervises the play of youth soccer under specialized rules and regulations, including that team membership be determined in a random manner, without specific considerations of a player's ability. Youth compete at seven levels: Pre-school (ages 4–5), Passers (ages 6–7), Wings (ages 8–9), Strikers (ages 10–11), Kickers (ages 12–13),

Minors (ages 14–15), and Seniors (ages 16–18). More than 75,000 players are organized in 14 states.

United States Youth Soccer Association (1974)

2050 N. Plano Road, Suite 100
Richardson, TX 75082
Dr. Robert Contiguglia, Chairman
800/4-SOCCER (800/476-2237)
214/235-4499
FAX: 214/235-4480

U.S. Youth Soccer is the Youth Division of the United States Soccer Federation, the governing body for soccer in the United States. Annually, more than 1.9 million young players are organized and compete through 55 member state associations. U.S. Youth Soccer provides rules and guidelines and other program supports; holds an annual exhibit show and workshop for administrators and coaches.

U.S.A. CUP (1985)

1700 105th Avenue, N.E.
Blaine, MN 55449
Teri Rolfes, Communications Director
800/535-4730
612/785-5656
FAX: 612/785-5699

An international soccer tournament for teams of youth ages 12–19 held annually in July. 650 teams from across the U.S. and 17 other countries competed in 1993. Program stresses making worldwide friendships based on a common interest in soccer. Independently incorporated.

Surfing

National Scholastic Surfing Association (1978)

P.O. Box 495
Huntington Beach, CA 92648
Janice Aragon, Executive Director
714/536-0445
FAX: 714/960-4380

Promotes the sport of surfing among students in elementary school through college; organizes competitive events. Stresses "scholar-surfer" as an ideal; recognizes students with high GPAs.

Swimming/Diving

United States Diving, Inc.

Pan American Plaza, Suite 430
201 S. Capitol Avenue
Indianapolis, IN 46225
317/237-5252
FAX: 317/237-5257

Sponsors competitive diving program for youth ages 5–18; youths register through one of 42 affiliated associations.

United States Swimming, Inc. (1980)

One Olympic Plaza
Colorado Springs, CO 80909
Ray B. Essick, Executive Director
719/578-4578
FAX: 719/575-9606

National governing body for competitive swimming in the U.S.; selects U.S. national teams for international competitions. Conducts programs for people ages 5 and up; sanctions local, state, regional, national, and international competitions.

U.S. Synchronized Swimming, Inc.

Pan American Plaza, Suite 510
201 S. Capitol Avenue
Indianapolis, IN 46225
Betty Watanabe, Executive Director
317/237-5700
FAX: 317/237-5705

Most young people interested in the sport belong to an affiliated club in their local areas; national organization conducts age-graded competitive program for youth ages 10 and up. National governing body for synchronized swimming in the U.S.

Table Tennis

U.S. Table Tennis Association

One Olympic Plaza
Colorado Springs, CO 80909
Linda Gleeson
Operations Administrator
719/578-4583
FAX: 719/632-6071

Youth program is used in schools and Boys and Girls Clubs of America around the U.S.; Association runs graded competitive program leading to the Junior Olympics.

Taekwondo

United States Taekwondo Union (1981)

One Olympic Plaza
Colorado Springs, CO 80909
Robert Fujimura, Executive Director
719/578-4632
FAX: 719/578-4642

Graded program for children as young as 2; junior competitive events involve youth ages 6–16, and culminate in U.S. Taekwondo Junior Olympics. Conducts junior training camps. Is governing body for the sport in the U.S.; affiliated with the World Taekwondo Federation. Taekwondo, introduced in the U.S. in the 1950s, was admitted to the Amateur Athletic Union in 1974.

Tennis

National Junior Tennis League (1969)

United States Tennis Association
70 W. Red Oak Lane
White Plains, NY 10604-3602
Dave Abrams
Recreational Tennis Coordinator
914/676-7000
FAX: 914/696-7167

Recreational team tennis for youths under age 18; program based on participation, skills development, and low-key team matches. Teams are composed of young people of similar ability. A program of the United States Tennis Association, Inc.

United States Tennis Association, Inc. (1881)

70 W. Red Oak Lane
White Plains, NY 10604
M. Marshall Happer
Executive Director and COO
914/696-7000
FAX: 914/696-7167

The national governing body for the sport of tennis in the U.S., USTA promotes amateur tennis, sets and maintains rules of play, and sanctions and conducts tournaments. It runs programs for juniors and seniors, circuits for amateurs and professionals, and amateur and professional international competitions for men and women of all ages. Conducts national championships for juniors at age levels 14, 16, and 18.

Track and Field

U.S.A. Track & Field (1979)

One Hoosier Dome, Suite 140
Indianapolis, IN 46225
Ollan Cassell, Executive Director
Martin E. Weiss
Junior Olympics Administrator
317/261-0500
FAX: 317/261-0481

The national governing body for track and field, long-distance running, and race walking. Selects U.S. national teams for international competitions. Conducts programs for boys and girls in five age divisions: 10 and under, 11–12, 13–14, 15–16, and 17–18. USATF Junior Olympics is a nationwide series of some 350 competitions progressing from Preliminary Meets to Association Championships, Regional Championships, and a National Championship; USATF Youth Athletics represents attainment of qualifying standards for entry into a National Championship.

Twirling/Cheerleading

International Cheerleading Foundation (1964)

10660 Barkley
Shawnee Mission, KS 66212
Randolph L. Neil, President
913/649-3666
FAX: 913/341-6031

National Baton Twirling Association, International (1945)

P.O. Box 266
Janesville, WI 53545
Don Sartell, President
608/754-2238
FAX: 608/754-1986

The original national and international baton twirling organization, NBTA International is dedicated to the advancement of baton twirling as a wholesome, worthwhile, and beneficial youth activity.

National Cheerleaders Association (1948)

P.O. Box 660359
Dallas, TX 75266-0359
800/527-4422

Conducts camps and competitive events for youth ages 7–15, in cheerleading, drill, and pom-pom throughout the U.S. Has some high school and college-level programs.

United States Twirling Association, Inc. (1958)

P.O. Box 24488
Seattle, WA 98124
Kathy Forsythe, Executive Director
206/623-5623
FAX: 206/623-2847

Promotes baton twirling as both a recreational and competitive sport in the U.S. and internationally; members are twirlers, coaches, and judges; organization sanctions competitive events for members, and certification seminars for coaches and judges.

See also:

Pop Warner Football, pages 37–38.

Volkssport

American Volkssport Association (1976)

Phoenix Square, Suite 101
1001 Pat Booker Road
Universal City, TX 78148
David Stewart, Executive Director
210/659-2112
FAX: 210/659-1212

The governing body for regional, state, and local Volkssport Clubs; groups sponsor noncompetitive sports events including walking, bicycling, swimming, and cross-country skiing. Not primarily a youth organization, but youth are encouraged to join; those under age 12 must be accompanied by an adult.

Volleyball

U.S.A. Youth Volleyball Program

U.S.A. Junior Olympic Volleyball
United States Volleyball Association
(1928)
3595 E. Fountain Boulevard
Colorado Springs, CO 80910-1740
John Carroll, Executive Director
719/637-8300
FAX: 719/597-6307

The USVBA is the national governing body for the sport of volleyball in the U.S.; in response to increased interest following the success of the U.S. team in the 1984 and 1988 Olympic Games, youth programs were developed. Youth Volleyball has three divisions: Setters (ages 7–8), Diggers (ages 9–10), and Spikers (ages 10–12). Junior Olympic volleyball has eight divisions: Boys (18 and under, 16 and under, 14 and under, 12 and under), and Girls (18 and under, 16 and under, 14 and under, 12 and under).

Weightlifting

U.S. Weightlifting Federation (1971)

One Olympic Plaza
Colorado Springs, CO 80909
George Greenway, Executive Director
719/578-4508
FAX: 719/578-4741

The national governing body for the sport of weightlifting in the U.S. Sanctions meets for members throughout the country. Provides support for the National Junior, Senior, and Women's Teams that compete nationally and internationally.

Wrestling

U.S.A. Wrestling (1982)

6155 Lehman Drive
Colorado Springs, CO 80918
Mark Scott, Director of State Services
719/598-8181
FAX: 719/598-9440

Offers U.S.A. Wrestling Kids Division for youth ages 14 and under, Cadet (ages 15–16), Junior (high school), Espoir (ages 17–20), and Senior Division (19 and up). Kids compete up to regional level; other divisions have competitions up to the national level. Athletes who represent the U.S. in international competitions are selected for national teams from the four older divisions. Sponsors camps and clinics throughout the U.S.

Sports Programs for Youth With Disabilities

U.S. Olympic Committee

Disabled Sports Services
One Olympic Plaza
Colorado Springs, CO 80909
Jan Wilson
Coordinator for Disabled Sports
719/578-4818
FAX: 719/632-5852

The U.S. Olympic Committee's Disabled Sports Services office serves as a clearinghouse of information on sports programs for persons with disabilities. The following six organizations are sanctioned by the USOC. A seventh organization, The American Athletic Association for the Deaf, does not currently sponsor activities for youth.

These groups serve as governing bodies for the selection of U.S. teams for international competitions. The Paralympic Games for disabled athletes were first conducted in connection with the Olympic Games of 1960 in Rome. With each succeeding Olympiad, the number of nations participating in the Paralympics has grown.

Dwarf Athletic Association of America (1985)

418 Willow Way
Lewisville, TX 75067
Janet Brown, Executive Director
214/317-8299
FAX: same

Conducts futures program for children ages 4–7; Junior competitions for youths ages 7–15; and open division for those age 16 and above. Chooses U.S. teams for World Dwarf Games for individuals 4'10" or shorter in which athletes from 165 countries participate. Affiliated with Little People of America.

National Handicapped Sports

451 Hungerford Drive, Suite 100
Rockville, MC 20850
Kirk Bauer, Executive Director
301/217-0960
FAX: 301/217-0968

Sports include winter skiing; sitting/standing swimming; volleyball; power lifting; table tennis, etc. Conducts annual Learn to Ski and Learn to Race Clinics in which youths may take part. Local chapters have additional youth opportunities. Is the sanctioning body for the U.S. Disabled Ski Team.

National Wheelchair Athletic Association

3595 E. Fountain Boulevard, Suite L-1
Colorado Springs, CO 80910
Patricia I. Long, Operations Manager
719/574-1150
FAX: 719/574-9840

Junior programs for athletes ages 16 and over. Sports include swimming; track and field, archery, weight-lifting, table tennis, and basketball. Local chapters may have additional programs.

Special Olympics International (1968)

1350 New York Avenue, N.W., Suite 500
Washington, DC 20005
Sargent Shriver, Chairman
Eunice Kennedy Shriver, Founder
202/628-3630
FAX: 202/737-1937

Sponsored by the Joseph P. Kennedy, Jr. Foundation, Special Olympics offers a year-round worldwide program of training and competition in 22 sports for persons with mental retardation ages 8 and over. The program culminates in quadrennial International Summer and Winter Special Olympic Games.

United Cerebral Palsy Athletic Association

500 South Ervay, Suite 452-B
Dallas, TX 75201
Mike King, Executive Director
214/761-0033
FAX: 214/761-0035

Arranges youth competitions at national events; programs include track and field, swimming. Will make referrals to local programs.

U.S. Association for Blind Athletes

33 N. Institute Street
Colorado Springs, CO 80903
Charlie Huebner, Executive Director
Mark Lucas
Assistant Executive Director
719/630-0422
FAX: 719/630-0616

Sports include swimming, Alpine/Nordic skiing, track and field, goal ball, power lifting, tandem cycling, wrestling, and judo. Training programs available for youth range from developmental through elite. Will make referrals to local groups.

See also:

American Sledge Hockey Association, page 39; **American Hearing Impaired Hockey Association**, page 38; **Little League Baseball**, page 32; **Pony of the Americas, Inc.**, page 119.

Resources

See:

American Camping Association, page 141; **American Coaching Effectiveness Program**, pages 141–142; **Melpomene Institute for Women's Health Research**, page 151; **North American Youth Sports Institute**, page 158.

Civic Education and Political Organizations

Partisan

These associations are related to specific political parties or philosophies. Program content is directed toward the understanding and promotion of a partisan viewpoint.

Note: Many of the organizations in the Peace and Global Understanding Groups (pages 55–62) and Ethnic Heritage Groups (pages 106–114) sections also have strong political agendas.

FRONTLASH (1968)

815 16th Street, N.W.
Washington, DC 20006
Cheryl Graeve, Executive Director
202/783-3993
FAX: 202/783-3591

An organization of college students and young workers that seeks to educate youth in the principles of the labor movement and unite their energies in support of social progress. FRONTLASH is a support group of the AFL-CIO; chapters work closely with state and local union leaders. Education efforts direct particular attention to issues that affect youth, such as the sub-minimum wage, child labor laws, cuts in education funding, and importance of buying American products. The organization encourages active participation in the political process.

Lead...or Leave (1992)

1100 Connecticut Avenue, N.W.
Suite 1300
Washington, DC 20036
Nick Nyhan, Deputy Director
202/857-0808
FAX:202/457-1453

A national pressure campaign the organizes young people to hold Washington responsible for cutting the $300 billion federal deficit in half by 1996 and eliminating it entirely by the year 2000. Works with youth groups around the country using grass-roots activities such as demonstrations, teach-ins, Congressional town-meetings, and concerts to cultivate a political voice for a new generation of voters.

National Teen Age Republican Headquarters (1965)

10620 C Crestwood Drive
P.O. Box 1896
Manassas, VA 22110
Barbara Wells, National Director
703/368-4214
FAX: 703/368-0830

Educates teens in principles of free enterprise, constitutional government, and patriotism; offers training in the techniques of precinct organization to help elect Republican candidates for office; holds annual Leadership Conference in Washington, DC. Sub-teen Age Republicans (STARS) groups for youth ages 9–12 exist in some regions.

National Traditionalist Caucus (1970)

P.O. Box 971, G.P.O.
New York, NY 10016
Don Rosenberg, National Chairman
212/685-4689
FAX: 212/689-4012

A program for junior and senior high and college students that stresses patriotism, conservative values, anti-Communism, and pro-free enterprise. The Reach for the Stars program awards young Hollywood entertainers who promote positive role model images. Publishes *Excalibur* (quarterly).

Spartacus Youth League (1971)

c/o Spartacus Youth Publications
P.O. Box 3118
New York, NY 10007
Alison Spencer, Secretary
212/732-7860

Committed to building a revolutionary Socialist movement of working-class youth. The youth group of the Spartacus League/U.S. Spartacus Youth Clubs are sponsored by local branches of the Spartacist League, and are for young men and women ages 15–30.

Young Communist League of the United States of America

235 W. 23rd Street, 6th Floor
New York, NY 10011
John Bachtell, National Coordinator
212/741-2016
FAX: 212-645-5436

A multi-racial organization that provides high school and college students ages 14 and older, both young workers and unemployed, with opportunities to learn about socialism and why capitalism cannot solve the problems of unemployment, racism, war, hunger, homelessness, lack of educational opportunities, and the many other ills young people face; fights for a socialist alternative in the U.S. Seeks to unite young people in the struggle for social equality, the well-being of working people, an end to the international arms race, and the preservation of the world's endangered ecological system.

Young Democrats of America (1932)

c/o Democratic National Committee
430 S. Capitol Street, S.E.
Washington, DC 20003
Leigh Pate, YDA Liaison
202/863-8000
FAX: 202/863-8012

Seeks to foster the aims of the Democratic Party among young men and women ages 35 and under.

Young Republican National Federation (1931)

310 First Street, S.E.
Washington, DC 20003
Irv Bisnov, National Chairman
202/662-1340
FAX: 202/393-2640

Seeks to further the aims of the Republican Party among young men and women ages 18–40. Holds an annual Spring Leadership Conference in Washington, DC.

Young Socialist Alliance (1912)

214 Avenue A
New York, NY 10009
National Secretary
212/388-9346

A national revolutionary socialist youth organization of workers and students who fight in the interests of working people and the oppressed worldwide. Organization remains a part of the worldwide fight for socialism.

Youth Section of the Democratic Socialists of America (1982)

15 Dutch Street, Suite 500
New York, NY 10038
Ginny Coughlin, Youth Organizer
212/962-0390
FAX: 212/227-4205

An organization of students and youth to age 31. Works to protect and expand the rights of workers, women, minorities, and all people; to encourage democratic social planning; and to achieve a more equitable distribution of the nation's wealth.

Nonpartisan

American Student Council Association (1987)

National Association of Elementary School Principals
1615 Duke Street
Alexandria, VA 22314-3483
Margaret Evans
Director of Student Services
703/684-3345
FAX: 703/548-6021

Promotes participative government by helping elementary and middle schools establish and maintain effective student councils that can help create a better school environment and, at the same time, help students achieve goals and learn skills that will last a lifetime. Young people write their own constitutions, nominate candidates, and elect their own leaders. Publishes handbooks on starting a student council, a newsletter, and other supporting materials for students, advisors, and schools.

Boys State
Boys Nation (1935)

American Legion
Contact State Legion Headquarters

A model government program for high school juniors, chosen through their schools, to acquaint youth with political processes and the way American government functions from the local up to the state level. Boys State programs are sponsored by each state department of the American Legion, and inquiry should be made there. Two representatives from each state program are chosen to attend Boys Nation, held annually in Washington, DC.

Girls State (1938)
Girls Nation (1947)

American Legion Auxiliary
Contact State Legion Auxiliary Headquarters

A youth citizenship training program to provide practical experience in the processes of governments. While participants are high school juniors recommended by their schools, final selection is made by the local American Legion Auxiliary Unit. Girls State programs are sponsored by each state Auxiliary, and inquiry should be made through the state headquarters.

Two representatives from each state program are chosen to attend Girls Nation.

Junior Statesmen of America (1934)

Junior Statesmen Foundation
650 Bair Island Road, Suite 201
Redwood City, CA 94063
Richard Prosser, Executive Director
800/334-5353
415/366-2700
FAX: 415/366-5067

An organization of high school students committed to preparing young leaders for active participation in democratic self-government. Through school-based chapters, regional conferences, and academic summer programs, this student-run organization helps young people develop the knowledge and skills necessary for active participation in public affairs. Also known as The Junior State.

NAACP Youth and College Division (1936)

4805 Mount Hope Drive
Baltimore, MD 21215-3297
Yvonne L. Finnie
Director, Youth and College Division
410/358-8900, Ext. 9134
FAX: 410/764-7357

The Youth and College Division of the NAACP—National Association for the Advancement of Colored People (1909)—consists of over 50,000 youth members nationwide. It has approximately 600 youth councils, college chapters, and young adult councils that work to motivate and train youth for leadership, provide understanding of issues pertinent to social conditions, and develop organizational skills for community related activities.

National Association of Student Councils (1931)

National Association of Secondary
School Principals
1904 Association Drive
Reston, VA 22091
Dale D. Hawley
Director, Division of Student Activities
703/860-0200
FAX: 703/476-5432

A federation of student councils in secondary and middle level schools. Promotes student government, provides direction for student activities, and fosters the improvement of student-teacher relationships.

YMCA Teen Leadership Programs (1936)

YMCA of the USA Program Services
101 N. Wacker Drive
Chicago, IL 60606
Don Kyzer, Associate Director, Program Services Division
800/USA-YMCA (800/872-9622)
312/269-1140
FAX: 312/977-9063

Youth and Government is a program for high school men and women stressing that democracy must be learned by each generation. Youth participate in model state legislatures and the annual Youth Governors Conference held in Washington, DC each summer. The top debaters from each state may participate in the annual Youth Conference on National Affairs. Also sponsors Model United Nations, Black/Minority Achievers, Counselor-In-Training programs, and YMCA Earth Service Corps.

Resources

The Center for Democracy and Citizenship

Humphrey Institute
301 19th Avenue S.
Minneapolis, MN 55455
Harry C. Boyte, Director
612/625-0142
FAX: 612/625-6351

The Center for Democracy and Citizenship, based at the University of Minnesota's Humphrey Institute, is dedicated to the study and advancement of democracy in the United States and abroad, and to the study and advancement of citizenship and civic education—understood as education for effective, public-spirited action by citizens on public problems. In the Land Grant tradition, the Center undertakes projects in areas of research, teaching, and outreach through civic leadership training.

Public Achievement is the Center's civic education initiative for developing the capacity of young people to become effective players in our democracy. Working in existing youth organizations with trained coaches and institutional leaders in semester or year-long projects, young people address issues that directly affect their lives. In the process they learn that politics is found in the daily actions people take to solve problems around them and to make changes in their communities and their own lives—while discovering connections to larger issues and arenas.

Guides and other publications are available. Project Public Life also publishes a quarterly newsletter that explores, in depth, the concepts and lessons of the work. Contact the Center for information.

Close Up Foundation (1970)

44 Canal Center Plaza
Alexandria, VA 22314
800/336-5479
703/706-3300
FAX: 703/706-0000

A nonprofit, nonpartisan organization dedicated to the ideal that active, aware citizens are essential to a responsive government and a healthy community. Seeks to increase understanding of government operation and individual participation through becoming involved in the democratic process.

Programs include the Close Up Washington Program, a series of week-long programs which enable high school students and teachers to study the process of government in Washington, DC. Program for New Americans, a similar study visit complete with service-learning projects for recently immigrated students; The Citizen Bee, an educational program and competition; and the Civic Achievement Award Program for students in grades 5–8 (see page 140).

Close Up also produces educational programs for the C-SPAN cable network and publishes instructional materials for civic education classes.

Young America's Foundation

110 Elden Street
Herndon, VA 22070
Ron Robinson, President
703/318-9608
FAX: 703/318-9122

A service organization for politically conservative high school and college students. Provides free books and posters; gives assistance in bringing speakers to campuses; holds an annual essay contest; conducts nationwide lecture program and annual National Conservative Student Conference.

Peace and Global Understanding Groups

AFS International Intercultural Programs (1947)

220 E. 42nd Street, Third Floor
New York, NY 10017
Jennifer Froistad, Executive Director
800/AFS-INFO (800/237-4636)
212/949-4242
FAX: 212/949-9379

Promotes international exchange of high school students from over 40 countries; offers year-long, semester, and summer programs. Most students live with host families; some programs include group living based on a specific interest such as language or cultural study, outdoor activities, or environmental study. AFS is supported by a network of more than 5000 local chapters worldwide. Also offers programs for adults.

American Friends Service Committee Youth Programs

1501 Cherry Street
Philadelphia, PA 19102
Hilda Grauman, Coordinator
215/241-7295
FAX: 215/241-7275

AFSC offers summer work camps and service opportunities in Mexico and Cuba for young adults ages 18–26; must speak Spanish. Volunteers work in remote villages, improving and constructing schools and other community facilities and helping with agricultural projects. Work lasts about seven weeks in Mexico and three weeks in Cuba. Participants are responsible for all travel costs and a contribution of $700 (Mexico) or $300 (Cuba) that covers the cost of training, health and accident insurance, meals, and accommodations. Limited scholarship aid may be available. Annual application deadline is April 1.

Amigos de las Americas (1965)

5618 Star Lane
Houston, TX 77057
Celdie Sencion, Director of Recruiting
800/231-7796
713/782-5290
FAX: 713/782-9267

Amigos de las Americas is an international, nonprofit, private voluntary organization that provides leadership development opportunities for the young people of the U.S., improved community health for the people of Latin America, and a better cross-cultural understanding between people of both hemispheres.

Through AMIGOS, young volunteers experience unparalleled leadership training opportunities while serving in community health projects in Mexico, the Caribbean, and Central and South America. Living and working in remote villages and urban communities, the volunteers inoculate people against communicable diseases, vaccinate dogs against rabies, teach community sanitation, construct latrines, teach dental hygiene, and distribute toothbrushes. Since its beginning in 1965, more than 17,000 AMIGOS volunteers have performed more than 11 million health services in 14 Latin American countries.

Amnesty International Youth Program (1990)

Amnesty International
1118 22nd Street, N.W.
Washington, DC 20037
Janice Christensen, National Youth
Program Coordinator
202/775-5161
FAX: 202/775-5992

An academic-year youth/student human rights program organized through clubs in more than 1,700 high schools nationwide. Program consists of a variety of campaign activities from which groups may choose each year; the Urgent Action program for ongoing letter-writing activities (see page 57), and special summer youth education programs. Interested campus groups sign up through regional offices and begin receiving monthly mail. Participants receive *SAY* magazine (available to others by subscription). Interested individuals may contact the national office at the above address, or, for a more rapid response, should contact Amnesty International regional offices (in San Francisco, Atlanta, Chicago, Boston, or Washington, DC.).

Anti-Defamation League of B'nai B'rith (1913)

823 United Nations Plaza
New York, NY 10017
Catherine Tremko Friedberg
Director of Marketing and Sales,
A World of Difference Institute
212/490-2525
FAX: 212/867-0779

The Anti-Defamation League is dedicated to the ideal of democracy and the fight against bigotry and discrimination. It is involved in all areas of civil rights and intergroup relations, including legal briefs, research studies and investigations, conferences, colloquia and educational efforts with school systems, and community and youth organizations.

As part of its national prejudice awareness effort, the ADL A World of Difference Institute has developed a program specifically geared to youth groups. It contains activities that relate to the American democratic, pluralistic society and to the evils of prejudice. Special training on combatting and confronting prejudice is available to the leaders and staff of youth organizations as well as youth group members.

The ADL produces and distributes a wide variety of books, curricula, and audiovisual materials. A free catalog of human relations materials is available from the headquarters in New York or from any of the regional offices.

Children's Campaign for Nuclear Disarmament (1979)

14 Everit Street
New Haven, CT 06511
Naomi Bernstein, President

A completely youth-run organization dedicated to ending the arms race. Children and youths under the age of 18 may join as individuals or as groups. Provides materials giving suggestions for forming local chapters and information about what youth can do.

Children's Edition

Urgent Action Network (1987)
Literacy Edition/Urgent Actions
Amnesty International
P.O. Box 1270
Nederland, CO 80466-1270
Ellen Moore
Assistant Program Coordinator
303/440-0913
FAX: 303/258-7881

An ongoing letter-writing program for young people in grades 4–8. Groups are organized through Sunday schools, youth organizations, school classes, etc.; middle school and junior high school students may also join as individuals. Leaders receive a specially-written *Urgent Action Case Sheet* monthly (where possible, cases involve children or youth, or those who work on their behalf). Also available: *Literacy Edition*, a plainly-written case sheet concerning victims in danger of maltreatment by police or military, usually for their nonviolent union, community, or political work. Amnesty International provides supporting materials that supplement the case sheets.

Council on International Educational Exchange (1947)

205 E. 42nd Street
New York, NY 10017
Jack Egle, President Executive Director
212/661-1414
FAX: 212/972-3231

A nonprofit membership organization that develops and administers a wide variety of study, work, travel, and volunteer service programs for American and international students at the secondary, undergraduate, graduate, and professional levels. Publishes *Going Places: The High School Student's Guide to Study, Travel and Adventure Abroad*, which describes over 200 opportunities worldwide for youth ages 12–18. Also publishes *Work, Study, Travel Abroad: The Whole World Handbook*; *Smart Vacations: The Traveler's Guide to Learning Adventures Abroad*; and *Volunteer! The Comprehensive Guide to Voluntary Service in the U.S. and Abroad*. A new magazine, *Student Travels*, is published twice annually.

Through its subsidiary companies, Council Travel and Council Charter, and affiliated and cooperating organizations, the Council also provides a wide range of services to facilitate student and youth travel.

Creative Response (1992)

International Performing Arts
Exchanges
9502 Lee Highway
Fairfax, VA 22031
800/275-7231
703/385-4494 (DC area)
FAX: 703/273-6568

Programs for youth ages 14–19 designed to promote cross-cultural understanding through use of the performing arts. These 4–6 week exchanges take place during the summer either in the U.S. or abroad. Countries traditionally hosting such programs are Russia, Japan, Hungary, South Africa, Czechoslovakia, and more. During each program, participants (roughly 15 Americans and 15 international youths) work to write and perform their own original musical play focusing on issues of international peace and cooperation. Students with widely varying performance skills are encouraged to apply. Creative Response emphasizes the process by which each performance is derived, not the performance itself.

Applications are accepted until the Spring of each year; selection is based on references and a brief essay, not on performance skill.

City at Peace, a project of Creative Response, uses the performing arts as a tool to effect change in the lives of youth in the U.S. Designed to bring together teenagers of all racial and socioeconomic backgrounds, City at Peace is being used in schools, theaters, and communities nationwide. Each group develops an original play based on the experiences of the participants. Through creation of the music and script, and through exercises that promote team-building, issues such as drugs, violence, gangs, abuse, etc., are explored and possible solutions are examined. City at Peace is a positive program through which youth can deal with the daily frustrations common in their lives and can communicate with peers and the community at large.

Fellowship of Reconciliation (1915)

P.O. Box 271
Nyack, NY 10960
Jo Becker, Executive Director
Francine Blume, Coordinator,
Peacemaker Training Institute
914/358-4601
FAX: 914/358-4924

The FOR is an interfaith organization concerned with nonviolent responses to conflict, peace, and social justice. FOR is not primarily a youth organization. However, it maintains the Peacemaker Training Institute, which enables young people to become more effective change agents through a full-time program of study, reflection, and action. It also sponsors Skills for Change, a one-week intensive organizing and leadership development program held during the summer, as well as occasional nonviolence training workshops for youth.

Grace Contrino Abrams Peace Education Foundation (1980)

2627 Biscayne Boulevard
Miami, FL 33137
Fran Schmidt, Chairman of the Board
800/749-8838
305/576-5075
FAX: 305/576-3106

The Foundation teaches youths how to "fight fair" how to manage conflicts without using violence. To this end, it provides teaching guides and audio-visual materials, including an 18-minute, award-winning video, *Fighting Fair: Dr. Martin Luther King, Jr., for Kids.* Also trains students to be peer mediators to whom other students can take their disputes and arrive at a fair agreement. The organization strives to build conflict resolution skills as life skills, useful at home, at school, and on the job. These skills are part of peace education that seeks to learn and teach nonviolent solutions to all problems threatening the human family and our fragile planet. List of publications and materials available.

Heifer Project International (1944)
International Office
1015 S. Louisiana
Little Rock, AR 72202
800/422-0474
501/376-6836

The Heifer Project is a nonprofit, interfaith organization helping to alleviate world hunger, one family at a time. It works by providing animals to organized groups of farmers who request assistance. The basic unit of HPI work is a community project which is shaped and driven by the expressed needs of the participants. Projects also help the environment through tree- and grass-planting and soil conservation.

Typically, a project consists of three essential components: livestock and other material goods, training and extension work, and organization development. Each person who receives an animal also receives training in its care. Each participant must "pass on the gift" by giving one of the animal's offspring to a needy neighbor, or share his or her new skills in animal care with others in the community.

There are currently more than 290 Heifer Projects in 37 countries and the United States.

International Christian Youth Exchange (1949)
134 W. 26th Street
New York, NY 10001
Andrea Spencer-Linzie
Executive Director
Heather Hutchens
Director of Outbound Programs
Kirsten Bunch
Director of Inbound Programs
212/206-7307
FAX: 212/633-9085

ICYE sponsors both year-long and 6-month international experiences for young people ages 16–30 in 30 countries around the world. Participants attend high school and/or volunteer with community agencies in hundreds of fields, ranging from environmental and health issues to literacy and construction projects. Participation is open to all persons, regardless of religious affiliation, who subscribe to ICYE's goal of addressing issues of injustice in a global context. Short-term programs include ecumenical work camps. Participants return to the U.S. with new perspectives on the U.S., worldwide friendships, and a wealth of personal skills to apply to college and life-long careers.

Legacy International (1977)
Route 4, Box 265
Bedford, VA 24523
Mary Helmig, Recruitment Coordinator
703/297-5982
FAX: 703/297-1860

An educational organization offering programs for youth ages 11–18 and adults from more than 25 different countries. Participants receive training in cross-cultural understanding, global issues, lead-

ership, community action, conflict resolution, and environmental awareness.
Summer workshops and exchange programs are offered.

Little Friends for Peace
4405 29th Street
Mount Rainier, MD 20712
Mary Joan Park, Director
301/927-5474

A peace-making skills education program
for young children, available to churches,
schools, and community organizations;
includes day and resident camp programs. Provides consultation and
resources including *Peacemaking for Little Friends*, *Creating a Peace Experience*,
*A Guide to Children's Peacemaking: Skills
for Building a Hopeful Future*, and *Family
Peacemaking*.

MADRE (1983)
Women's Peace Network
121 W. 27th Street, Room 301
New York, NY 10001
Lilliana Cortes, Program Director
212/627-0444
FAX: 212/675-3704

MADRE seeks to foster friendships among
children in the United States and abroad.
Youth Leadership Through the Arts is a
school-based program that addresses
racism, sexism and violence in the U.S.
Artists and performers conduct multidisciplinary residencies featuring leadership training and skills development.
Sponsors Voices of the Children/Voces de
los Ninos, a travelling collection of draw-
ings by children in Nicaragua, El Sal-
vador, Guatemala, Panama, the Occupied
Territories, and cities in the U.S. that give

glimpses of contemporary life through
young people's eyes.

The National Student Campaign Against Hunger and Homelessness (1985)
29 Temple Place
Boston, MA 02111
Jennifer Jones, Director
617/292-4823
FAX: 617/292-8057

The Campaign was launched in 1985 as
a cooperative venture among twenty Public Interest Research Groups (PIRGs) and
USA for Africa. Today it is the nation's
largest network of student activists seeking to alleviate hunger and homelessness.
Primarily for high school and college students, it will also work with highly motivated junior high school groups.
Sponsors annual Hunger Cleanup, a
work-a-thon through which students
improve their own communities as well as
raise funds for the impoverished, and
Hunger and Homelessness Week; holds
national conference. Publishes organizing
manuals and *Students Making a Difference* newsletter (quarterly).

Open Door Student Exchange (1963)
839 Steward Avenue, Suite D
Garden City, NY 11530-4857
Dr. Frank Tarsitano
Executive Vice President
516/745-6232
FAX: 516/745-6233

An international educational exchange
organization that provides intercultural
learning opportunities for American and
foreign high school students and their

families. Programs for U.S. students include overseas school/intern/home stays
of varying length with host families in over
30 countries. Scholarships available.

World Federalist Association (1947)

418 7th Street, S.E.
Washington, DC 20003
Aaron Knight
Student Programs Director
800/WFA-0123 (800/932-0123)
202/546-3950
FAX: 202/546-3749

WFA has 70 active adult and 20 student
chapters around the country and is part
of a worldwide movement promoting a
just world order through a strengthened
and more democratic United Nations.
Low-cost student memberships are available; members receive four newsletters
from the national and international
offices each year.

World Learning (1932)

Kipling Road
P.O. Box 676
Brattleboro, VT 05302-0676
Alan Carter, Acting President
Michael Koonce
Director of Summer Abroad
802/257-7751
FAX: 802/258-3248

A worldwide organization whose mission
is to enable participants to develop the
knowledge, skills, and attitudes needed to
contribute effectively to international
understanding and global development.
Programs include summer stays for high
school students through Summer
Abroad; undergraduate and graduate

degrees and semesters abroad for college
students offered at the School for International Training; and work-study opportunities abroad as *au pairs* through
AuPair/Homestay Abroad.

World Vision (1950)

919 W. Huntington Drive
Monrovia, CA 91016
News and Information Services
818/357-7979
FAX: 818/305-0248

An international Christian relief and
development agency with more than
6,000 projects in over 94 countries.
Through 15 support offices in North
America, Europe, Asia, Australia, and
New Zealand, World Vision provides
emergency relief for victims of national
and human-made disasters. The agency
also offers development assistance for
individuals and communities with the
aim of promoting self-reliance.

World Vision donors help more than one
million children enrolled in sponsorship
projects around the globe. Its overall aim
is to convey Christian love in actions and
Christian witness in deeds and words.

Conducts the 30 Hour Famine, an international hunger-fighting program
through which participants, mostly teens,
recruit family members and friends who
sponsor them to go without food for 30
hours. During this time, young people
experience firsthand the reality of hunger
while they learn about the issues of
hunger and poverty through educational
activities, videos and resource materials
provided by World Vision. Schools,

churches, youth groups, community organizations, families, and individuals have participated in the program.

Youth Exchange Program

Rotary International
1560 Sherman Avenue
Evanston, IL 60201-3698
Edward Omohundro, Program Coordinator, Intercultural Programs Section
708/866-3421
FAX: 708/328-8554

For more than 30 years, the Youth Exchange Program has offered young people ages 15–19 opportunities for long- and short-term exchanges between any two countries in which there are Rotary Clubs. Long-term programs last for an academic year during which the student lives with more than one family and attends school in the host country; short-term exchanges vary from several days to several weeks, often during periods when schools are not in session. In 1993, about 9,000 young people were hosted by more than 50 different countries. Applicants for Youth Exchange programs are selected by a sponsoring Rotary Club on the basis of a written application and a personal interview. For information about other youth programs of Rotary International, see page 97.

Youth for Understanding International Exchange (1951)

International Center
3501 Newark Street, N.W.
Washington, DC 20016-3167
William M. Woessner, President
800/TEEN-AGE (800/833-6243)
202/966-6800

A nonprofit international exchange program for high school students ages 15–18 in approximately 30 countries around the world. Ten regional offices in the U.S. and national offices in other countries provide support services to youth and families involved in the program. Has developed a series of training programs in volunteer management and program promotion techniques; originally intended to improve the skills of Youth for Understanding volunteers who work with students and host families, the training videos and materials may be purchased for use by other agencies. The programs focus on increasing intercultural sensitivity and awareness; each involves 35–40 hours of training.

See also:

World Future Society, page 161; **Youth for Christ/U.S.A., Inc.**, page 74.

Character-Building Organizations

These groups provide comprehensive programs aimed at the development of the "whole child." They are open to all members of the community.

Boy Scouts of America (1910)

1325 W. Walnut Hill Lane
Irving, TX 75015-2079
Jere B. Ratcliffe, Chief Scout Executive
214/580-2000

An educational program for boys and young adults to build character, to train in the responsibilities of participating citizenship, and to develop personal fitness. Community groups receive national charters to use the Scouting program as part of their own youth work. These groups, which have goals compatible with those of the BSA, include religious, educational, civic, fraternal, business, and labor organizations, government bodies, corporations, professional associations, and citizens groups.

Camping, high adventure, and international opportunities are available. Includes Tiger Cubs (grade 1), Cub Scouts (grades 2–3), Webelos (grades 4–5), Boy Scouts (ages 11–18), Varsity Scouts (ages 14–18), and Exploring, for young men and women ages 15–20 (see page 17).

The BSA also operates a wholly-owned subsidiary, Learning for Life, that offers a curriculum designed as a supplemental school program for character development through helping to build confidence, motivation, and self-esteem.

Boys & Girls Clubs of America (1860/1906)

1230 W. Peachtree Street, N.W.
Atlanta, GA 30309
Thomas G. Garth, President

Comprised of over 1,450 member Clubs throughout the U.S., Puerto Rico, and the Virgin Islands, Boys & Girls Clubs of America is the nation's largest youth service organization with a primary focus on youth development directed especially toward young people from disadvantaged backgrounds. Programs and services are provided on a daily basis for boys and girls ages 6–18. Nominal membership dues are charged.

The organization program has six core areas: Social Recreation, Citizenship and Leadership Development, Cultural Enrichment, Health and Physical Education, Personal and Educational Development, and Outdoor and Environmental Education. The Clubs provide specialized services and programs focused on social issues dependent on community need and available resources.

Camp Fire Boys and Girls (1910)

4601 Madison Avenue
Kansas City, MO 64112-1278
K. Russell Weathers
National Executive Director/CEO
816/756-1950
FAX: 816/756-0258

Since 1975, this organization, dedicated to programmatic excellence, has served girls and boys (who now make up one-third of the participants). Five major delivery systems reach school-age youth with the Camp Fire program: clubs, camping, self-reliance courses, youth leadership/teens in action, and school-age child care. Youths participate in one or several of these programs, which focus on teaching self-reliance skills and good citizenship.

Co-Ette Club (1941)

2020 W. Chicago Boulevard
Detroit, MI 48206
Mary-Agnes Miller Davis, M.S.W.,
C.S.W., Executive Sponsor
313/867-0880

An organization for leadership training and community service for African-American high school girls that stresses involvement in national and local charitable, civic, educational, and cultural causes through an active program of charity, cultural, civic, and educational activities. The club was founded in Detroit, where its national headquarters remains. Currently operations are mainly in the Detroit area; sponsors an annual Teen Conference and provides service to an adopted inner-city elementary school.

Cooperative Extension Service

4-H Youth Development (1914)
U.S. Department of Agriculture
Washington, DC 20250
Dr. Susanne G. Fisher
Interim Deputy Administrator
202/720-5853

A coeducational program for urban as well as rural youth ages 9–19. This partnership of the USDA, land-grant universities, local governments, and the private sector is committed to strengthening the nation's food and fiber agricultural systems, and the American family through helping youth attain the knowledge, human skills, and technology needed to create a satisfying quality of life with available resources.

The program is delivered in a variety of modes and will vary from state to state, but will always include leadership development, competitive events, demonstrations, and public speaking. Most groups offer camping and international programs and exchanges.

It is possible for other youth groups to obtain services through the Cooperative Extension Service. Contact your local county extension agent, or the 4-H Youth Development Office at your state's land-grant university.

Girl Scouts of the U.S.A. (1912)

420 Fifth Avenue
New York, NY 10018-2702
Mary Rose Main, Executive Director
212/852-8000
FAX: 212/852-6509

An education program that seeks to prepare girls ages 5–17 for life in a changing and pluralistic society. Programs emphasize the development of individual potential and relationships with others; the development of values to guide action and decision making; and the importance of contributing to the betterment of society. The Contemporary Issues program provides information and activities to help girls cope with daily life.

Camping programs, wider opportunities, and international experiences are available. Includes Daisy Girl Scouts (ages 5–6 or grades K–1), Brownie Girl Scouts (ages 6–8 or grades 1–3), Junior Girl Scouts (ages 8–11 or grades 3–6), Cadette Girl Scouts (ages 11–14 or grades 6–9), and Senior Girl Scouts (ages 14–17 or grades 9–12).

Girls Incorporated (1945)

30 East 33rd Street
New York, NY 10016
Isabel C. Stewart
National Executive Director
212/689-3700
FAX: 212/683-1253

National Resource Center

441 W. Michigan Street
Indianapolis, IN 46202
Heather Johnston Nicholson, Director
317/634-7546

Girls Incorporated is a national organization serving more than 250,000 girls and young women ages 6–18 through nearly 300 centers. Programs include Preventing Adolescent Pregnancy, a multifaceted approach that motivates girls to avoid early pregnancy; Friendly PEER-suasion, which deters elementary and junior high school age girls from alcohol, tobacco, and other drug use; Operation SMART, which enhances girls' interest in science, math, and relevant technology; Sporting Chance, which encourages girls' participation in sports and fitness; AIDS/HIV Education Project, which integrates information about AIDS/HIV into health and sexuality education programs; and Kid-Ability, which works to prevent child sexual abuse.

The National Resource Center serves as the research, training, and distribution arm of Girls Incorporated; it is the main organization's repository for information on girls' needs, concerns, and programs.

Hugh O'Brian Youth Foundation (1958)

10880 Wilshire Boulevard, Suite 900
Los Angeles, CA 90024
Douglas H. Barr, President and CEO
213/474-4370
FAX: 213/475-5426

HOBY has been providing leadership seminars to outstanding sophomores since 1958. The seminars are designed to allow future leaders—the HOBY Ambassadors—to interface in a meaningful way with recognized leaders in business, government, science, education, and the professions. Seminars take place at the community, state, and international levels. An alumni association carries on the same format in many locations and

through travel and tours. Core programs are provided at no cost to the student, family, or school. HOBY does not accept United Way or government funding.

Jack and Jill of America, Inc. (1938)

346 Commerce Street
Alexandria, VA 22314
Barbara Hofman, Executive Secretary
703/683-9663

Memberships are held by mothers with children ages 2–19 (who are automatically enrolled); local chapters select member families from their geographic areas. The program promotes awareness of community needs and stimulates cultural, civic, recreational, and social growth.

Lions-Quest

Lions Clubs International
300 22nd Street
Oakbrook, IL 60521-8842
Denise Whistler
Drug Awareness Coordinator
708/571-5466, Ext. 330
FAX: 708/571-8890

Lions-Quest is a flexible program designed for implementation in schools and communities; there are three levels: Skills for Growing (for grades K–5); Skills for Adolescence (for grades 6–8); and the high-school-age initiative to be introduced in 1994. These programs promote a positive life-style that includes social competence, citizenship, ethical behavior and service to others. They also seek to counteract student alienation and apathy and prevent self-destructive and antisocial behaviors through fostering a commitment to healthy living and responsible behavior and strengthening decision-making, communication, language, and writing skills. High school program helps students prepare for the transition from school to work or from high school to higher education.

See also:

Leo Club Program, page 98.

National Association of Youth Clubs (1930)
5808 16th Street, N.W.
Washington, DC 20011
Carole A. Early, Headquarters Secretary
202/726-2044

These community-based clubs for boys and girls ages 8–18 are sponsored by local affiliates of the National Association of Colored Women's Clubs. Individual club programs are developed locally within national guidelines. The organization promotes character development and service to the community and sponsors oratorical, fashion, talent, and arts and crafts contests at the state, regional, and national levels.

National Tots and Teens, Inc. (1954)
P.O. Box 1517
Washington, DC 20013-1517
Gwendolyn H. Joe
Acting Executive Director
301/292-4999
Jacqueline Richardson
Director of Publications
301/894-2734

National Tots and Teens, Inc. is an organization of families—parents and youth—who believe that the family is the critical

setting for influencing positive pursuits and instilling values which produce full and effective participants in society. Generally youth of the organization are ages 3–18. In addition to being actively involved in community service projects, youth members are encouraged to develop leadership and public speaking skills. Membership is received through local chapters, most in major U.S. cities.

Woodcraft Rangers (1902)
2111 Park Grove Avenue
Los Angeles, CA 90007
James Van Hoven, Executive Director
213/749-3031
FAX: 213/749-0409

Provides youth groups and camps for children in Southern California area, with focus on multicultural and underprivileged communities.

YMCA of the USA (1851)
101 N. Wacker Drive
Chicago, IL 60606
David Mercer, Executive Director
800/USA-YMCA (800/872-9622)

YMCAs are dedicated to putting Christian principles into practice through programs that build a healthy body, mind, and spirit for all. Local Y's are autonomous, so programs will vary. National youth programs include parent-child Guide (boys) and Princess (girls) programs for youngsters in kindergarten through grade 3, and Trailblazers for youth in grade 4 through junior high. High school club programs emphasize leadership development (see YMCA Teen Leadership Programs, page 53).

In addition, most Y's now offer school-age child-care programs emphasizing total development; year-round and/or summer camping programs; aquatics; and fitness (see YMCA Youth Sports, page 30).

YWCA of the USA (1855)

726 Broadway
New York, NY 10003
Jo Sachiko Uehara
Interim National Executive Director
212/614-2700

A membership movement of women from diverse backgrounds, faiths, ages, and experiences who are committed to empowering women and eliminating racism. Local YW associations are autonomous, and programs will vary. Most offer opportunities for personal growth and self-development, education, health, and fitness.

Youth development is a theme of the YWCA core program. Peer education programs available to both young men (who may join as associate members) and women emphasize self-esteem building, decision making, adolescent sexuality, and personal development. Available programs and materials include *Choices or Chances? A Life Options Program for Teens*; *PACT: Peer Education in Sexuality and Health*; and videos relating to teen pregnancy prevention.

See also:

NULITES, page 112.

Social Welfare and Community Betterment Groups

American Red Cross

421 18th Street, N.W.
Washington, DC 20006
Donna M. Feeley, M.P.H., Director
Division of Youth Involvement
National Office of Volunteers
202/639-3039
FAX: 202/639-6165

The American Red Cross Youth Program celebrated its 75th anniversary in 1992. Nationally, the Youth Office has been reestablished to renew support for the development, training, and volunteer participation of youth. The program mission is to promote training of children and youth to:

- Enhance self-reliance, cope with challenges, and improve the quality of life;

- Develop concern for others, and contribute to family and community welfare;

- Serve and be served, thereby developing a commitment to a lifetime of community service; and

- Become caring and capable adult citizens by developing their sense of competence, usefulness, belonging and empowerment.

The program themes to promote the youth development philosophy over the next five years include Volunteer Service; Leadership Development; Youth/Adult partnerships; School-Based Partnerships; and International Awareness. Pathways of education, training, leadership development and volunteerism are offered through local Red Cross programs and services including: Health and Safety, HIV/AIDS education, Disaster, Military and Social, Blood, and International services. Materials, training, and opportunities for volunteerism are available through local Red Cross chapters, schools, and communities.

Big Brothers/Big Sisters of America (1977)

230 N. 13th Street
Philadelphia, PA 19108
Thomas McKenna
National Executive Director
215/567-7000
FAX: 215/567-0394

Formed through the merger of separate Big Brother (1904) and Big Sister (1908) organizations, BB/BS helps meet the challenges of growing up through matching school-aged children, most from single-parent homes, with adult volunteers who serve as mentors and role models. These informal one-to-one friendships are monitored, guided, and supported by professional caseworkers. Local affiliates also provide an array of counseling, referral, and family support services to parents and children; some have additional programs focusing on children with special needs, including those who have been abused and neglected. Special prevention and intervention programs at agencies address the problems of drug abuse, teen pregnancy, and juvenile delinquency.

Programs developed by the national organization include senior mentors for youth at risk; Alternatives, drug and alcohol abuse prevention and education, and

EMPOWER, a child sexual abuse prevention and education program.

Guardian Angels (1979)

982 E. 89th Street
Brooklyn, NY 11236
Curtis Sliwa, Founder
718/649-2607

An organization of trained volunteers who seek to deter crime through unarmed street patrols in more than 65 American cities; has several chapters overseas. Although open to individuals older than 16, about two thirds of the members are ages 16–20.

Junior Guardian Angels

5891 S. Military Trail, Suite 5A
Lake Worth, FL 33463
Sean P. Kelley, Director/Junior Angels

Junior Guardian Angels programs are inactive at the national level, although some local programs for youth ages 7–15 are in operation. Younger members are not permitted to patrol, but are encouraged to understand the value of community involvement through service to the elderly and others who need their help.

National Network of Runaway and Youth Services, Inc. (1974)

1319 F Street, N.W., Suite 401
Washington, DC 20004
Della M. Hughes, Executive Director
202/783-7949
FAX: 202/783-7955

The National Network of Runaway and Youth Services is a national, nonprofit organization that represents approximately 1,000 agencies, state and regional networks, and affiliates that serve runaway, homeless, and other youth in high-risk situations. With a mission to "ensure that young people can be safe and grow up to lead healthy and productive lives," the Network advocates on behalf of youth; develops and disseminates information about model programs; provides training, educational materials and technical assistance; conducts an annual conference in Washington, DC; and operates YOUTHNET™, a nationwide telecommunications system. *Network News*, published quarterly, and *Policy Reporter*, published eight times per year, are available for a $25 membership fee.

Volunteers of America, Inc. (1896)

3939 N. Causeway Boulevard, Suite 400
Metairie, LA 70002
Clint Cheveallier, President
504/837-2652
FAX: 504/837-4200

A wide range of youth services are provided through the auspices of the VOA. Programs will vary considerably from one office to another. Inquire locally.

YouthBuild USA (1988)
YouthBuild Coalition (1988)

58 Day Street
P.O. Box 440322
Somerville, MA 02144
Dorothy Stoneman, President
617/623-9900
FAX: 617/623-4331

YouthBuild Coalition engages low-income young people in building housing for homeless people in their own communities. Trainees alternate between on-site supervised construction work and off-site academic studies, leading to a GED.

YouthBuild programs are comprehensive. In addition to education and job skills training, they include leadership development, counseling, and cultural and recreational activities. In some communities, YouthBuild programs are expanding to include skills development in the areas of environmental technologies and child-care. At the end of the program, staff help trainees find employment in construction or other fields, attend college, or join an apprenticeship program.

YouthBuild USA provides technical and fundraising assistance to program sites. The YouthBuild Coalition, composed of more than 375 organizations, lobbies for YouthBuild USA's federal and state legislative initiatives.

Religious Organizations

Protestant

All of the organizations in this section were Protestant at the time of their founding, although some have since broadened their membership bases. Those marked "(C)," while Christian in mission, offer comprehensive programs designed to develop the physical, mental, and social dimensions as well as the spiritual.

Nondenominational

Some of these are organized through individual churches or parishes of many denominations, while others are not connected with any particular church or parish.

Athletes in Action (1966)

P.O. Box 588
Lebanon, OH 45036
Wendel Deyo, National Director
513/933-2421
FAX: 513/933-2422

The athletic program of Campus Crusade for Christ. Maintains a speakers' bureau; sponsors competitions; and runs a summer program of sports camps for junior high and high school students. Provides assemblies for middle and high schools addressing drug and alcohol issues.

Awana Clubs International (1950) (C)

One East Bode Road
Streamwood, IL 60107
Dr. Art Rorheim, President
708/213-2000
FAX: 708/213-9704

A Christ-centered organization for youth ages 3 through high school that operates in the United States and 59 foreign countries. Promotes training in Christian living and service.

Boys' and Girls' Brigades of America (1980)

P.O. Box 9863
Baltimore, MD 21284
Joseph Sauthoff, President
410/391-4331

Formed by a merger of United Boys' Brigades of America (1887) and United Girls' Brigades of America (1949). Serves young people ages 6–18 with a program of Bible and missions training, athletics, games, camping and outdoor activities; seeks to provide a healthy environment where youth can learn obedience, reverence, discipline, and self-respect.

Campus Crusade for Christ International (1951)

Student Venture
Sunport Center
100 Sunport Lane
Orlando, FL 32809
Dr. Bill Bright, Founder and President
407/826-2000
FAX: 407/826-2120

Campus Crusade for Christ International is an evangelical student outreach organization. Student Venture emphasizes evangelism and discipleship in weekly meetings of Bible study, fellowship, and recreation for high school students.

Center for Youth Ministry YouthQuest Ministries (1971)

c/o Liberty University
Box 20000
Lynchburg, VA 24506
Dr. David F. Adams, Executive Director
804/582-2310
FAX: 804/582-2589

Based at Liberty University, the Center provides an academic program emphasizing field training for college students preparing for vocational youth work in evangelical churches, camps, counseling centers, cross-cultural ministries, and schools. The CYM serves as a consultation and resource center for these youth workers.

YouthQuest operates national and regional programs and projects that facilitate the mentoring process between college students and middle and high school teens. Programs include youth rallies, church internships, public school assemblies, inner-city ministry, student conferences, camps and retreats, and cross-cultural ministry trips.

Child Evangelism Fellowship (1937)

P.O. Box 348
Warrenton, MO 63383
Reese Kauffman, President
314/456-4321
FAX: 314/456-5000 or 314/456-2078

An international organization that seeks to reach children through Bible classes, camps, rallies, and other programs throughout the U.S. and in 121 countries overseas. Publishes training materials for use in religious education programs. Catalog available.

Christian Endeavor International (1881)

3575 Valley Road
P. O. Box 820
Liberty Corner, NJ 07938-0820
Rev. David G. Jackson
General Secretary
908/604-9440

Christian Endeavor is a Christ-centered, youth-oriented ministry which assists local churches in reaching young people with the Gospel of Jesus Christ, discipling them in the Christian faith, and equipping them for Christian ministry and service in their church, community, and world. Multi-church, cross-cultural, and global in its outreach, it produces materials for program enrichment, provides seminars for equipping youth leaders for effective ministry, and holds conferences and conventions for Christian inspiration, spiritual growth, and fellowship.

Christian Service Brigade (1937) (C)

P.O. Box 150
Wheaton, IL 60189
Kenneth F. Keeler, President
708/665-0630
FAX: 708/665-0372

An evangelical Christian organization that provides local churches with leadership and fathering training for men, father/child programs for fathers with children ages 2–7, and programs for boys ages 6–18, through weekly meetings, special events and camps.

Coalition for Christian Outreach (1971)

6740 Fifth Avenue
Pittsburgh, PA 15208
Rev. Robert R. Long, President
412/363-3303
FAX: 412/363-1005

An interdenominational and evangelistic student ministry working in Pennsylvania, eastern Ohio, and northern West Virginia. Challenges students to develop a Christian perspective in their areas of study so they can develop direction in the vocation to which God calls them, and commitment to outworking of the gospel relative to vital social and political issues of the day.

Fellowship of Christian Athletes (1954)

8701 Leeds Road
Kansas City, MO 64129
Dal Shealy, President
816/921-0909

A Christ-centered, Bible-based program for student athletes and coaches in junior and senior high schools and colleges. Sponsors sports camps, rallies, and special events.

High School Evangelism Fellowship (1939)

P.O. Box 7
Bergenfield, NJ 07621
Andy Nelson, International Director
201/387-1750
FAX: 201/387-1348

Evangelizes and disciples high school students through Bible clubs; operates in the United States and Japan.

The International Order of the King's Daughters and Sons (1886)

34 Vincent Avenue
P.O. Box 1017
Chautauqua, NY 14722
Mrs. Eugene R. Smith
Director, Junior Department
2215 Allison Avenue
Indianapolis, IN 46224-5024
317/244-9149

An interdenominational and international organization of Christian men and women dedicated to service in Christ's name. Its three-fold program (Religious, Educational, and Philanthropic) trains members and others for Christian service. The youth program of the Junior Department is open to all and seeks to develop the spiritual life and stimulate Christian activities. Stresses service to others and provides leadership development opportunities. Local chapters will vary.

The Logos System Associates (1962)

The Logos System Associates, Inc.
1405 Frey Road
Pittsburgh, PA 15235
Dr. Dale K. Milligan, Executive Director
412/372-1341
FAX: 412/372-8447

Works with churches to fulfill their responsibilities for effective Christian education of children and youth. Uses a midweek afternoon format to incorporate four types of quality relational experience: Recreation/Activities, Worship Skills/Choir, Family Time/Dinner, and Bible Study Hour. The program enables the local church to enroll a large percentage of children and youth in grades 1–12 in a positive, enjoyable experience.

Patch the Pirate Clubs (1983) (C)

Majesty Music, Inc.
P.O. Box 6524
Greenville, SC 29606
Ken Pujdak, Vice President, Operations
800/334-1071
FAX: 803/370-3877

A nondenominational organization, organized through local congregations, for young people in grades 1–6. Promotes the development of Godly character through daily devotional guide. Music lessons further promote such values as obedience, trustworthiness, honesty, having a tender heart, etc. Seeks to develop healthy social relationships and ideals of Christian service.

Pioneer Clubs (1939) (C)

Pioneer Ministries
27 W. 130 St. Charles Road
P.O. Box 788
Wheaton, IL 60189-0788
Virginia Patterson, Ed.D., President
708/293-1600
FAX: 708/293-3053

An international, activity-based program for Christian youth enrolled through their churches. Seeks to help children and youth put Christ in every phase of their lives to nurture healthy relationships and develop a positive self-image. Originally for girls only, the organization has included boys since 1980. The program for ages 2–18 may be offered in boys', girls', or coeducational groups. The Explorers group for high school students is coed. Offers summer camping program.

Pro-Teens (1969)

Positive Action for Christ, Inc.
833 Falls Road
P.O. Box 1948
Rocky Mount, NC 27802-1948
Mark Farnham
Director of Youth Ministries
Rev. Frank Hamrick, President
800/688-3008 (Outside NC)
919/977-9977
FAX: 919/977-2181

A church-based, Christian training program for junior and senior high youth. Promotes personal devotions, Bible study and memorization, recreation, and services. Publishes a complete Bible curriculum for Christian schools, grades K–12. Introduced a youth group ministry project in 1992. Discipleship materials available.

Sonlight Ministries, Inc. (1981)

5950 Spring Creek Road
Rockford, IL 61114
Jerome Green, President
815/877-4040
FAX: 815/877-4096

A club-type, Christ-centered program for grades K–6; uses a system of advancement and an awards program based on Bible knowledge and growth in Christian life.

Success with Youth (1951)

Christian Education Publishers
Box 261129
San Diego, CA 92196
Arthur L. Miley, Publisher
800/854-1531
619/578-4700

A nondenominational, evangelical, club-based ministry that works through local churches. Programs include Honeybees (ages 2–3); Space Cubs (ages 4–5); Whirleybirds (grades 1–3); Jet Cadets (grades 4–6); Alpha Teens (grades 7–9); and Omega Teens (grades 10–12). Catalog available.

Teen Missions International, Inc. (1970)

885 E. Hall Road
Merritt Island, FL 32952
Robert M. Bland, Director
407/453-0350
FAX: 407/452-7988

An interdenominational, evangelical organization that promotes the involvement of young people in world missions; in the summer of 1993, 1,370 North American youth ages 13–25 were trained and sent to 45 countries on work and evangelism projects. Runs ten programs throughout the year in ten different countries that provide similar mission exposure to national youth. A pre-teen Boot Camp for ages 8–12 gives young people an opportunity to do service projects and evangelism in the U.S. Teams learn to do light construction, puppetry, music and drama, and to minister in local churches and nursing homes.

Word of Life Fellowship (1942)

Schroon Lake, NY 12870
George Theis, Executive Director
Jack Wyrtzen, Founding Director
Harry Bollback, Senior Director
518/532-7111
FAX: 518/532-7421

An international, fundamentalist, evangelistic organization for teens. Conducts Bible clubs; radio, television, and Bible Institute programs; and rallies. Operates several camps in various parts of the world.

Young Life (1941)

720 W. Monument Street
P.O. Box 520
Colorado Springs, CO 80901
Denny Rydberg, President
719/473-4262
FAX: 719/389-0856

A nondenominational, community-based program that seeks to introduce young people to the gospel of Christ by establishing and maintaining friendships with them. Originally for high school students, the program now works with junior high age adolescents as well, and has a growing ministry for youth with disabilities as well as urban and international work.

Young Life has recently ventured into a new area of church partnership relationships in several hundred communities in the U.S., providing youth workers who divide their work between church and high school settings. Summer program includes outreach camping for teens at a wide variety of Young Life resorts around the country. Campaigners are groups of young people organized for Bible study and committed to adapting faith into everyday life. Young Life has had a significant Catholic membership for several years.

Youth for Christ/U.S.A., Inc. (1945)

Box 228822
Denver, CO 80222
Roger Cross, Chief Executive Officer
303/843-9000
FAX: 303/843-9002

A mission organization with the goal of presenting the life-changing message of Christ to every young person. Uses a variety of methods to reach youths in junior high and high schools, neighborhoods, inner cities, and juvenile institutions. Offers teenagers across the country high adventure and residential camps, local events, regional conferences, and national conventions. Provides opportunities for teens to serve overseas in short-term work projects in underdeveloped countries.

Denominational

These organizations are part of the youth programs of specific denominational bodies.

Alliance Youth Fellowship (1954)

Christian and Missionary Alliance
P.O. Box 35000
Colorado Springs, CO 80935
Rev. Dan Bergstrom
National Youth Director
719/599-5999

A program for youth ages 14–18 that endeavors to bring them to Christ, bring them up in Christ, and send them forth for Christ. Activities include Operation Good News, an evangelism program; Bible quizzing; and overseas mission trips. Together, they seek to create "Teen-Age World Christians" who will be uncharacteristically unselfish with their time, service, money, and prayer, and who will demonstrate concern for those who do not know Christ and a willingness to go beyond the secure peer group into the uncertainties of outreach.

Berean Youth Fellowship (1902)

5823 Trammell Road
P.O. Box 100,000
Morrow, GA 30260
James Graham, Director
FAX: 404/362-9307

The youth program of the Church of God of the Abrahamic Faith General Conference works year-round to foster spiritual development. Sponsors a summer camping program; holds a National Youth Congress annually in July.

The Caravan Program (1950)

Nazarene Youth International (NYI)
The Church of the Nazarene
6401 The Paseo
Kansas City, MO 64131
Kathy Hughes, Caravan Coordinator
Fred Fullerton, Director, NYI
816/333-7000

The Caravan Program offers scouting-type activities for children ages 4 through grade 6. Individual congregations may also offer other types of teen programs. There are active Bible quizzing programs for both children and teens.

Christian Life Clubs
Free Methodist Youth Ministries

Free Methodist Church of North America (1860)
P.O. Box 535002
Indianapolis, IN 46253-5002
317/244-3660
FAX: 317/244-1247
Dottie Miller
Director of Children's Ministries
517/589-9924
Myke Merrill
Director of Youth Ministries
716/392-4178
FAX: 716/392-5792

Christian Life Clubs provide an activity-oriented program promoting Christian values among youth in grades 1–6. Also conducts the Joybell program for children ages 4–5. Free Methodist Youth Ministries encourage lives of Christian commitment through witness and service to others.

Church Education Ministries (C)
Women's Ministries Department (C)

c/o International Pentecostal
Holiness Church
P.O. Box 12609
Oklahoma City, OK 773157
Rev. Paul Howell, Church Education
Ministries Executive Director
Doris Moore
Director, Women's Ministries
405/787-7110
FAX: 405/789-3957

The program seeks to put youth into action for Christ. Weekly youth meetings in local churches center around local T.E.A.M. (Teaching, Equipping, And Mobilizing) chapters. T.E.A.M. 2000 is the broad concept under which the youth ministry is organized. Organizations and activities include The Royal Rangers for boys ages 5–17; The National Talent Program; and the National Bible Quiz Program for junior and teen levels. The Women's Ministries Department sponsors the GEMS (Girls Entering the Master's Service) for girls in kindergarten through grade 12.

Free Church Student Ministries (1941)

Evangelical Free Church
901 E. 78th Street
Minneapolis, MN 55420
Rev. Steve Hudson
Director of Student Ministries
612/854-1300

An organization for youth in grades 7–12 that encourages a personal relationship with Christ and unites youth in a bond of Christian love and fellowship. The biennial conference includes ministry development and outreach activities.

Girl Guards (1916) (C)
Adventure Corps (1984) (C)

Salvation Army National Headquarters
P.O. Box 269
615 Slaters Lane
Alexandria, VA 22313
Sherrill J. Benson, Lt. Colonel,
National Consultant for Evangelism
and Christian Education
703/684-5530
FAX: 703/684-5538

These outreach programs of the Salvation Army stress mental, physical, social, and spiritual development and service to others. Girls are Sunbeams in grades 1–5, Girl Guards in grades 6–12. The Adventure Corps is the indoor-outdoor skills and achievement program for boys, who become Explorers (grades 1–4), Rangers (grades 5–8), and Adventurers (grades 9–12). Some Salvation Army centers continue to use the program of the Boy Scouts of America. All of these programs are open to everyone.

Within the Salvation Army membership, Junior Soldiers (grades 1–6) pursue Bible study, Salvation Army history, and leadership development. The Corps Cadets (ca. 1890) is a Bible study and leadership development program for teen members.

Girls in Action/Acteens (1970)

Women's Missionary Union
Auxiliary to the Southern Baptist
Convention
P.O. Box 830010
Birmingham, AL 35283-0010
Sylvia DeLoach
Girls in Action Specialist
Marti Solomon, Acteens Specialist
205/991-8100
FAX: 205/995-4841

These missions education organizations have roots going back to 1817. Girls in Action members are in grades 1–6; Acteens are in grades 7–12.

Junior Daughters of the King (1896)

c/o National Order
Daughters of the King
P. O. Box 2196
Marietta, GA 30061-2196
National Chairwoman (elected annually)
404/419-8580
FAX: 404/419-0686

Junior Daughters chapters are formed in Episcopal churches where there are three or more baptized girls (ages 7–20) who promise to pray daily and work toward the spread of Christ's Kingdom and strengthening the spiritual life of the church. The purpose is Christian fellowship, growth, and evangelism. Girls of other denominations may join.

Luther League Federation (1963)

Association of Free Lutheran
Congregations (AFLC)
3110 E. Medicine Lake Boulevard
Minneapolis, MN 55441
Rev. Dennis Gray
AFLC Youth Resources Director
P.O. Box M
Greenbush, MN 56726
218/782-2249

A program in AFLC congregations for evangelizing boys and girls ages 9 to young adult and teaching them discipleship. AFLC Youth Resources serves as a clearinghouse of information and materials, and provides problem-solving assistance and counseling for adult leaders, youth pastors, and other youth workers.

Lutheran Girl Pioneers (1954) (C)

7611 Caledonia Street
LaCrosse, WI 54603
Barbara Wolff, National Counselor
608/781-5232

This character-building program for girls in grades 1–8 includes physical fitness and skills training. "Caravans" are organized in individual congregations of the Wisconsin Evangelical Lutheran Synod (2929 N. Mayfair Road, Milwaukee, WI 53222).

Lutheran Pioneers (1951) (C)

P.O. Box 66
Burlington, WI 53105
Dale Lorfeld, National Commander
414/763-6238
FAX: 414/534-2892

An organization for boys in grades 1–12. Stresses character building, physical fitness, and skills training through "trains" groups organized through individual congregations. Affiliated with the Wisconsin Evangelical Lutheran Synod (2929 N. Mayfair Road, Milwaukee, WI 53222).

Lutheran Youth Fellowship (1979)

Lutheran Church Missouri Synod
1333 S. Kirkwood Road
St. Louis, MO 63122
Rev. Terry Dittmer
Director of Congregational Services
314/965-9000

Maintains Christian fellowship among junior and senior high school youth; promotes Bible study, religious and social activities, interest in missions, and service to others. Succeeded the Walther League.

Lutheran Youth Organization (1987)*

Evangelical Lutheran Church
in America
8765 W. Higgins Road
Chicago, IL 60631
Mark Knutson and Becky Von Fischer,
Co-Directors
312/380-2700

Organization conducts a variety of programs for youth from junior high age through young adult. Programs stress the development of Christian leadership and service to others; service activities include building homes, working with children, cleaning fields, and the like. *Unable to obtain current information.*

Missionettes (1957)

Assemblies of God
1445 Boonville Avenue
Springfield, MO 65802
Linda Upton
National Missionettes Coordinator
417/862-2781
FAX: 417/862-8558

An advancement program of Bible memorization, missions education, and other aspects of religious education. Stages include Rainbows (girls and boys ages 3–4); Daisies (kindergarten and first grade girls); Prims (girls grades 2–3); Stars (girls grades 4–8); and Ys (girls grades 9–12).

National Youth Ministry Organization (1976)

United Methodist Church
Box 840
Nashville, TN 37202
Angela Gay Kinkead, Executive Director
615/340-7184
FAX: 615/340-7006

The youth advocacy agency for the United Methodist Church. Members (80 percent youth) are elected through church jurisdictions. Areas of endeavor include advocacy for youth; empowerment of youth for leadership; outreach to youth through the Youth Service Fund and the Youth Serving Youth Mission Fund; and providing a forum for the expression of youth concerns. An additional youth outreach of the church is the United Methodist Youth Fellowship, organized through local congregations.

Ongoing Ambassadors for Christ (1970)

103 N. Main Street
P.O. Box 41
Athens, IL 62613-0041
Rev. Erwin Ruhlig, Executive Director
217/636-7729

Trains youth to share their faith in Christ at monthly weekends through song, drama, puppets, testimony, Bible study, and door-to-door witnessing. National training course held each July; travel teams spread the training to new areas. OAFC is affiliated with the Lutheran Church—Missouri Synod.

Pentecostal Young People's Association (1928)

Pentecostal Church of God, Inc.
P.O. Box 705
Joplin, MO 64802
Robert E. (Eddie) Vansell
General PYPA President
417/624-7050, Ext. 351/352
FAX: 417/624-7102

The denomination's programs include Junior PYPA for ages 5–12, and PYPA for youth and young adults ages 13–35. Ministries include Bible Quizzing, Christian Pathlighters (a Scouting-type program), YEA (Youth Evangelism in Action), YLD (Youth Leadership and Development), and Merge (a young-married's ministry. Sponsors a biennial National Youth Leadership Conference, Seasons of Service (SOS, short term mission trips) and an annual National Teen Talent Expo.

Presbyterian Youth Ministry

Presbyterian Church (U.S.A.)
100 Witherspoon Street
Louisville, KY 40202-1396
Rodger Nishioka, National Director
Presbyterian Youth Ministry
502/569-5497
FAX: 502/569-5018

Youth programs are organized throughout the 13,000 local congregations of the Presbyterian Church (U.S.A.). The national denomination office publishes curriculum resources and provides training for youth workers.

The Primary Association (1878)
The Young Men (1875)
The Young Women (1869)

The Church of Jesus Christ
of Latter-Day Saints
76 N. Main Street
Salt Lake City, UT 84150
Michaelene Grassli
President, The Primary Association
Jack H. Goaslind
President, The Young Men
Janette C. Hales
President, The Young Women
800/453-3860
FAX: 801/240-5458

The Primary Association (ages 18 months-12 years), the Young Men (ages 12–18) and the Young Women (ages 12–18) follow age-appropriate curricula; groups meet on Sundays and during the week. Churches also sponsor Boy Scout troops which non-members are invited to join.

Royal Rangers (1961) (C)

Assemblies of God
1445 Boonville Avenue
Springfield, MO 65802
Ken Hunt, National Commander
417/862-2781, Ext. 4181
FAX: 417/862-0416

An advancement program for boys ages 5–17. Seeks to promote physical, spiritual, mental, and social growth through a program of education in Christian living.

The Seventh-day Adventist Church in North America (1914) (C)

12501 Old Columbia Pike
Silver Spring, MD 20904-6600
Noelene Johnsson, Children's Ministries
301/680-6424
Norm O. Middag, Adventurers (Grades 1–4), Pathfinders (Grades 5–10)
301/680-6426
Ted Wick, Teen Ministries (High School), Young Adult Ministries (ages 19–30)
301/680-6434
FAX: 301/680-6464

Primary program focus is the salvation of children and youth through Jesus Christ. Programs seek to:

- lead youth to understand their individual worth;

- discover and develop their spiritual gifts and abilities;

79

- equip and empower them for a life of service within God's church and the community;

- foster an appreciation of the Creator; and

- help them enjoy, preserve and protect the world of nature.

Skylarks (C)
Oriole Girls (C)
O-Teens (1915) (C)

Reorganized Church of Jesus Christ of Latter-Day Saints
Box 1059, The Auditorium
Independence, MO 64051
Jerry Ashby, Youth Director
816/833-1000

A scouting-type advancement program that helps girls develop understanding of self, an appreciation for others, and a strong Christian faith. Since 1980, the World Community program for all youth ages 8–18 has been the official religious emblem program, replacing the God and Country award of Scouting. The Boy Scouts of America is the denominational organization for boys.

Teen World Outreach

Elim Fellowship
7245 College Street
Lima, NY 14485
Jim Porter, Director
Teen World Outreach
716/582-2790
FAX: 716/624-1229

Teen World Outreach is a ministry of Elim World Missions. There are three branches: Teen World Outreach (TWO) is a summer missions project for teens and adult leaders; Adult Mission Project (AMP) is a 2–3-week program designed to give missions exposure to adults; and Short Term Enlistment Program (STEP) is a Missions discipleship ministry for individual adults.

United Calvinist Youth (1919)

1333 Alger Street, S.E.
P.O. Box 7259
Grand Rapids, MI 49510
Joanne Ilbrink, Director, Calvinettes
Richard Broene, Director, Cadets
Brian Bosscher
Director, Young Calvinist Federation
616/241-5616

Calvinettes (girls ages 8–14), Cadets (boys ages 8–14), and the Young Calvinist Federation (high school students) promote Christian living and service to others and the church. Programs for younger members include scouting-type advancement and camping.

Victory Leaders Band
Gleaners Band (1933)

The Church of God
National Headquarters
P.O. Box 13036
Huntsville, AL 35803
Bishop Bullen, General Overseer
205/881-9629

Promotes Christian growth and service to others; trains young people ages 5–35 to accept leadership in the church. Seeks to enroll unchurched youth and bring them into the fullness of Christian life. Has summer camping program; offers service opportunities outside of the U.S.

World Changers (1990)
Royal Ambassadors (1908)
Challengers (1994)

The Brotherhood Commission of the
Southern Baptist Convention
1548 Poplar Avenue
Memphis, TN 38104
901/272-2461
FAX: 901/726-5540

World Changers is a coeducational missions education opportunity for youth in
grades 9–12. Summer missions work projects are used by World Changers to help
youth grow spiritually as they become
aware of the needs of others around
them. The Royal Ambassadors missions
education programs for boys includes
Lads (grades 1–3), and Crusaders (grades
4–6). Challengers is a missions education
program for youth.

Young People Love Joy Band
(1920) (C)

Apostolic Overcoming Holy Church
of God, Inc.
1120 N. 24th Street
Birmingham, AL 35234
Dr. Jaunita R. Arrington
Christian Counselor and
National Executive Secretary
205/324-2202

Seeks to provide youth with wholesome
activities in a Christian environment
while they are learning about the love of
the Heavenly Father. Pledges to develop
the "whole child" so that young people
may become useful and productive assets
to themselves and to their families, communities, and country. Specific programs
may vary from one church to another.

Young Religious Unitarian
Universalists

Unitarian Universalist Association
25 Beacon Street
Boston, MA 02108
Rev. Jory Agate
Director of Youth Programs
617/742-2100
FAX: 617/523-4123

A fourfold program that encourages learning, worship, fellowship, and social action.
Provides a communications network for
local and district groups; promotes
youth leadership development. Publishes
Synapse; holds annual North American
Conference. This organization has roots
extending back to the 19th century.

Youth and Children's Ministries
(1928)

The Church of God of Prophecy
Bible Place
P.O. Box 2910
Cleveland, TN 37320-2910
William M. Wilson
International Director
615/559-5205
FAX: 615/559-5202

The youth ministry arm of the Church of
God of Prophecy; seeks to evangelize
youth and train them for Christian service. Seeks to enlist them in getting the
message of Christ and the Church to the
world; members must show interest and
participate in church services and activities. Groups raise money for the printing
of literature for worldwide distribution.

Zioneers

Zion's League (1937)
Reorganized Church of Jesus Christ
of Latter-Day Saints
Box 1059, The Auditorium
Independence, MO 64051
Jerry Ashby, Youth Director
816/833-1000

Zioneers (junior high) and Zion's League (senior high) groups are organized through individual congregations. Programs will vary, but all seek to foster recreation, worship, study, and service.

Catholic

There is considerable variety in the way these groups are organized. Some are independent organizations, while others are organized through parishes or parochial schools, or are youth divisions of adult organizations.

Additional youth organizations affiliated with national churches may be found in the Ethnic Heritage Groups section (pages 106–114).

Cadet Commanderies, Knights of St. John

Knights of St. John Supreme
Commandery (1886)
6517 Charles Avenue
Parma, OH 44129
216/845-0570
Brig. Gen. Salvatore LaBianca
Supreme Secretary
Brig. Gen. James Howard Young
Supreme Cadet Organizer
Knights of St. John
2612 Shirley Avenue
Baltimore, MD 21215

Membership is open to Catholic young men ages 8–16. Cadet units are affiliated with parish-based adult commanderies. Dedicated to promoting faith, hope, and charity through service to church and humanity. Sponsors sports program; holds biennial convention.

Catholic Big Brothers of New York, Inc. (1911)

1011 First Avenue
New York, NY 10022
Ed Remson, Executive Director
Merrie Teitel-Greene
Director of Social Services
Steve Becker, Deputy Director
212/371-1000, Ext. 2256
FAX:212/319-8265

Matches inner-city young people ages 9–17, most residing within single-parent families, with adult Big Brothers, Big Sisters and Mentors who spend about 3–5 hours weekly with their young person for at least a year. These adults act as friends, role models and sources of support to the young people with whom they are matched. CBB's Mentoring Project for junior and senior high-school students also includes a peer support/world of work group component.

For information about Catholic Big Brothers/Big Sisters programs in other U.S. cities, contact the archdiocesan office in that area.

Colombian Squires (1925)
Knights of Columbus Supreme Council
1 Columbus Plaza
New Haven, CT 06510-3326
Ronald J. Tracz, Vice President
Fraternal Services
203/772-2130
FAX: 203/772-1923

A program for boys ages 12–18 sponsored by the Knights of Columbus. Seeks to develop leadership through emphasis on intellectual, civic, spiritual, and physical qualities. Membership is drawn from the U.S., Canada, Mexico, and the Philippines.

High School Young Christian Students (1938)
7436 W. Harrison Street
Forest Park, IL 60130
Ed Buck, Director

Works with young people to develop Christian leadership.

Junior Daughters of Peter Claver (1930) (C)
Junior Knights of Peter Claver (1917) (C)
1825 Orleans Avenue
New Orleans, LA 70116
Elmo J. Pratt
Director General, Jr. Knights
Anetta Wilson
National Counselor, Jr. Daughters
504/821-4225
FAX: 504/821-4253

A program for youths ages 7–17. Seeks to motivate youth to gain skills and provide service for church and community; holds biennial convention. Peter Claver (1581–1654) was a Spanish Jesuit who devoted himself to aiding the victims of the African slave trade. He was canonized in 1888.

League of Tarcisians of the Sacred Heart (1917)
3 Adams Street
P.O. Box 111
Fairhaven, MA 02719
Father Alphonsus Mitchell, S.S., C.C.
National Director
508/999-2680

Seeks to increase love for Jesus and His Body the Church, for family, and for all; encourages prayer, the Mass, Communion, sacrifices, and joyful service. For children and youth of elementary through high school age.

National Catholic Forensic League (1952)
21 Nancy Road
Milford, MA 01757
Richard Gaudette, Secretary-Treasurer
508/473-0438

A speech and debate league for students in parochial, private, and public high schools. Organized through local diocesan auspices; holds annual national tournament.

National Christ Child Society, Inc. (1887)
5101 Wisconsin Avenue, N.W., Suite 304
Washington, DC 20016
Mrs. Angie Kopf, President
202/966-9250
FAX: 202/966-2880

An all-volunteer, nonprofit Catholic organization that provides multiple services to needy children and youth, regardless of race or creed. Local chapters are autonomous.

National Federation for Catholic Youth Ministry (1982)

3700-A Oakview Terrace, N.E.
Washington, DC 20017
Fr. Len Wenke, Executive Director
202/636-3825

Not an organization of youth members, but a regional federation of diocesan youth offices and key teenage leaders in each region. It is the coordinating body for all diocesan youth work and convenes regular meetings of its constituency. Sponsors biennial conferences for youth and adults; publishes resources for youth ministries. Associate memberships are available to individuals.

National TEC Conference (1965)

3501 State Street
Omaha, NE 68112
Michael Ellis, Executive Director
402/453-4077
FAX: 402/451-2147

TEC (Teens Encounter Christ) is a 3-day retreat experience. The core of the TEC movement is the proclamation of the central Christian Message—the Paschal Mystery—death, resurrection and mission. Youth not only hear about death, resurrection and mission in Christ, but explore the meaning of these mysteries.

Jewish

Agudath Israel of America

84 William Street
New York, NY 10038
Rabbi Joshua Silbermintz, National Director, Perchei Agudath Israel
Rabbi Avraham N. Perl, Menahel
Devorah Streicher and Leah Zagelbaum Directors, Bnos Agudath Israel
212/797-9000

The youth organizations of Agudath Israel are for othodox Jewish youth. Their programs foster knowledge and fulfillment of Torah and its values and way of life. Boys' and girls' groups meet separately.

Bnos Agudath Israel is the youth movement for girls. On the local level, programming takes the form of *Oneg Shabbos* groups inculcating a love of Torah and *mitzvos*, and a sense of communal responsibility. *Chesed* projects for the elderly and homebound are a particular focus. The national office coordinates publications, interbranch activities, essay contests, and other projects.

Perchei Agudath Israel is the youth movement for boys. Programs create a Torah-based environment for *yeshiva* children ages 8–15 during their extracurricular hours. Program goals are to imbue youngsters with an independent, personal commitment to and love of Torah values, learning, and observance, and to guide them toward an effective application of their study in their daily lives. Activities include *Oneg Shabbos* get-togethers, youth *minyanim*, interbranch conventions, and publications. Conducts a series of national Torah-knowledge competitions; awards prizes and citations for achievements in independent study.

Agudath Israel also conducts the Jewish Education Program (JEP), a release-time program for youngsters with limited Judaic knowledge, who attend New York City public schools. (Contact: JEP National Office, 425 E. 9th Street, Brooklyn, NY 11218, Rabbi Mutty Katz, Director, 718/941-2600.)

American Zionist Youth Foundation (1963)

110 E. 59th Street
New York, NY 10022
Don Adelman, Executive Vice Chairman
212/339-6925
FAX: 212/755-4781

AZYF is a coordinating service agency for member organizations; sponsors large number of educational programs to Israel.

Betar (1923)

218 E. 79th Street
New York, NY 10021
Glenn Mones, Director
212/650-1231
FAX: 212/650-1413

A Zionist Jewish organization for youth ages 12–22 that offers educational activities on a year-round basis, including a summer program in Israel. College students may join Tagar, a politically active Zionist student movement with chapters on over 70 college campuses in the U.S. and Canada. Offers educational materials, summer and winter programs in Israel.

B'nai B'rith Youth Organization (1929) (C)

1640 Rhode Island Avenue, N.W.
Washington, DC 20036
Sam Fisher, International Director
202/857-6633
FAX: 202/857-1099

An international Jewish youth-led organization for teens. Provides opportunities for Jewish youth to develop their leadership potential, a positive Jewish identity, and commitment to their personal development. Includes Aleph Zadik Aleph (AZA) for high school boys, B'nai B'rith Girls for high school girls, and the coeducational Teen Connection for 7th and 8th graders. Recent programs include Project E.A.R.T.H. (Everyone has A Responsibility To our Home) and Project R.E.A.C.H. (Responsibility Everywhere to Aid and Care for the Homeless). Organization offers summer recreational camping and leadership training; Israel Summer Institute; Judaic studies.

Ezrah Youth Movement (1948)

Poale Agudath Israel of America
4405 13th Avenue
Brooklyn, NY 11219
Rabbi Y. Wudowski
Director of Special Projects
718/435-5449
FAX: 718/435-8003

A Zionist movement for youth ages 9–25. Seeks to educate members to Jewish and Torah values and lifestyle.

Habonim-Dror Labor Zionist Youth Movement (1946)

27 W. 20th Street, 9th Floor
New York, NY 10011
Seth Brysk, National Director
212/255-1796
FAX: 212/929-3459

A Zionist youth movement that provides spiritual, cultural, and physical training to increase appreciation of the Jewish heritage and of Israel. Sponsors a summer camping program for youth ages 9–16, a North American training tour for youth who have completed 11th grade, and Workshop, a one-year kibbutz-based program in Israel for high school graduates.

Hashomer Hatzair (1913)

224 W. 35th Street
New York, NY 10001
Avshalom Vilan, Director
212/868-0388, Ext. 77
FAX: 212/868-0364

An international Zionist youth movement for ages 9–23 that educates towards secular Judaism and promotes traditional kibbutz values and lifestyle. Sponsors a summer camping program, the Yedid on Kibbutz, and Yedid Plus Program offering summer experience in Israel for youth ages 15–18. Fosters *garinim* ("seeds") groups among graduates who strengthen existing *kibbutzim* and establish new ones.

Histadruth Ivrith of America (1916)

47 W. 34th Street, Room 600
New York, NY 10001
Dr. Aviva Barzel
Executive Vice President
212/629-9443
FAX: 212/629-9472

The general membership includes youth of all ages throughout North America. Dedicated to the advancement of Hebrew language and culture; provides assistance to schools and camps and sponsors a recognition program for students doing outstanding work in Hebrew. Publishes *Lamishpaha*, an illustrated monthly in simple Hebrew; *Hadoar*, a weekly newspaper in Hebrew; *Tov Lictov*, collected creative work in Hebrew by young people; and *Hebrew in America* in English.

JCC Association/NA (1890)

Jewish Community Centers Association of North America
15 E. 26th Street
New York, NY 10010-1579
Leonard Rubin
Assistant Executive Director
212/532-4949

The Jewish Community Centers Association of North America has 275 affiliated Jewish Community Centers and YMHAs/YWHAs and their branches and camps in the U.S. and Canada. It provides a wide variety of planning, management, and program services to member agencies.

Lubavitch Youth Organization (1955)

770 Eastern Parkway
Brooklyn, NY 11213
Rabbi D. Raskin, Executive Director
718/953-1000

For youth ages 12 and up. Seeks to educate and inspire youth of all ages and from all walks of life; seeks to rescue the estranged and uncommitted, revitalize their spirits, and bring them back into communication with their Jewish heritage and the foundation of the faith.

Masada of the Zionist Organization of America (1933)

4 E. 34th Street
New York, NY 10016
Yuval Koren, Director
212/481-1500

A Zionist organization open to all Jewish youth ages 13–23. Promotes Jewish identity and culture; encourages *aliyah* (immigration of Jews to Israel). Operates summer programs in Israel, including a 6-week stay. Garin Masada is a program for young adults contemplating *aliyah*. Programs for younger children are in the planning stage.

National Conference of Synagogue Youth (1953)

Union of Orthodox Congregations
of America
333 7th Avenue, 18th Floor
New York, NY 10001
Rabbi Raphael Butler, National Director
Chavie Hagler, Director, Jr. Yachad
212/563-4000
FAX: 212/564-9058

A program of educational, cultural, social, and recreational activities for youth ages 13-high school that promotes commitment to a traditional, meaningful Torah lifestyle. Conducts *shabbaotonim* (weekend retreats), U.S. summer tours, recreational camps, New York Torah Experience, and summer programs in Israel. Includes the Our Way program for the hearing impaired.

Conducts Yachad program for the developmentally disabled. Three program levels include: Junior Yachad (ages 9–16), Senior Yachad (ages 16–30), and Rayim (adults). The program encourages mainstreaming and seeks not only to provide a Jewish experience of fun for the disabled, but helps their peers to understand the special needs of persons with disabilities.

National Council of Young Israel Youth (1912)

3 W. 16th Street
New York, NY 10011
Richard Stareshefsky, Director
212/929-1525
FAX: 212/727-9526

This program includes first-graders through collegiate young adults throughout North America and Israel. Promotes traditional Judaism and education in the heritage and culture of the Jewish people; promotes fitness through basketball leagues; sponsors Achva, summer programs in Israel, and Shayara, a year-long program of advanced Jewish studies and community service, with college transfer credits available. Each summer, the National Council runs two cross-country tours in the United States.

NCJW Junior Council (1972)

National Council of Jewish Women
53 W. 23rd Street
New York, NY 10010
212/645-4048
FAX: 212/645-7466

Local sections of the National Council of Jewish Women sponsor Junior Councils. Members of the Junior Councils provide service to the organization and community and raise funds for community service projects.

North American Aliyah Movement (1986)

7 E. 59th Street, Suite 201
New York, NY 10022
Louis Schaeffer, President
212/319-5397
FAX: 212/535-6446

A national Zionist grassroots movement that serves to promote and encourage *aliyah* (immigration of Jews to Israel) from North America. Local support groups around the country, known as Chugei Aliyah, meet on a regular basis to exchange information and hear speakers on a wide range of topics related to Israel and to moving there. In addition, NAAM sponsors a variety of programs to Israel including study programs and student internships. NAAM also assists in job searches in Israel.

North American Federation of Temple Youth (1939)

Union of American Hebrew
Congregations (Reform)
P.O. Box 443
Warwick, NY 10990
Rabbi Allan Smith
Director, Youth Division
914/987-6300
FAX: 914/986-7185

Sponsors youth groups for high school-age members of Reform congregations; a program for junior high youth is under development. Offers recreational camping program for youth ages 8–17 and a variety of summer programs for high school

students in Israel. Holds annual Teenage Leadership Academy for leadership development. College-level program available.

The Religious Zionist Youth Movement—Bnei Akiva of the United States and Canada (1931)

25 W. 26th Street, 4th Floor
New York, NY 10010
Jerry Morgenstern, National Director
212/889-5260
FAX: 212/213-3053

The religious Zionist youth movement for youth ages 7–27, with educational programs that promote Jewish culture and a love of Israel. Promotes *aliyah* (immigration of Jews to Israel) and operates six summer camps in the U.S. and Canada, and a summer tour in Israel. Bnei Akiva sponsors a year-long post-high school Yeshiva and kibbutz work-study program, Midrash U'Maaseh.

Tzivos Hashem—Lubavitch (1980)

332 Kingston Avenue
Brooklyn, NY 11213
Rabbi Yerachmiel Benjaminson
Executive Director
718/467-6630
FAX: 718/467-8527

A worldwide organization of more than 300,000 members from all walks of Jewish life, affiliated and non-affiliated. Girls are members to age 12, boys to age 13.

United Synagogue Youth—Kadima (1951)

United Synagogue of Conservative Judaism (Conservative Movement)
155 Fifth Avenue
New York, NY 10010
Jules Gutin, Director
212/533-7800

An organization for youth (pre-teens through high school) offering religious, social, and cultural educational programs in Israel and the U.S. Summer programs include intensive educational and touring programs in Israel and across the U.S. and Canada.

Young Judaea (1901)
Hashachar (1967)

50 W. 58th Street
New York, NY 10019
Doron Krakow, National Director
212/355-7900
FAX: 212/303-8282

The largest of the Zionist youth organizations, Young Judaea represents the youth arm of the Hadassah Zionist Youth Commission and includes members from grades 4–12. Hamagshimim is the related organization for youth of college age. Groups are sponsored by Hadassah chapters and promote Jewish identity, education about Israel, leadership development, and service education. Programs offered include summer camping for youth in grades 3–12; summer programs in Israel for high school students; and a year-long program in Israel for students just completing high school. Hashachar is the umbrella organization for Young Judaea and Hamagshamim.

Yugntruf Youth for Yiddish (1964)

200 W. 72nd Street, Room 40
New York, NY 10023
Dr. Adina Singer and Binyamen Schaechter, Co-Chairpersons
David Braun, Editor-in-Chief
212/787-6675

Promotes the use of the Yiddish language among young adults 17–40; publishes *Yugntruf*, a quarterly magazine written in Yiddish by members; helps develop Yugntruf groups through the U.S.; maintains a resource center for information on Yiddish culture. Sponsors classes, conversation groups, a yearly week-long retreat, and the Pripetchik Playgroup, a Yiddish children's school in New York City.

Other Religious Organizations

Baha'i National Youth Task Force (1950)

National Teaching Committee Office
Baha'i National Center
Wilmette, IL 60091
Kathleen Colucci
Coordinator, Youth Desk
708/869-9039, Ext. 237
FAX: 708/869-0247

For youth of the Baha'i faith ages 12–24. Concerned with development of positive attributes such as love, unity and humility; promotes world peace and service to humanity; creates an environment that encourages personal and collective responsibility for establishing racial, ethnic, religious and national unity and the equality of women and men. Works in collaboration with youth and adults to further the Baha'i Faith and develop models of Baha'i community life. Older youth are encouraged to devote a year to full-time domestic or international service to the Faith in the Baha'i Youth Service Corps.

Moslem Youth of North America

P.O. Box 38
Plainfield, IN 46168
317/839-8157
FAX: 317/839-8140

Organization of young people of the Moslem faith, ages 12–18.

Western Young Buddhist League (1948)

Buddhist Churches of America
1710 Octavia Street
San Francisco, CA 94109
National Youth Coordinator
415/776-5600

Coordinates the activities of young Buddhists of the Jodo Shinshu denomination.

Resources

Programs of Religious Activities with Youth (1973)

8520 MacKenzie Road
P.O. Box 6900
St. Louis, MO 63123-3433
Mark P. Hazlewood, Executive Director
314/638-1017

Provides religious program materials to supplement Girl Scout, Boy Scout, and Camp Fire programming in local churches. Its major resource, *God and Country*, focuses on Christian growth for church members who are involved in these youth programs. The organization also sponsors conferences to link churches and youth agencies. Publishes *Youthscope* three times a year (free), with information about the Commission and resources available for building church-youth agency relationships.

Reach Out Ministries, Inc. (1977)

3961 Holcomb Bridge Road, Suite 201
Norcross, GA 30092
Barry St. Clair, Founder/Executive Director
404/441-2247
FAX: 404/449-7544

Provides training for church youth workers to assist them in communicating effectively with students. Through training modules, personal encouragement, and resource equipping, youth workers discover and learn how to develop a strategy to reach youth, set and accomplish priorities, recruit additional leadership, and maintain a vibrant personal faith.

Youth Leadership, Inc.

122 W. Franklin Avenue, Suite 510
Minneapolis, MN 55404
Rev. Dennis McLuen, Executive Director
612/870-3632
FAX:612/870-4885

A nondenominational training organization committed to preparing adults to serve adolescents and their families. Services include an accredited Graduate School of Youth Ministry that offers a Masters Degree in youth ministry through two cooperating Minnesota seminaries. Offers in-service seminars for youth workers, training for volunteers, and workshops for parents of teenagers.

See also:

The Center for Youth Studies, page 146; **Group Publishing, Inc.**, page 149; **Youth Specialties, Inc.**, page 163.

Conservation and Humane Education Groups

At present, many of the organizations listed in this section do not sponsor club programs for youth at the national level. However, many of their local affiliates have active programs for youth members, and inquiry should be made locally. Some of the groups sponsor expedition and summer programs for high school youth. Write to the national offices for descriptions of these programs.

These organizations publish relatively low-cost conservation or nature study materials appropriate for use by other youth groups. Catalogs or publication lists are available from the national offices.

American Society for the Prevention of Cruelty to Animals (ASPCA) (1866)

424 East 92nd Street
New York, NY 10128
Director of Education
212/876-7700

America's oldest humane society provides assistance and resources on humane education to teachers and youth group leaders. Humane education teaches empathy and respect for all animals, humans, and the environment. A consultation with an ASPCA specialist on how to incorporate animal-related materials throughout the curriculum will result in a richer lesson plan and students with an educated concern for the world around them.

Children's Action for Animals (1985)

American Humane Education Society
350 S. Huntington Avenue
Boston, MA 02130
Judith Golden, Director
617/541-5095
FAX: 617/983-5449

A classroom-based program to aid young people in their understanding of animal life. Pet Protection Kits are also available to teach care and safety and other aspects of responsible pet ownership. Distributes other curricular materials. Contact for further information.

Children's Alliance for the Protection of the Environment (1989)

P.O. Box 307
Austin, TX 78767
Patricia Scharr, Executive Director
512/476-2273
FAX: 512/476-2301

CAPE is an international network of young people throughout the U.S. and in 35 other countries that seeks to empower them to take action to preserve, conserve, and protect the environment locally and globally. Young people may join as individuals, clubs, schools or scout troops. Facilitates pen pal relationships; encourages young people to form partnerships to make a project happen. Publishes newsletter, *Many Hands*, and program guide for schools.

EARTHWATCH (1972)

680 Mount Auburn Street, Box 403
Watertown, MA 02172
Brian A. Rosborough, President
617/926-8200
FAX: 617/926-8532

The nonprofit EARTHWATCH recruits volunteers for field research expeditions in disciplines ranging from archaeology to zoology. People 16 years of age or older are able to join any of the over 100 expeditions in 36 countries and 16 states. Some of the current projects include working with Australian scientists studying the kangaroo, helping with archaeological excavations in Majorca or Israel, or investigating reasons for infant malnutrition in Zimbabwe. Two- to three-week-long research sessions are directed by noted university scholars, and volunteers pay a share of the costs of the research. Membership in EARTHWATCH costs $25.00 per year, which includes subscriptions to *EARTHWATCH Magazine* and the *Expedition News*. Catalog available.

Inner City Outings (1971)

Sierra Club (1892)
730 Polk Street
San Francisco, CA 94109
Debra Asher
Inner City Outings Coordinator
415/923-5628
FAX: 415/776-4868

Inner City Outings is a community outreach program of the Sierra Club. Trained volunteer leaders provide wilderness adventures and environmental educational experiences for people who wouldn't otherwise have them, including urban youth of diverse cultural and ethnic backgrounds, seniors, hearing or visually impaired individuals, and the physically disabled. Specific programs will vary; contact your local Sierra Club chapter for information.

The Izaak Walton League of America (1922)

1401 Wilson Boulevard, Level B
Arlington, VA 22209
Karen Firehock
Save Our Streams Director
703/528-1818
FAX: 703/528-1836

Save Our Streams (SOS) is a citizen-action program for protecting surface water in which individual young people and organized youth groups can take part. By "adopting" a stream, youth commit themselves to its care on a year-round basis. The League publishes other materials related to the protection and wise use of natural resources. Many local affiliates have Uncle Ike programs for youth. SOS adoption kits and materials are available at low cost. List available. Write for a free brochure on how young people can save streams.

Kids for a Clean Environment (1989)

P.O. Box 158254
Nashville, TN 37215
Trish Poe, Director
800/952-FACE (800/952-3223)
615/331-7381
FAX: 615/333-9879

An environmental action organization for young people ages 9 and up. Local chapters and individual members of Kids F.A.C.E. are encouraged to create environmental programs that fit the needs of their own schools and communities. Such projects have included recycling programs, planting trees, keeping "energy logs" of the energy they use, and writing plays and commercials about the environment. Members share ideas through a newsletter.

Kids for Saving Earth (1990)

P.O. Box 47247
Plymouth, MN 55447-0247
612/525-0002

The first Kids for Saving Earth (KSE) Club was started by a young Minnesotan named Clinton Hill, who, with his classmates, believed that young people can make a difference in saving the environment. When Clinton died of cancer in 1989, his parents, with the help of many sponsors, carried on his mission of establishing KSE Clubs all over the world. KSE publishes a guidebook and a youth-written quarterly newsletter. Send SASE for more information.

Kids in Bloom

ECO-RENEWAL
P.O. Box 344
Zionsville, IN 46077
Kay Grimm, Director
317/290-6996

A company that deals in "heirloom" seeds—strains of vegetables and garden and wild flowers that have been passed on from generation to generation, adapting naturally to their environments along the way. Seeks to maintain biodiversity through the use of these old varieties. Seeds are packaged for young people; each packet comes with instructions and "blooming tips," as well as a history of the plant and how it has been used through the years. Seed catalog available.

National Association for Humane and Environmental Education (1974)

P.O. Box 362
East Haddam, CT 06423-0362
203/434-8666
FAX: 203/434-9579

NAHEE is the youth education division of the Humane Society of the United States. Promotes kindness toward people, animals, and the Earth through sponsorship of Kids In Nature's Defense (KIND) Clubs at the elementary level. Publishes *Kind News*, a monthly newspaper for children available at three reading levels, covering grades K–6. Each issue is sent to the classroom in bundles of 32 copies with a 3-page teaching guide and a Kind Club packet. Each class that receives *Kind News* automatically becomes a KIND Club. Individuals, civic groups, and businesses can supply teachers with subscriptions through the Adopt-a-Teacher program. NAHEE also publishes materials for secondary-level students, including the *Student Action Guide*, *Student Network News*, and the teaching packet, *Alternatives to Dissection*.

National Audubon Society (1905)*

National Education Office
RR #1, Box 171
Sharon, CT 06069
Marshall Case
Vice President for Education
203/364-0520
FAX: 203/434-9579

93

The Audubon Adventures program provides curricular materials for in-school use (ages 10–11). Special materials have been developed for Native American youth. Audubon Expedition Institutes are available for youth ages 12–15; other expedition programs are available for those 16 and over (age limits will vary). Sponsors summer educational programs, with academic credit available. In addition to the programs of the national office, local affiliates offer many other opportunities for youth participation. *Unable to obtain current information.*

National Bird-Feeding Society

2218 Crabtree
P.O. Box 23
Northbrook, IL 60065-0023
Sue Wells, Executive Director
708/272-0135

A society of individuals of all ages who enjoy feeding their backyard birds. NBS funds research and educational projects that promote improved feeding techniques, better housing, and more effective ways to attract and keep birds coming to feed; promotes bird-feeding as a family activity. Publishes newsletter, *Birds-eye reView.*

National Energy Foundation (1973)

5160 Wiley Post Way, Suite 200
Salt Lake City, UT 84116
Edward A. Dalton, Ed.D.
President and CEO
801/539-1406

The National Energy foundation creates and distributes economical instructional materials dealing with energy, water, mining, science, technology, conservation,

the environment, and other national resource topics. NEF is a unique non-profit educational organization devoted to the development of instructional materials and the implementation of innovative teacher training and student programs. NEF is supported by businesses, government agencies, associations and the education community. The Foundation's materials and programs enhance and supplement existing curricula. NEF invites all to join in the quest to improve education and prepare a scientifically and technologically literate public.

National Wildlife Federation (1936)

1400 16th Street, N.W.
Washington, DC 20036-2266
Dr. Gary San Julian, Vice President
for Research and Education
800/432-6564

Publishes magazines and books for children and adults; produces a nationally acclaimed environmental education activity series, *NatureScope*, for educators; and sponsors National Wildlife Week. Current publications are offered for a nominal fee; call and ask for an information directory and publications list. Subscribers to *Ranger Rick* magazine automatically become members of Ranger Rick's Nature Club. Local clubs meet independently of the National Wildlife Federation. The Federation has discontinued the Discovery Club program.

PETA Kids
People for the Ethical Treatment of
Animals
P.O. Box 42516
Washington, DC 20015
Jeanne Roush, Executive Director
301/770-7444
FAX: 301/770-8969

PETA Kids are young activists under age
13 who are concerned with the rights of
animals and their use in laboratories and
the meat industry. The organization also
provides support to young people who
object to animal dissection in the classroom, and provides materials for teachers
suggesting alternative ways of learning.
Members receive a membership card and
twice-yearly issues of *PETA Kids*. Youths
age 13 and over may become regular
members of PETA.

Student Action Corps for Animals (1981)
P.O. Box 15588
Washington, DC 20003
Rosa Feldman, Director
202/543-8983

An advocacy and educational organization that seeks to empower high school
students to work on behalf of animal
rights. Provides individual assistance and
telephone counseling to students refusing
to perform dissections. Sporadically publishes *SACA News*, a newsletter for students that serves as a forum for animal
rights issues while encouraging networking and activism.

The Student Conservation Association, Inc. (1957)
P.O. Box 550
Charlestown, NH 03603
Scott D. Izzo, President
603/543-1700
FAX: 603/543-1828

Involves student volunteers ages 16 and
up in the stewardship of national parks,
forests, and wildlife refuge areas. Offers
educational opportunities for volunteers
to pursue personal and career goals in
conservation. Most of the high school
work groups run for 4–5 weeks during the
summer months; Resource Assistant
positions for those 18 and older run for
12–14 weeks year-round. Conducts conservation exchange programs involving
youth from Mexico, the Soviet Union, and
the U.S. Publishes *Earth Work*, a monthly
magazine for and about current and
future conservation professionals.

Student Environmental Action Coalition (1988)
P.O. Box 1168
Chapel Hill, NC 27514-1168
800/700-SEAC (800/700-7322)
919/967-4600
FAX: 919/967-4648

A coalition that brings a sense of unity
to the many existing environmental
groups on high school and college campuses throughout the nation. Provides
training for grass-roots organizing; publishes monthly magazine, *Threshold*.

Touch America Project (TAP) (1983)

U.S. Forest Service
P.O. Box 96090
Washington, DC 20090
Don Hansen, Manager
Volunteer Programs
703/235-8858
FAX: 703/235-1597

A volunteer program through which youth ages 14–17 learn about the nation's natural resources. Young people work on conservation projects on public lands. This is a partnership program with major youth organizations and other groups interested in conservation.

Youth for Environmental Sanity (1990)

706 Frederick Street
Santa Cruz, CA 95062
Ocean Robbins, Director
408/ 459-9344
FAX: 408/458-0255

A project of the EarthSave Foundation, YES! Tours bring young environmental crusaders to local communities to make presentations on environmental and social issues in assemblies, workshops, and hands-on training sessions. Week-long environmental leadership summer camps train young people to start local clubs, take action for the protection of the environment.

See also:

National Gardening Association, page 14; National Junior Horticultural Association, page 15.

Service Organization Youth Programs

Anchor Clubs (1952)
Pilot International

Pilot International Building
P.O. Box 4844
Macon, GA 31213-0599
Cynthia Mills, Executive Director
Gina Wyatt, Anchor Coordinator
912/743-7403
FAX: 912/743-2173

A voluntary service organization (of primarily high-school-aged youth) sponsored by local Pilot Clubs. Anchors work with Pilot members on projects to assist and increase awareness of those affected by brain-related disorders.

C.L.A.S.S. Program (1991)

International Training in Communication
2519 Woodland Drive
Anaheim, CA 92801
Muriel Bryant, Executive Director
714/995-3660
FAX: 714/995-6974

The Communication, Leadership, and Speaking Skills Program is an eight-week training program for junior and senior high school students. Program is in use in the U.S., Australia, and South Africa. C.L.A.S.S. replaces the Zenith Club program.

Excel Clubs (1929)

National Exchange Club
3050 Central Avenue
Toledo, OH 43606-1700
Neal Davis, Executive Vice President
419/535-3232
FAX: 419/535-1989

Sponsored by local Exchange Clubs for high school youth, Excel works to promote responsible American citizenship and service to the community. Sponsors the One Nation Under God program and the National Youth of the Month and Year awards.

Interact (1962)

Rotary International
1560 Sherman Avenue
1 Rotary Center
Evanston, IL 60201
Jennifer L. Mehlan, Program Coordinator, Partners in Service Section
708/866-3296
FAX: 708/328-8554

Clubs for young men and women ages 14–18 dedicated to service and international understanding. The program aims to develop constructive leadership and personal integrity, as well as develop an attitude of individual responsibility. Clubs may be school- or community-based. Rotary International also sponsors Rotaract, a worldwide organization for young men and women ages 18–30, that improves the lives of others through community and international service projects.

Rotary International also sponsors several other programs for youth. Write or call for more information.

See also:

Youth Exchange Program, page 62.

Junior Civitan International (1935)

Civitan International
P.O. Box 130744
Birmingham, AL 35213-0744
Mary M. Luck, Staff Director
800/CIVITAN (800/248-4826)
205/591-8910

A service club for youth in junior and senior high schools. Seeks to promote good citizenship in the home, school, and community; encourage high standards of scholarship and respect for the law; support good government; and develop leadership through service. Junior Civitan members also aid persons with physical and mental disabilities on the local, district, and international levels. Clubs may be all male, all female, or coed, and are sponsored by adult Civitan Clubs.

Junior Optimist Octagon International (1920)

Optimist International
4494 Lindell Boulevard
St. Louis, MO 63108
Barbara Lehocky, Director
314/371-6000
FAX: 314/371-6006

Civic service organizations for elementary students (Alpha Clubs), junior high students (Jr. Optimist Clubs) and high school students (Octagon Clubs). They promote active interest in good government and civic affairs; leadership through service; self-discovery; appreciation of aesthetic, cultural, and spiritual values; and civic betterment.

Key Club International (1925)
Builders Clubs

Kiwanis International
3636 Woodview Trace
Indianapolis, IN 46268
David A. Wohler, Administrator
317/875-8755

Key Club International is a high school student organization that promotes service to school and community, citizenship, and leadership training. Builders Clubs for junior high students have the same aims.

Leo Club Program (1967)

Lions Clubs International
300 22nd Street
Oakbrook, IL 60521-8842
Rose Mary Ozga, Manager
Youth Programs Department
708/571-5466, Ext. 323
FAX: 708/571-8890

Promotes leadership development among young men and women ages 12–28. Encourages them to assume leadership roles within their clubs and to provide service to others.

See also:

Lions-Quest, pages 65–66.

Rotary Youth Leadership Awards

Contact your local Rotary Club for information.

RYLA is a leadership training program open to qualified young people ages 14–30; Participants are chosen by local Rotary clubs; applicants must be well-organized and demonstrate good listening and problem-solving skills, administrative aptitude, friendly rapport with others and a willingness to master public speaking. Participants attend an all-expense-paid three- to ten-day workshop with other young people from communities in their area. Seminars are organized and run by Rotarians and include a wide range of educational topics tailored to the age group in attendance. Program stresses exchange of ideas, career exploration, leadership skill development, conflict resolution, and personal responsibility as role models in their communities.

S Clubs (1958)

Soroptimist International
of the Americas
1616 Walnut Street
Philadelphia, PA 19103
215/732-0512
FAX: 215/732-7508

An organization for junior and senior high school students who wish to serve their schools and communities. S Clubs are sponsored by local Soroptimist Clubs.

School Safety Patrols

American Automobile Association
1000 AAA Drive
Heathrow, FL 32746
Dean Childs, Director, Traffic Safety Services

For students in grades 5–8 in U.S. schools and 30 foreign countries. The national organization publishes policies and standards developed collaboratively with several national organizations such as the national Congress of PTAs and the

National Safety Council. Patrols are organized in schools and assisted by local AAA affiliates. In some cities, patrols are supported by several sponsoring organizations. Activities will vary from one jurisdiction to another. Belts, badges, rain wear, awards, membership and parent-consent cards, handbooks and manuals, and much more are provided by local AAA affiliates. For more information, contact local AAA offices.

Serteen Clubs (1971)

Sertoma International
1912 E. Meyer Boulevard
Kansas City, MO 64132
Terri McCaffrey, Director of
International Sponsorship
816/333-8300
FAX: 816/333-4320

For high school youth in grades 9–12; sponsored by local Sertoma Clubs. Youth provide service and raise funds for projects related to the needs of their own communities.

Self-Help Organizations

Alateen (1957)

Al-Anon Family Group
Headquarters, Inc.
P.O. Box 862, Midtown Station
New York, NY 10018-0862
Alateen Administrator
800/356-9996
212/302-7240
FAX: 212/869-3757

Alateen is a fellowship of young Al-Anon members, usually teenagers, whose lives have been affected by someone else's drinking. In Alateen they learn that they are not the cause of anyone else's drinking or behavior; they cannot change or control anyone but themselves; they have spiritual and intellectual resources with which to develop their own potentials, no matter what happens at home; and they can build satisfying and rewarding life experiences for themselves. At Alateen meetings, young people share their experiences, strength, and hope with one another but offer no advice. Meetings are conducted by the young people themselves and guided by an Al-Anon member.

Cocaine Anonymous World Services

P.O. Box 2000
Los Angeles, CA 90049-8000
310/559-5833
FAX: 310/559-2554

Cocaine Anonymous is not a youth organization, but they welcome young members who are recovering from cocaine addiction or who are significant others of such individuals. The national organization is a federation of state and local chapters who use the traditional Twelve Step program of recovery.

Daughters and Sons United (1972)

232 E. Gish Road, First Floor
San Jose, CA 95112
Patti-Ann Bossert, M.S.W., Coordinator
408/453-7616
FAX: 408/453-9064

DSU, with more than 100 local chapters across the country, is the children's component of Garrette Institute, assisting sexually abused children and their families.

Affiliated with Parents United. Internationally, DSU offers professionally-led counseling programs and a guided self-help program designed to help children support each other and speak out to break the cycle of child abuse.

Gay/Lesbian Youth Hotline (1990)

The Indiana Youth Group
P.O. Box 20716
Indianapolis, IN 46220-0716
800/347-TEEN (800/347-8336)
317/546-8336 (In Indianapolis)

The Gay/Lesbian Youth Hotline is a peer counseling and informational line for self-identified gay and lesbian youth under 21. It seeks to help reduce their feelings of isolation and rejection, build self-esteem, offer social support, and provide information that will reduce high risk behavior and the spread of HIV infection and AIDS. The line is open year-round on Thursday through Sunday nights from seven p.m. to midnight (EST).

Hug-a-Tree and Survive (1981)

6465 Lance Way
San Diego, CA 92120
Ab Taylor, President and Founder

A safety education program for children ages 5–12 designed for presentation in school assemblies and to youth organizations. It teaches youngsters how not to get lost, how to stay safe and comfortable if they do get lost, and how to increase their chances of being spotted and found. Please send SASE for information.

Narcotics Anonymous (1953)

World Service Office
P.O. Box 9999
Van Nuys, CA 91409
818/780-3951
FAX: 818/785-0923

Narcotics Anonymous is a fellowship of recovering addicts who help each other stay clean. There are no dues or fees for NA services, and NA is open to any addict regardless of age, race, sexual orientation, creed, religion or lack of religion.

National Self-Help Clearinghouse (1977)

25 W. 43rd Street, Room 620
New York, NY 10036
Dr. Frank Riessman, Director
212/642-2944
FAX: 212/642-1956

Provides information and referral to self-help groups and clearinghouses throughout the country; runs conferences and fairs, trains professionals, and helps to facilitate start-up of self-help groups. Publishes a quarterly newsletter and other materials on how to organize self-help groups.

RAINBOWS (1983)

1111 Tower Road
Schaumburg, IL 60173
Suzy Yehl Marta, Founder and President
708/310-1880
FAX: 708/310-0120

A 12-week support program for youth from elementary school through high school who are experiencing grief following a loss through death or divorce. RAINBOWS materials are available for use in religious and secular settings. RAINBOWS uses trained volunteer facilitators, who work with small groups of youth to help them work through the grieving process.

Youth Suicide National Center

445 Virginia Avenue
San Mateo, CA 94402
Charlotte Ross, Executive Director
415/342-5755
FAX: 415/342-6615

Coordinates and mobilizes efforts to prevent youth suicide among young people; provides information to lay and professional public regarding youth suicide and how to prevent it. Membership is open to all ages.

Substance Abuse Prevention and Temperance Organizations

America's PRIDE Program (1977)

National Parents' Resource Institute for Drug Education
10 Park Place S., Suite 340
Atlanta, GA 30303
Dr. Thomas Gleaton
Executive Director/Founder
Michelle Basket
National Youth Director
404/577-4500
FAX: 404/688-6937

Dedicated to creating an international generation of drug-free youth. Offers a comprehensive range of drug prevention programs and services to parents, youth, community organizations, and educators

throughout the U.S. and in nine other nations. Presents energetic weekend retreats for youth that emphasize education, leadership, communication, and performance. Program levels include PRIDE Junior (elementary student); Club PRIDE (junior high students); and America's PRIDE (high school students).

International Good Templars Youth Fellowship

International Organization of
Good Templars National Council
of the USA (1851)
National Office and Museum
2926 Cedar Avenue
Minneapolis, MN 55407
612/721-7606
Arlene Melton
National Director of Youth Work
221 10th Street
Wilmette, IL 60091

The International Organization of Good Templars (IOGT) is one of the pioneer organizations educating youth to total abstinence from alcohol or other drugs. IGTYF holds a national conference, an International Congress, and a worldwide cultural conference, all triennially.

"Just Say No" International (1985)

2101 Webster Street, Suite 1300
Oakland, CA 94612
Ivy Cohen, President
800/258-2766
510/451-6666
FAX: 510/451-9360

Provides materials, technical assistance, and training to help children and teens ages 5–18 lead healthy, productive, drug-free lives. Researched, developed, and introduced Youth Power program (1993) to foster young people's resiliency, drawing on and encouraging the skills and attributes that allow young people to cope with challenges and adversity. Four separate projects of the program provide a framework for empowering youth to discover and hone their assets so as to succeed in all areas of their lives.

Loyal Temperance Legion (1877)

Youth's Temperance Council
Tots for Temperance
White Ribbon Recruits
Woman's Christian Temperance Union
1730 Chicago Avenue
Evanston, IL 60201
Natalie Wilson
National Executive Director, LTL
3789 Northland Drive
Los Angeles, CA 90008
Mrs. Rita Wert
National Executive Director, YTC
2250 Creek Hill Road
Lancaster, PA 17601

These youth groups are dedicated to total abstinence as the most effective means of avoiding the abuse of alcohol and other drugs. The WCTU pioneered in the education of youth against substance abuse. Groups include White Ribbon Recruits (infants through age 3 dedicated by their parents); Tots for Temperance (ages 3–5); Loyal Temperance Legion (ages 6–12); and Youth's Temperance Council (teens through young adults). The WCTU's Signal Press (Evanston address) publishes extensive materials on substance abuse prevention that are available at very low cost. Catalog available.

National Association of Teen Institutes (1984)

c/o CCACD
100 Billingsley Road
Charlotte, NC 28211-1072
John King, Administrator
704/376-7447
FAX: 704/376-2172

A coalition of nearly 100 autonomous state and local organizations that conduct Teen Institutes designed to train teenagers in substance abuse prevention skills. Trained teens return to their communities and implement prevention programs. Individuals and organizations that support the Teen Institute concept may join as "Interested Others." NATI annually conducts a national Teen Training Institute and a national conference on prevention.

National Family Partnership (1980)

11159-B South Towne Square
St. Louis, MO 63123
Phyllis Dettman, Executive Director
314/845-1933
FAX: 314/845-2117

The National Family Partnership (NFP) is a national nonprofit organization dedicated to the formation and support of local parent and youth groups. NFP sponsors the National Red Ribbon Celebration which promotes drug awareness and prevention of the illegal use of tobacco, alcohol, and other drugs. NFP also sponsors Advanced Youth Leadership Training conducted during the annual conference. Students who attend this training return to their own communities with specific skills and plans for working towards a supportive drug-free environment as well as drug-free youth. CODE RED (formerly

REACH and Lifers) is a two-day seminar with separate training programs for middle/junior high and high school students; emphasizes a strong "no use" message, and informs young people with current information on tobacco, alcohol, and other drugs, addresses the impact of advertising on behavior, teaches peer pressure reversal skills and peer leadership skills. Also trains students in how to conduct drug education presentations for younger elementary-school students and other teen groups in their communities.

Students Against Driving Drunk (SADD) (1982)

P.O. Box 800
Marlboro, MA 01752
William F. Cullinane, Executive Director
508/481-3568
FAX: 508/481-5759

An organization of students united to combat underage drinking, drug abuse and impaired driving, the nation's number one killer of youth. Provides a community awareness program; promotes the use of the student-parent contract and the party guide. School-based programs include Students Against Doing Drugs (middle school), Students Against Driving Drunk (high school), and Student Athletes Detest Drugs, a program for athletes. College program encourages contracts among friends.

Students To Offset Peer Pressure (STOPP) (1984)

STOPP Consulting Services
P.O. Box 103
Hudson, NH 03051-0103
Peter M. Jean, Executive Director
603/889-8163

An organization of high school-aged youth dedicated to promoting a drug-free environment by providing alternatives to drugs. Junior STOPP (for grades 5–8) and STOPP-A-TEER Clubs (preschool through grade 5) offer youth-led education programs. Individual clubs plan and sponsor alternative activities such as plays, dances, field trips, programs, and speakers. Proceeds from activities support educational programs designed by the club members themselves. Adult groups work with the community to inform the public of related issues. Organization offers training programs and assistance in organizing and sustaining clubs.

Youth to Youth International (1982)

CompDrug (1971)

700 Bryden Road
Columbus, OH 43215
Lori Frantz, Jill Povoli, Directors
614/224-4506
FAX: 614/224-8451

A comprehensive youth leadership and community-based drug prevention program for middle and high school students. Provides a summer conference training series for teams of adults and youths. Provides leadership and Speakers Bureau training for teens. Offers "drug-free gear"—T-shirts, buttons, manuals, etc. Has continuous programming throughout the year.

See also:

Alateen, page 99; **Cocaine Anonymous World Services**, page 99; **Narcotics Anonymous**, page 100.

Resource

Do It Now Foundation (1968)
P.O. Box 27568
Tempe, AZ 85285
James Parker, Executive Director
602/491-0393
FAX: 602/491-2849

The Do It Now Foundation publishes a wide variety of low-cost booklets, leaflets, posters, and reports on drug, alcohol, and health-related issues. Not a membership organization. Catalog available.

Hereditary, Veterans, Military, and Patriotic Groups

American Legion and Auxiliary Youth Programs

The American Legion and the American Legion Auxiliary sponsor a broad range of youth services, including Boys State/ Boys Nation (see page 52), Girls State/ Girls Nation (see pages 52–53), and American Legion Baseball (see page 32). They hold annual oratorical contests and other competitive events. Local posts often sponsor troops or clubs affiliated with other national youth organizations.

Junior Members, American Legion Auxiliary (1919)
777 N. Meridian Street
Indianapolis, IN 46204
National Secretary
317/635-6291
FAX: 317/636-5590

Membership is open to female descendants (up to age 18) of Legion members and men or women who saw active duty in WWI, WWII, the Korean and Vietnam Wars, Grenada, Lebanon, Panama, and the Persian Gulf War. Activities stress service to the community and the organization. Write for additional details on membership criteria.

Sons of the American Legion (1932)
P.O. Box 1055
Indianapolis, IN 46206
John W. Kerestan, SAL Staff Liaison
317/635-8411

Membership is open to male descendants, adopted sons, and stepsons of members of the American Legion, and such male descendants of veterans who died in service during WWI, WWII, the Korean and Vietnam Wars, Grenada, Lebanon, Panama, and the Persian Gulf War. The program is devoted to perpetuating a true spirit of Americanism and inculcating a sense of obligation to community, state, and nation.

Veterans of Foreign Wars and Ladies Auxiliary Youth Programs

In addition to their youth organizations, the VFW and the Ladies Auxiliary sponsor several competitive scholarship programs. Voice of Democracy, an audio/ essay competition, is a script-writing contest in which over 300,000 youth participate annually through their schools; 53 finalists compete for scholarships. They also sponsor the Young American Creative Patriotic Art Awards and the Outstanding Young Volunteer of the Year Awards. Members of Junior Girls Units of the Ladies Auxiliary to the VFW are also eligible to compete for the Junior Girls Scholarship.

The VFW encourages local posts to sponsor youth sports and scouting programs.

Sons of the Veterans of Foreign Wars (1930)
VFW Building, 7th Floor
34th and Broadway
Kansas City, MO 64111
Gordon R. Thorson
Director of Youth Activities
816/756-3390

Membership is open to males through age 18 whose fathers or grandfathers are eligible for membership in the VFW (i.e., have received a campaign ribbon for overseas duty). The program is designed to build rapport between fathers and sons. Youth units are sponsored through local VFW posts.

Additional Organizations

Children of the Confederacy (1955)
United Daughters of the Confederacy
328 North Boulevard
Richmond, VA 23220-4057
804/355-1636

For boys and girls from birth to age 18 who are lineal descendants of Confederate men and women who served honorably in the War between the States.

Children of the Republic of Texas (1891)
The Daughters of the Republic of Texas
510 E. Anderson Lane
Austin, TX 78752
Lee Spencer, CRT Director
512/339-1997
FAX: 512/339-1998

For youth under age 21 who are descended from men and women who were citizens of, or soldiers for, Texas before February 19, 1846. Program emphasizes the study of Texas history, preserving historical artifacts, and cherishing the cultural heritage of Texas.

Devil Pups, Inc. (1954)
1 Wilshire Boulevard, Suite 2000
Los Angeles, CA 90017
Duncan Shaw, Jr., President
213/629-7743

A program for young men ages 14–17 conducted at Camp Pendleton during the month of July. Stresses physical fitness and the development of good citizenship, including self-control, discipline, self-confidence, respect for others, and national pride.

Junior American Citizens Committee (1906)

Daughters of the American Revolution
1776 D Street, N.W.
Washington, DC 20006-5392
Mrs. Burt T. Weyhing
National Chairwoman
202/628-1776

This organization seeks to "instill good citizenship in youth of all races, creeds, and economic backgrounds, by teaching loyalty to the U.S.A., giving practical ideas for service to home, community, school, and country." Membership is open to all youth from pre-school through high school.

Junior Sons of America (1847)

Patriotic Order, Sons of America
1547 Pratt Street
Philadelphia, PA 19124
Harvey Stoehr, Executive Secretary
215/289-2646

A civilian patriotic order devoted to promoting an appreciation for our heritage of freedom. Sponsors educational tours, study of the Constitution, etc. Youth up to age 16 may belong to the junior order; between ages 16–18 they may transfer to the adult organization.

National Organization, Sons of Union Veterans of the Civil War (1881)

411 Bartlett Street
Lansing, MI 48915
James T. Lyons
National Secretary-Treasurer

This is not primarily a youth organization, but males ages 14 and over who are direct lineal descendants of Union Veterans of the Civil War are eligible for membership.

National Society, Children of the American Revolution (1895)

1776 D Street, N.W.
Washington, DC 20006
Administrator
202/638-3153

For lineal descendants, from birth to age 22, of patriots of the American Revolution.

Ethnic Heritage Groups

The organizations in this category exist to preserve and promote the material culture and traditions of a particular ethnic heritage. Some are restricted to youth of a specific ethnic background; others are open to all who are interested. Some have insurance functions as fraternal or mutual benefit societies. Many offer scholarship programs.

American Carpatho-Russian Youth (1939)

American Carpatho-Russian
Orthodox Diocese
312 Garfield Street
Johnstown, PA 15906
814/536-4207
Very Rev. John R. Fedornock
National Spiritual Advisor
211 Cable Avenue
East Pittsburgh, PA 15112
412/824-0246

Seeks to foster, perpetuate, uphold, protect, learn, and maintain the Faith of their Fathers, the Holy Eastern Orthodox Greek Catholic Faith; promotes the healthy, clean, spiritual, social, cultural, educational, and athletic development of the young people of the Carpatho-Russian diocese; fosters true Americanism, loyalty and allegiance to the government of the United States. Junior Groups are for youth ages 10–16; Senior Groups are for ages 16 and up. Supports the institutions of the Diocese such as the Seminary, Monastery, Youth Camp, and Church Schools.

American Romanian Orthodox Youth (1950)

Romanian Orthodox Episcopate
of America
2522 Grey Tower Road
Jackson, MI 49201-9120
Nicholas Gibb, IV, National President
(elected annually)
517/522-4800

For youth in their teens to age 30 who are members of Romanian Orthodox parishes. Youths support projects of the church and assist with summer camping and church-school programs. Sponsors sports tournaments in football, soccer, basketball, volleyball and softball. Raises funds for Project Hope, which is providing education for medical professionals in Romania.

American Sokol Organization (1865)

6424 W. Cermak Road
Berwyn, IL 60402
Charles R. Borvansky, President
708/795-6671
FAX: 708/795-0539

Promotes Czech culture, customs, and language, but membership is open to all. Fosters physical fitness through gymnastics instruction and competitions, as well as through other sports such as golf, swimming, volleyball, and track.

ARCAYD

Fellowship (1948)
Association of Romanian Catholics of America Youth Department
1700 Dale Drive
Merrillville, IN 46410-1340
George Stroia, Director
219/980-0726

ARCAYD (for youth to age 21) and the Fellowship (young adults ages 18–35) promote religious and cultural traditions of Romanian Byzantine Catholic usage; holds annual conference. Groups provide service for the Church and individual parishes. They have recently re-established contacts with the Church in Romania.

Armenian Church Youth Organization of America (1946)

Armenian Church of America
630 Second Avenue
New York, NY 10016
212/686-071
FAX: 212/779-3558

The youth program of the Armenian Apostolic Orthodox Church in America.

ASPIRA Association, Inc. (1961)

1112 16th Street, N.W., Suite 340
Washington, DC 20036
Dr. Janice Petrovich
National Executive Director
202/835-3600

Dedicated to encouraging and promoting education and leadership development among Latino youth as a means of fostering the socioeconomic development of the Hispanic community. Provides counseling and educational services; conducts research; operates pilot programs and related advocacy projects. ASPIRA has been at the forefront of the effort to focus attention on the crisis of Latino students who drop out of school.

Association of American Youth of Ukrainian Descent (1950)

4004 Roanoke Circle
Minneapolis, MN 55422
Anatoly Lysyj, M.D., President
612/377-4031

For youth ages 7–35 of Ukrainian birth or descent. Promotes Ukrainian language, arts, and music and the study of Ukrainian history and culture; operates a summer camping program. Members take part in international festivals and public exhibitions.

Byelorussian-American Youth Organization (1950)

P.O. Box 1123
New Brunswick, NJ 08903
George Azarko, President
908/560-8610

For youth ages 15–35 of Byelorussian descent. Promotes culture; sponsors folk-dancing groups. Seeks to inform the American public about the struggles of the Byelorussian people. The scholarship program supports graduate study in Eastern European area studies.

Cherokee Nation Youth Leadership Program (1982)

P.O. Box 948
Tahlequah, OK 74465
Diane Kelley, Director of Tribal Services
Londa Cox, Coordinator
Youth Programs (Tribal Services)
918/456-0671
FAX: 918/456-6485

Seeks to develop the potential of Cherokee youth ages 16–21. Programs provide guidance and direction to prepare them for the work force. Conducts Summer Youth Employment Program and holds annual Indian Youth Vocational Conference to develop leadership skills and expose participants to various vocations and careers. Summer Youth Tribal Internship program includes work in a professional setting, workshops on Cherokee history and tribal cultural heritage, etc. Additional youth activities take place throughout the summer.

Federated Russian Orthodox Clubs (1927)

10 Downs Drive
Plains, Wilkes Barre, PA 18705
John Kruchok, President
717/825-3158

For youth of the Russian Orthodox faith. The program includes cultural, religious, athletic, and social activities; promotes service to others. Conducts summer camping program and other activities.

Fraternal Department, Polish Roman Catholic Union of America (1897)

984 N. Milwaukee Avenue
Chicago, IL 60622
Dolores Spejewski, Vice President
Fraternal Department
312/278-3210
FAX: 312/278-4595

The Polish Roman Catholic Union of America (PRCUA) is a fraternal benefit society maintaining a life insurance department for the benefit of its members. The Fraternal Department sponsors Polish language classes, dance and choral groups, presentation balls, gymnastics, junior bowling, fishing derby, and other activities for youth; also conducts national softball, basketball, bowling, and golf tournaments. PRCUA offers student loans and student scholarships.

Greek Orthodox Young Adult League (1951)

8 East 79th Street
New York, NY 10021
Father Angelo Artemas
National Youth Director
212/570-3560
FAX: 212/861-2183

A program for youth of the Greek Orthodox faith. Activities include leadership development, religious education, and athletic and camping programs.

Hermann Sons Youth Activities (1953)

Order of the Sons of Hermann in Texas
P.O. Box 1941
San Antonio, TX 78297
Lee Vogel, Fraternal Director
210/226-9261
FAX: 210/226-3055
Allan "Buddy" Preuss, Camps Director
P.O. Box 629
Comfort, TX 78013-0629
210/995-3223

A fraternal benefit society; originally, lodge members were German, but current membership is open to everyone. Local lodges sponsor youth chapters that raise money for charitable causes and provide service. The Grand Lodge sponsors dance classes, and conducts two summer camps. Most members are from the state of Texas.

Indian Youth of America (1978)

609 Badgerow Building
P.O. Box 2786
Sioux City, IA 51106
Patricia Trudell Gordon
Executive Director
712/252-3230
FAX: 712/252-3712

Dedicated to improving the lives of Native American children and youth; builds self-esteem and pride in Native American culture. Encourages members to take advantage of opportunities and experiences that will foster career, cultural, and personal growth. Conducts summer camping program.

Junior Cultural Federation of America

Junior Tamburitzans (1966)
Croatian Fraternal Union of America
100 Delaney Drive
Pittsburgh, PA 15235
Bernard M. Luketich, National President
412/351-3909

Local lodges throughout the U.S. and Canada sponsor youth activities that promote Croatian language and culture; music and dance groups perform at an annual Tamburitzan festival. Groups are open to all youth with an interest in Croatian culture.

Junior Division, Ancient Order of Hibernians in America (1836)

31 Logan Street
Auburn, NY 13021
Thomas McNabb, National Secretary
315/252-3895

Separate groups for junior boys and girls ages 9–16 are sponsored by local lodges. The groups promote Irish history and culture, step-dancing, choral groups, and tin whistle instruction. Youth provide service to adult lodges and to people in need in the community.

Junior Order of the Serb National Federation (1901)

One Fifth Avenue, 7th Floor
Pittsburgh, PA 15222
Robert Rade Stone, President
412/642-7372
FAX: 412/642-1372

Junior division programs for youth up to age 16 are sponsored through local lodges. Promotes Serbian customs and language and the welfare of the Serbian Orthodox Church. Members of this fraternal benefit association are primarily Americans of Serbian descent.

Junior Ukrainian Orthodox League of the U.S.A. (1962)

1 St. John's Parkway
Johnson City, NY 13790
Fr. Myron Oryhon, Spiritual Advisor
607/797-1584
Daria A. Pishko
Youth Commission Chairwoman
64 Coleman Avenue
Chatham, NJ 07928

An organization of young members (through age 17) of the Ukrainian Orthodox church; most activities are planned within local congregations. Runs summer camping program; holds annual national convention and Teen Conference. Promotes interest in Ukrainian spiritual and cultural heritage. Maintains communication with youth in Ukraine and Ukrainian youth throughout the world.

Knights of Lithuania Juniors (ca. 1940)

3420 South Lithuanica Avenue
Chicago, IL 60608
Robert A. Martin, Jr.
Vice President, Youth Activities
312/434-7785

Youth of Lithuanian descent through age 18 are members of junior groups; youth ages 18 and up belong to young adult councils. Fosters interest in Lithuanian culture, language, and traditions.

Lithuanian Catholic Federation Ateitis (1910)

1209 Country Lane
Lemont, IL 60439
Juozas Polikaitis, President
708/257-2022

A federation of four organizations including the Association for Lithuanian Catholic Children (grade school) and the Lithuanian Catholic Youth Association/Ateitis (high school). These youth groups foster the traditions and values of the Lithuanian Catholic heritage; stress the value of a strong family life; and encourage higher education and the development and use of intellect in active service to others, both in the immediate community and the world at large. Will assist free peoples of Lithuania to regain their moral compass and traditions, and recover their religious heritage.

Maids of Athena (1930)

Daughters of Penelope
1909 Q Street, N.W., Suite 500
Washington, DC 20009
Helen Pappas, Executive Director
202/234-9741

Promotes high ethical standards, patriotism, democratic traditions, and an appreciation of Greek culture. Youth assist the adult Order of the Daughters, who are their sponsors, and support health-related philanthropies.

National Indian Youth Council (1961)

318 Elm Street, S.E.
Albuquerque, NM 87102
Kenneth Tsosie, Executive Director
505/247-2251

Not primarily a youth organization, but provides services to youth. Assists Native American people in attaining civil rights, promotes social and economic development, and encourages education and employment through a program for recent high school graduates.

National Indian Youth Leadership Project (1983)

650 VandenBosch Parkway
Gallup, NM 87301
McClellan Hall, Founder and Director
505/722-9176
FAX: 505/722-9794

Created to provide opportunities to Native American youth to become capable individuals and positive contributors to their communities; holds leadership training camps in five states. Is currently operating year-round demonstration programs for middle and high school students, their parents, and communities that seek to develop appropriate leadership models growing from the traditional cultures of Native American peoples. Young participants in both the camps and demonstration programs develop service projects that they carry out in their home communities. NIYLP also operates the Native American office for the National Service Learning Initiative through support from the Kellogg Foundation and the National Native American Technical Assistance Center under a grant from the Commission on National and Community Service.

NULITES (1991)

National Urban League Incentives
to Excel and Succeed
National Urban League
Youth Services Department
500 E. 62nd Street
New York, NY 10021
Renita E. Carter, Coordinator
212/310-9084
FAX: 212/593-8250

NULITES, sponsored by the Urban League for youths ages 10–18, is designed to reflect the positive aspects of urban youth in today's society while promoting and developing leadership characteristics and providing opportunities for community service by young people.

NULITES chapters are run by local Urban League affiliates which provide the program's structure, leadership development activities, educational seminars and community service opportunities. For additional information about the National Urban League, see page 157.

PLAST, Ukrainian Youth Organization (1911)

144 2nd Avenue
New York, NY 10003
Olha Kuzmowycz, President
212/475-6960

A coeducational organization based on scouting principles. Promotes character development, physical fitness, skill building, and service; seeks to perpetuate Ukrainian cultural heritage. Reorganized in Ukraine in 1991.

Polish National Alliance of the United States of North America Youth Programs (1880)

6100 N. Cicero Avenue
Chicago, IL 60646
Anthony F. Piwowarczyk
Vice President and Chairman
of Sports and Youth Commission
312/286-0500

A fraternal insurance association; conducts sports programs and national bowling, golf and softball tournaments. Local lodges have activities that promote Polish language, dance, and music.

Slovak Catholic Sokol (1905)

205 Madison Street
P.O. Box 899
Passaic, NJ 07055
Steven M. Pogorelec, Supreme Secretary
800/886-7656
201/777-2605

For American Catholics of Slovak descent. Promotes gymnastics as well as other sports including bowling, golf, basketball, and softball. Holds biennial track and field meet; offers scholarships to youth.

Sokol USA (1896)

276 Prospect Street
P.O. Box 189
East Orange, NJ 07019
John Sopoci, Executive Secretary
201/676-0280

Slovak fraternal benefit organization. Promotes gymnastics and other sports; sponsors tournaments in bowling, gymnastics, volleyball, and golf. Provides scholarships for study of physical education to deserving members. Local lodges promote Slovak culture. The organization is also known as the Slovak Gymnastic Union of the U.S.A.

Sons of Norway Youth Club (SNYC) (1986)

Sons of Norway
1455 W. Lake Street
Minneapolis, MN 55408
Orlyn A. Kringstad
Chief Fraternal Officer
612/827-3611
FAX: 612/827-0658

SNYC is a fraternal program for youth of high school and college age; promotes Norwegian language and culture; publishes quarterly newsletter.

Sons of Pericles (1926)

Junior Order of AHEPA
1909 Q Street, N.W., Suite 500
Washington, DC 20009
Basil Mossaidis, Executive Secretary
202/232-6300
FAX: 202/232-2140

Promotes education, athletics, and service to others; seeks to create good citizens and capable leaders; promotes family life and a love and understanding of the ideals of both American and Hellenic cultures.

SPJST Youth Clubs (1934)

Slavonic Benevolent Order
of the State of Texas
P.O. Box 100
Temple, TX 76503
Howard Leshikar, President
817/773-1575
FAX: 817/774-7447

Youth clubs are organized through local lodges to promote fellowship and interest in Slavonic culture. Holds competitions at the lodge and state level. Membership is mainly from the state of Texas.

Ukrainian-American Youth Association, Inc. (SUM) (1949)

136 Second Avenue
New York, NY 10003 or
P.O. Box 211
Cooper Station
New York, NY 10276
212/477-3084
FAX: 212/505-2577

For youth of Ukrainian descent ages 5 and up; educates in the cultural, historical, and spiritual basis of Ukrainian society. Programs of more than 30 local branches in the U.S. include folk dancing, music, sports teams, and organizations; conducts summer camping programs in eight North American locations; just opened a new camp in Ellenville, NY.

United National Indian Tribal Youth, Inc. (UNITY) (1976)

4010 Lincoln Boulevard, Suite 202
P.O. Box 25042
Oklahoma City, OK 73125
J.R. Cook, Executive Director
405/424-3010
FAX: 405/424-3018

United National Indian Tribal Youth, Inc. (UNITY) is a national nonprofit organization serving the individual and collective needs of American Indian and Alaska Native youth. UNITY's mission is to foster the spiritual, mental, physical and social development of Native youth and to build a strong, unified and self-reliant Native America through involvement of its youth. UNITY is designed to develop leadership, promote self-sufficiency, and instill cultural pride among Native youth in the spirit of unity.

Young Vikings of the Danish Brotherhood of America (1975)

3717 Harney Street
Omaha, NE 68131-3844
Jennifer Denning-Kock, Director,
Fraternal Services
402/341-5049
FAX: 402/341-5049

Local lodges of this fraternal benefit association sponsor youth groups and promote Danish language and culture.

Youth of Evrytania (1945)

Evrytania Association of America
121 Greenwich Road, Suite 212
Charlotte, NC 28211
Olga P. Kleto, Office Secretary
704/366-6571

For young descendants (ages 18–25) of men and women from the Greek province of Evrytania. Promotes interest in culture; sponsors trips to Greece; provides scholarships; holds annual convention.

See also:

Co-ette Club, pages 63–64; Junior Daughters/Junior Knights of Peter Claver, page 83; National Council of La Raza, pages 154–155; National Urban League, page 157; The Links Incorporated, page 151.

Youth Lodges and Orders

Included below are only those societies that meet regularly as youth lodges or orders. Many other fraternal and sororal orders also offer a variety of services for youth. Inquiry should be made at the local level.

Constellation of Junior Stars, Inc. (1949)

11 Mark Lane
New City, NY 10956
Joyce Bidnick
President of the Grand Council
914/638-3128
FAX: 914/639-1832

A charitable organization for girls ages 11–21, related to the Masons. Program stresses service to others.

Degree of Anona (1952)
Degree of Hiawatha (1952)

Great Council of the United States
Improved Order of Red Men
4521 Speight Avenue
Waco, TX 76711
Robert E. Davis, Great Chief of Records
817/756-1221
FAX: 817/756-4828

The youth programs of the Order of Red Men, Degree of Anona is for girls, Degree of Hiawatha for boys. Both promote freedom, friendship, and charity.

Degree of Honor Protective Association Junior Clubs (1925)

445 Minnesota Street, Suite 1600
St. Paul, MN 55101-1080
Wilma Williams, National President
612/224-7436
FAX: 612/224-7446

Clubs promote civic responsibility through educational, social, and service activities; members belong to the Degree of Honor national fraternal insurance society.

International Order of Job's Daughters (1920)

Promotes spiritual and character development among girls ages 11–20 who are related to Master Masons. For information about the Job's Daughters organization, contact your local Masonic or Eastern Star Order office.

Junior Lodge, Independent Order of Odd Fellows (1923)

Sovereign Grand Lodge Office
422 Trade Street
Winston-Salem, NC 27101
Norman Gleason
Sovereign Grand Secretary
919/725-5955

Young men may join the order between ages 8–18 and remain members through age 21. Junior units are sponsored by local adult lodges and promote community service and fund-raising for various health and education philanthropies. Members learn parliamentary procedures and how to conduct a meeting.

Junior Order, Knights of Pythias (1938)

Supreme Lodge, Knights of Pythias
2785 E. Desert Inn Road, Suite 150
Las Vegas, NV 89121
Jack R. Klai, Supreme Secretary
702/735-3302

Open to all young men ages 12–18. Promotes the virtues of friendship, charity, and benevolence; prepares young men to reaffirm their commitment to the Order, Knights of Pythias. Enacted by Congress, February 19, 1864.

Junior Service Clubs (1942)
Teen Clubs (1974)

Modern Woodmen of America
Mississippi River at 17th Street
Rock Island, IL 61201
Rita Johnson, Assistant Manager
Youth Division, Fraternal Department
309/786-6481

Youth clubs are organized through local lodges of the sponsoring fraternal benefit society. Seeks to train youth in parliamentary procedure; promotes patriotism and service to others.

National Grange Junior (1888)
National Grange Youth and Young Adults (1945)

1616 H Street, N.W.
Washington, DC 20006
Emalee Colver, National Junior Director
Jeff Wetzel, National Youth and Young Adult Director
202/628-3507
FAX: 202/347-1091

The National Grange (1867) is an agricultural, community and family fraternity;

youth ages 5–14 are members of Junior Grange; youth ages 14 and over may become full members. The youth programs are designed to build character, develop leadership, promote community betterment, instill on appreciation of high ideals, and teach the value of cooperation and service.

Order of DeMolay (1919)

10200 N. Executive Hills Boulevard
Kansas City, MO 64153-1367
Joe R. Manning, Jr., Grand Secretary
816/891-8333
FAX: 816/891-9062

A fraternity for young men ages 13–21 under Masonic sponsorship. The program seeks to instill an appreciation for and understanding of leadership.

Order of Pythagorans

A youth fraternity for boys ages 8–18, whose purpose is to make better sons, brothers, men, and citizens of themselves and others. Sponsored by individual local lodges of Prince Hall Masons. Contact a local lodge for additional information.

Pythian Sunshine Girls (1930)

Pythian Sisters
RR #1, Box 159A
Hartman, AR 72840-9801
Muriel Lightfoot
Supreme Royal Princess
501/497-2171

Membership is open to girls ages 8–20 who are relatives of Knights of Pythias or Pythian Sisters, and to other individuals interested in the program. Promotes friendship and sociability among members and the inculcation of progressive moral and intellectual ideals; wishes to develop kindness, sympathy, and comfort among members. Organization is active in the U.S. and Canada.

Supreme Assembly, International Order of Rainbow for Girls (1922)

315 E. Carl Albert Parkway
P.O. Box 788
McAlester, OK 74502
918/423-1328

This group is under the sponsorship of Masonic, Eastern Star, and Amaranth orders. Membership is open to unmarried girls ages 11–20.

Theta Rho Girls' Club (1931)

International Association of Rebekah
Assemblies, IOOF
422 Trade Street, Suite R
Winston-Salem, NC 27101
Janet Simmonds
International Secretary
919/725-6037
FAX: 919/773-1066

Membership is open to all girls ages 8–21. Girls' units are sponsored by local lodges and programs vary, but all encourage participation in community projects for the benefit of others. In June and July, the United Nations Pilgrimage program offers one-week, behind-the-scenes study trips to the U.N. in New York.

William Penn Association (1886)

709 Brighton Road
Pittsburgh, PA 15233
E. Vargo, National President
412/231-2979

Youth join through local lodges of this fraternal benefit life insurance society.

Youth activities focus on perpetuating Hungarian culture and traditions. Sponsors bowling and golf tournaments for members. This association absorbed the Catholic Knights of St. George (1881) and the American Hungarian Catholic Society (1894).

Woodmen Rangers (1903)
Woodmen of the World
1700 Farnam Street
Omaha, NE 68102
John S. Manna
Fraternal Activities Manager
402/271-7258
FAX: 402/271-7269

Promotes and maintains a nationwide youth program for members. Provides meaningful monthly activities which stimulate physical and mental growth; conducts annual summer camping program. Rangers are ages 8–15; program is sponsored by Woodmen of the World, a fraternal benefit society.

Agriculture and Livestock Associations

These organizations are primarily junior programs of adult organizations dedicated to ensuring the future quality of breeding stock and accurate breeding records. Some groups meet as independent clubs, others work primarily through organizations such as 4-H or the National FFA (Future Farmers of America) Organization, and some do both.

In recent years, many agriculture and livestock-related youth programs have broadened in scope. Typical of the activities under their sponsorship are animal breeding and raising programs; junior divisional competitive events at stock shows; essay, public speaking, photography, or other contests; queen contests; and scholarship programs.

American Cavy Breeders Association (1943)
P.O. Box 7522
Eugene, OR 97401
Penny Deggelman, Secretary

American-International Junior Charolais Association (1967)
P.O. Box 20247
Kansas City, MO 64195
David Hobbs, Director of Activities
816/464-5977
FAX: 816/464-5759

American Junior Hereford Association (1956)
P.O. Box 014059
Kansas City, MO 64101
Linda Johnson, Head
Youth Activities Department
816/842-3757
FAX: 816/842-6931

American Junior Paint Horse Association (1971)
American Paint Horse Association
P.O. Box 961023
Fort Worth, TX 76161-0023
Youth Coordinator
817/439-3400
FAX: 817/439-3484

American Junior Quarterhorse Association (1961)

P.O. Box 200
Amarillo, TX 79168
Julie Kimball
Director of Youth Activities
806/376-4888
FAX: 806/376-8304

American Junior Shorthorn Association (1968)

8288 Hascall Street
Omaha, NE 68124
Tim Loudon, Junior Activities Director
402/393-7200

American Junior Simmental Association (1975)

One Simmental Way
Bozeman, MT 59715
Tom White, Director
Youth and Industry Relations
406/587-4531
FAX: 406/587-9301

American Milking Shorthorn Junior Society (1970)

P.O. Box 449
Beloit, WI 53512-0449
Betsy R. Bierdek, Executive Secretary
608/365-3332

American Rabbit Breeders Association, Inc. (1910)

1925 S. Main
P.O. Box 426
Bloomington, IL 61704
Glen C. Carr, Secretary
309/827-6623
FAX: 309/827-7011

The Holstein Junior Program

The Holstein Association of America
1 Holstein Place
P.O. Box 808
Brattleboro, VT 05301-0808
Jason E. Devino, Coordinator
Youth Programs
802/254-4551

International Arabian Horse Youth Association (1950)

P.O. Box 33696
Denver, CO 80233-0696
303/450-4774
FAX: 303/450-5127

International Junior Brangus Breeders Association (1977)

International Brangus Breeders Association
P.O. Box 696020
San Antonio, TX 78269-6020
Lea Weinheimer, Director of Promotions
& Youth Activities
512/696-8231
FAX: 512/696-8718

National Hampshire Junior Association

P.O. Box 9518
Peoria, IL 61612
Rick Maloney, Executive Secretary
309/692-1571
FAX: 309/691-8178

National Junior Angus Association

American Angus Association
3201 Frederick Boulevard
St. Joseph, MO 64506
James Fisher
Director of Junior Activities
816/233-3101
FAX: 816/233-9703

National Junior Polled Hereford Council (1974)

American Polled Hereford Association
c/o Youth Department
11020 N.W. Ambassador Drive
Kansas City, MO 64153
Dennis Schock
Director of Youth Activities
816/891-8400
FAX: 816/891-8811

National Junior Santa Gertrudis Association (1979)

Santa Gertrudis Breeders International
P.O. Box 1257
Kingsville, TX 78364
Robert Williams
Director of Youth Activities
512/592-9357
FAX: 512/592-8572

North American Junior Limousin Association

7383 S. Alton Way, Suite 100
P.O. Box 4467
Englewood, CO 80155
303/220-1693
FAX: 303/220-1884

Pony of the Americas, Inc. (1954)

5240 Elmwood Avenue
Indianapolis, IN 46203
Clyde Goff, Executive Secretary
317/788-0107

Texas and Southwestern Cattle Raisers Association (1877)

1301 W. 7th Street
Fort Worth, TX 76102
Don C. King
Secretary-General Manager
817/332-7064

Resource

A full list of the livestock record associations may be obtained from:

National Pedigree Livestock Council

RR #2, Box 129A
Brattleboro, VT 05301
Zane Akins, Secretary
802/257-9396
FAX: 802/254-6290

Changed Status Organizations

The organizations that follow were listed in the fourth edition of this Directory (1992–1993). Since that time, they have changed status as shown.

Name Changes

Amateur Skating Union of the United States

See **Amateur Speedskating Union of the United States**, page 39.

American Double Dutch League

See **National Double Dutch League**, page 42.

The Athletics Congress of the U.S.A.

See **U.S.A. Track & Field**, page 46.

Baha'i National Youth Committee

See **Baha'i National Youth Task Force**, pages 89–90.

Bnei Akiva of North America

See **The Religious Zionist Youth Movement—Bnei Akiva of the United States and Canada**, page 88.

Business and Professional Women's Clubs

See **National Federation of Business and Professional Women's Clubs**, page 20.

Christian Youth Aflame and Christ's Helpers in Parental Strife

See **Teen World Outreach**, page 80.

Data Processing Management Association

See **DPMA, The Association of Information Systems Professionals**, page 16.

Free Methodist Youth Young Teen Program

See **Christian Life Clubs/Free Methodist Youth Ministries**, page 75.

Future Secretaries of America

See **Future Secretaries Association**, page 17.

General Christian Education Department

See **Church Education Ministries**, page 76.

Golden Gloves Association of America, Inc.

See **National Golden Gloves Association of America, Inc.**, page 35.

Hermann Sons Youth Chapters

See **Hermann Sons Youth Activities**, page 109.

High School Baptist Young Men

See **Challengers**, page 81.

The High/Scope Summer Camp for Teenagers

See **The High/Scope Institute for IDEAS**, page 149.

International Society of Christian Endeavor

See **Christian Endeavor International**, page 71.

"Just Say No" Clubs

See **"Just Say No" International**, pages 101–102.

The Logos Program Associates

See **The Logos System Associates**, page 72.

National Association for the Advancement of Humane and Environmental Education

See **National Association for Humane and Environmental Education**, page 93.

National Society for Internships and Experiential Education

See **National Society for Experiential Education**, pages 156–157.

The National VOLUNTEER Center

See **Points of Light Foundation**, pages 158–159.

NFP Reach America

See **National Family Partnership**, pages 102–103.

Peace Child Foundation

See **Creative Response**, pages 57–58.

Pilot Club International

See **Pilot International**, page 96.

Presbyterian Church (U.S.A.) Youth Club

See **Presbyterian Youth Ministry**, page 79.

Project Public Life

See **Center for Democracy and Citizenship**, page 54.

Sunrise Associates

See **Empowering People**, page 148.

United Way of America

See **YOUNG AMERICA CARES!**, pages 161–162.

U.S. Baseball Federation

See **USA Baseball**, page 33.

U.S. Experiment in International Living

See **World Learning**, page 61.

U.S. Gymnastics Federation

See **USA Gymnastics**, page 38.

USA Amateur Boxing Federation

See **USA Boxing**, page 35.

USA Karate Federation Junior Olympics

See **USA Karate Federation All American Youth**, page 40.

Victory Leaders Band

See **Youth and Children's Ministries**, page 81.

Young People Love and Joy Band

See **Young People Love Joy Band**, page 81.

Youth Communication North American Center

See **Youth Communication**, page 162.

Youth to Youth

See **Youth to Youth International**, page 103.

YouthQuest Clubs

see **Center for Youth Ministry**, page 70.

Other Changes

American Junior Rodeo Association

Unable to obtain current information.

Benjamin Franklin Junior Stamp Clubs

Defunct.

Bible Memory Association

Unable to obtain current information.

Center for Youth Development and Research

Defunct.

Christian Camping International/USA

Unable to obtain current information.

Children of War

Inactive.

EARTH KIDS

Unable to obtain current information.

Field Hockey Association of America

Defunct.

Global Nomads

Unable to obtain current information.

Human Environment Center

Unable to obtain current information.

Junior Guardian Angels

Inactive at the national level.

Lincoln Filene Center

Unable to obtain current information.

Mini-Hockey (MINKEY)

Defunct.

NAD Youth Programs
National Association for the Deaf

Defunct.

National High School Slavic Honor Society (1973)

Defunct.

National Youth Network

Defunct.

Star Blazers

Inactive.

Students and Youth Against Racism

Unable to obtain current information.

Yavneh

Defunct.

Young Americans for Freedom

Inactive at the national level.

Youth Against War and Fascism

Defunct.

Zenith Clubs

Replaced by **C.L.A.S.S. Program**, see page 96.

The following groups are active, but information is not carried in the Directory at the request of the organizations.

Health Occupations Student Association

Junior Auxiliary, Supreme Ladies' Auxiliary, Knights of St. John

Junior Girls Units, Women's Auxiliary to the Veterans of Foreign Wars

The Navigators

Tauettes, Tau Gamma Delta

BACKGROUND INFORMATION ABOUT YOUTH ORGANIZATIONS

A Brief History of American Youth Organizations

The information in this section and in A Special Note to Parents (pages 9–10) was drawn from lengthy study questionnaires returned by the organizations, from interviews with more than 100 members of national youth organization staffs, and from the available professional literature.

From Missionary Societies...

The first organizations designed by adults specifically for young people seem to have appeared in the 1830s. Prior to that time, churches, Sabbath and day schools, and singing societies accepted youth into their memberships, but there was little separation of the age groups. The only early "youth organizations" for which we found evidence were numerous local prayer, mutual improvement, and other kinds of societies organized by adolescents for their own benefit.

Then, in 1831, the Juvenile Missionary Society of the First Reformed Presbyterian Church of Philadelphia was formed. Despite the word "juvenile" in its name, members seem to have ranged in age from two up through the early 20s. (Like "child," "youth," and "young people," "juvenile" has had several different meanings over the years.) The missionary society idea spread to New York and perhaps elsewhere; its publication came from the Philadelphia "headquarters." By a stretch of definition, this society was the first indigenous "national" youth organization.

More in keeping with today's concept of a national organization were the Cold Water Armies that began their march under the temperance banner in 1836. Considering that many adults at that time still held that "idle hands are the devil's playthings" and approved of only limited types of recreation, the range of their activities was quite broad. In addition to parades, the young soldiers attended special talks, held picnics, formed choruses, and saved or collected funds for the less fortunate. Many of these activities are carried out by youth groups today. In fact, one of the newest organizations, "Just Say No" International, bears a remarkably strong resemblance to its early ancestor.

The oldest of the well-known organizations currently serving large numbers of American youth is the Young Men's Christian Association (YMCA), founded in Boston in 1851, seven years after the first "Y" was organized in London. The Young Women's Christian Association (YWCA) first appeared in New York in 1855. The

Young Men's and Women's Hebrew Associations (YMHAs and YWHAs) followed soon after. All of these were designed to meet the needs of young, unmarried working people, many of whom had left their families to come to the nation's cities. Working adolescents often belonged, but specific programs for boys and girls were not offered by the Y's until near the end of the nineteenth century.

In the period following the Civil War, a number of juvenile societies began to appear in conjunction with women's mission groups in the Protestant churches. There were similar developments in the Catholic schools and parishes, which organized youth sodalities. But even religious youth groups did not become widely popular until 1881, when the Society of Christian Endeavor was presented to the young members of the Williston Congregational Church in Portland, Maine. This nondenominational association spread rapidly through the small towns of America, spawning imitators and competitors. At least 50 similar programs were formed within various Protestant denominational bodies, who saw the idea as useful for keeping young people in the fold.

...to Meeting the Special Needs of Youth

The late nineteenth century was a period of rapid change in the worlds of children and adolescents. Where once they had been more-or-less integrated working members of their communities from about age 14 on, they were increasingly perceived as having special needs.

A variety of new institutional forms, from juvenile courts to age-graded Sunday schools, appeared as attempts to meet these needs. It soon became evident that these alone were not sufficient. Too much was happening. Young people, whose transition to adult roles once had been eased by learning and working alongside adults, were being displaced in the labor force. They were compelled to spend more of their time in schools. The West, long an outlet for adventuresome or disgruntled youth, was providing fewer options for the young person without capital. More immigrant families with scant knowledge of the realities of American life were arriving; more rural and small-town residents were migrating to the cities.

All of these factors contributed to widespread concern about the character of youth—the nation's future citizens. Suddenly young people had a lot of leisure time. Organizations appeared that set for themselves the task of developing "good character" during these potentially dangerous hours. Some of these groups saw themselves as taking over for the positive influences of the workplace and life on the frontier. In the single decade between 1910 and 1919, the Boy Scouts, Camp Fire, the Girl Scouts, 4-H Clubs, Junior Red Cross, Junior Achievement, the Pioneers of the YMCA, and the Girl Reserves of the YWCA were founded. These programs variously stressed health and recreation, camping and outdoor living, service to others, and the development of skills, good habits, and human virtues as the foundation for a productive and well-rounded adult life.

A number of other patterns are found in examining the development of organizations for youth. For example, many ethnic groups found their national heritages under assault during the Americanization drives of the World War I period. In response, they formed associations to help their youth preserve some of their valued ethnic traditions while accepting the new ways. Many lodges and orders, service clubs, political parties, occupational groups, and labor unions formed junior divisions as recruitment paths into the adult groups.

Organized athletic teams and programs offering guided skill development and regular play schedules came to replace the informal recreational life of the street, field, and playground. In fact, once it was recognized that youth organizations were settings in which learning could occur, they were put into place by just about any group of adults who believed they had something important to teach.

Not all adult-sponsored youth groups were equally successful. Those listed in this Directory are the survivors of well over 650 such groups. Some, long gone, once had as many as a half million members.

Local Autonomy

A few youth organizations were designed from the start to be national in their membership scope. Most, however, began with several adults who cared that a group of local children or adolescents had needs that were not being met through the activities then available.

Programs evolved during regular meetings and at first reflected the particular interests of the founding group. Organizations grew through the spread of information by word of mouth or the printed page. When similar programs existed in

several locations, they frequently coalesced into an organization with some form of central administration to which they sent membership dues and records and from which they received a common set of program directions. This pattern of development led to the very strong tradition of local autonomy that most youth organizations still retain.

Differences Among Organizations Today

Although youth organizations share many characteristics, they differ in several ways. The basic differences are defined in policies and recommendations set by national boards of directors and staff. It is at the local level, however, that these are translated into the practices that directly affect their members.

Most organizations have some type of chartering or franchising process that requires a commitment to national standards. In reality, organizations vary considerably in their enforcement of charter provisions, and local operations may deviate markedly from national expectations. Some of the ways in which programs differ are discussed below.

Membership Requirements

Some organizations are open to all youth; others have gender, skill, or interest requirements. (Most single-sex organizations have, to date, been exempted from Title IX sex-discrimination requirements.) In a few organizations, a parent or other relative must be a member of the sponsoring group.

Qualifications for membership are closely related to the group's mission. Where this involves bringing together youth with widely different backgrounds to foster mutual understanding and appreciation, membership requirements are generally few. Where an organization is dedicated to transmitting a particular social, religious, or ethnic heritage, they may be more restrictive.

Leadership Requirements

Most organizations have minimum age recommendations for their leaders; some have gender, skill level, or membership in the sponsoring organization as prerequisites. There is generally an expressed hope that the leader will possess "good character" and "work well" with youth. Otherwise, there are few absolutes in this area.

Actual recruiting practices vary widely both within and between organizations. With the discovery of the extent of the nation's child abuse problem, many organizations have developed safeguards through formal selection procedures complete with required application forms, references, and sometimes even police and FBI checks. It has become increasingly rare for on organization to settle for the first willing volunteer.

There are times when a particular leader simply doesn't work out. Youths who drop out of organizations persistently blame leadership that is uninspired ("We do the same thing all the time") or that does not conform to the membership's conception of its needs to be led ("He/she is too bossy").

For many reasons, leaders can become embroiled in power struggles with their groups. Although youths are sometimes unreasonable or in error, too often a leader's own needs for control over the group are not in harmony with the members' very normal needs for self-direction.

The removal of an unpopular leader who expresses no wish to retire is a sensitive issue under the best of circumstances. If the person is truly inflexible in leadership style, he or she is likely to be just as rigid in other forms of interaction. It is important that people within the organization, but outside of the local unit, be available to assist in such situations with discretion, firmness, and tact.

Youth Leadership

In Europe and many other parts of the world, the leadership of youth groups is in the hands of older teens and young adults. Historically, American youth organizations have rarely chosen this direction for long, and the increasingly litigious nature of our society makes it unlikely that they will do so in the near future. The growing youth service movement, however, is reminding adults of the valuable resources and skills that young people can provide. Many organizations have developed and expanded leadership and governance roles for adolescents.

Leadership Training

All organizations seem to express the hope that their leaders will be prepared. How such expectations are met varies considerably from one organization to another. Locally available training can be as informal as "having a talk" with a previous leader, or as formal as attending a well-designed sequence of sessions. Many of the larger organizations provide a range of conferences and advanced training opportunities for volunteers, including how to adapt programs to meet the special needs of disabled young people. A growing number also offer special youth leadership training.

Prepared leaders, regardless of age, are always important. They are absolutely crucial in sports and camping programs and other activities conducted away from home where safety is a factor.

Sponsorship

Generally, sponsors are expected to be committed to national organization goals and willing to maintain continuity of group leadership, membership, and program. Financial support is often expected as well, since this may reduce the necessity for group fundraising efforts and shield the young members from commercial exploitation.

Many youth organizations require a formal sponsorship agreement with an ongoing organized body such as a church, lodge, school, or parent-teacher organization. For others, an informal committee of interested adults is sufficient. In instances where the youth group is a junior division of an adult organization, sponsorship duties usually fall to an appointed committee of the board of directors.

Research suggests that formal sponsorship arrangements contribute to the stability and continuity of youth programs.

Because sponsoring organizations also participate in the screening of adults who will fill leadership positions, they play an important role in ensuring the safety of young members.

Program Scope

Scouting groups, neighborhood centers, the Y's, and several of the religious organizations offer a wide choice of program activities. At the opposite end of this continuum are groups such as sports teams or hobby clubs that focus activities on a single area. The latter groups may also encourage activities that they feel contribute to wider citizenship or character-building goals.

Most of the larger organizations have adapted programs or adjusted requirements where necessary to allow physically and mentally challenged youth to participate. Some also provide special training to help leaders work with children with learning differences. However, not all local councils have the resources or experience needed to accomplish these changes.

The Role of Competition

Most youth groups endorse activities that are in some way competitive. They may be central to the organization's program, or secondary to it. Participation may be compulsory or voluntary and may involve individual or group effort against one another, or against a stated set of standards.

Ongoing research continues to raise the alarm against the effects of early, highly competitive sports participation. The rate of physical injuries (some of them permanent) continues to rise in spite of efforts to develop more effective safety equipment and rules against "overplaying" the very able team members.

There is also growing concern about the psychological effects of competition. For example, young participants in highly competitive sports programs have been found to lag behind their peers in moral development; they tend to see others as obstacles to be overcome, rather than companions out to enjoy the game. While there are intervention strategies that can help to deal with this problem, some organizations have begun to re-evaluate the overall place of competition in their programs, replacing it with activities that require collaboration so that all may succeed.

The Role of Service

Helping others has been a vital part of youth organization programs since the very beginning. It is sometimes forgotten that these groups were the pioneers, encouraging service among generations of young Americans a century and a half in advance of the service-learning movement now gaining momentum in the nation's schools. Years ago, juvenile society members performed such acts of kindness as collecting wood for needy families, running errands for the elderly, and forgoing expensive treats such as butter or sweets so that the money saved could be donated for worthy causes. Today, nearly all organizations for youth give members some opportunity to help other people or their communities.

Although the heightened interest generated by the recent work of the Commission on National and Community Service and the availability of Serve America Service Learning grants is commendable, it also means that a lot of new players are entering the field. With their many years of experience, community-based organizations have much to offer the youth service movement. It is our hope that they will be full partners in national and local efforts to furnish youth with opportunities to make meaningful contributions to the well-being of their communities.

The William T. Grant Foundation Commission on Work, Family and Citizenship reviewed and summarized the findings of research on youth service in its publication, *The Forgotten Half* (see page 166). The Commission's findings remain valid. To be effective, they concluded, youth service programs "must be carefully crafted; given full support, administratively and financially; be based on an understanding of the developmental needs of young people; and make a genuine contribution."

Commitment to service also continues to grow on the nation's college and university campuses. Many of the young adults who are now active in this part of the movement began volunteering as children when they were members of community-based youth organizations. Many have chosen leadership positions in these same organizations as their current avenues of service.

Opportunity for Progression

Organizations that hope to retain members for several years have attempted to develop progressively more complex sets of program activities geared to age or skill levels. In addition to providing leadership training and opportunities to practice new skills with younger members, many organizations encourage their maturing members to exercise increasing control over group management.

Camping and Summer Programs

Outdoor living and camping have been integral to the programs of many organizations since their beginnings. Such groups typically own their sites and facilities and provide low-cost, well-designed day or resident camping for their members. Other groups, newer to the camping field and attracted by the advantages gained by a concentrated experience, rent sites—generally for less than full seasons.

Although many organization camping programs exceed the accreditation standards, many do not. Parents are well advised to find out the status of any camp to which they plan to send their children.

In attempting to retain the interest of older youth, many organizations conduct camp "counselor-in-training" programs. More recently, many camps have initiated "challenge courses" that encourage group effort and developmentally-appropriate risk-taking activities. Others have moved into the field of "high adventure," offering advanced wilderness camping or canoeing, scuba-diving, etc.

Several organizations, particularly those for high school youth, do not offer actual camping opportunities but do conduct travel, leadership development, and service programs during the summer months.

Some are open to all; for others, participation is by nomination or invitation. In some programs, attendance is an end in itself; in others, it is a prelude to a later leadership or training responsibility.

Some of the athletic organizations either sponsor or recommend concentrated summer training experiences for their members. Again, whether availability is general or confined to nominees will vary.

Costs of summer programs differ greatly, usually according to how heavily they are subsidized by the sponsoring organization. In a number of cases, selection for participation is an honor, and all costs are borne by the organization. For most programs, some aid is available to youth who would be prevented from participating for financial reasons.

International Emphasis

In recognition of the growing interdependence of the nations of the world, many youth organizations have developed programs to help young members understand other cultures and peoples. Several of the organizations are American branches of international federations. Others, although entirely national in their structure, have ties with overseas groups. Such international connections can broaden a young person's perspective.

Typical activities with an international emphasis include foreign travel, member exchanges, international service projects, and pen pal programs. A few organizations provide special services for American youth living outside the United States.

Product Sales

Youth organizations attain needed financial support in a number of ways. Many rely heavily on the income from product sales to meet local capital and operating costs.

There is considerable variation in the appropriateness of the products sold, the organization and management of sales campaigns, the percentage of profit the organization receives, the way profits are distributed, and the safety standards set for young salespersons.

Adherence to Standards

Most organizations foster a marked degree of local autonomy. This is a great source of strength for youth groups, but it can also be a source of problems. On the one hand, a local organization that is left relatively free to assess and adapt to the needs of youth in its own community may provide service more effectively. On the other hand, this same freedom makes it possible for local traditions and attitudes contrary to those of the national organization to intrude. Most organizations monitor local practices and have means to expel units that stray too far from national guidelines.

Still, organizations tend to vary in the extent to which they monitor adherence to standards set by the national organization. Appropriately chosen leadership, well prepared to undertake the particular activity at hand, remains the major assurance that youth groups and teams will be conducted in the best interests of the members.

Meeting standards set by relevant certifying and accrediting bodies is also essential for the welfare of program participants. Some areas in which compliance is important include:

- Maintenance of physical facilities at camp or program sites.

- Maintenance of vehicles in which members are transported; proper licensing of drivers.

- Availability of first-aid skills or, where appropriate, more complex medical expertise.

- Availability of well-rated insurance coverage for both routine and unusual group activities, and of adequate fiduciary coverage for adult governing bodies.

- Licensing or certification of coaches, referees, instructors, waterfront personnel, individuals who undertake counseling or other therapeutic programs, and so on.

Cost

The annual expense for organization participation will be affected by both national and local factors. At a minimum, there are usually national membership dues, local unit dues, insurance fees, and uniform costs. These may have to be paid by the individual member, or they may be provided by the sponsoring group.

Additional expenses may arise from transportation to events or places, admission fees, special project materials, camp registration, and so on. For older, highly active participants, costs may include expenses related to attendance at out-of-town conventions, fairs, leadership training courses, or group trips.

In summary: An awareness of organization differences may raise questions among prospective members and their parents. Discussion with a group leader may reassure some, but not others. An organization should be able and willing to provide additional sources of information as requested.

Volunteers: The Vital Ingredient

The importance of voluntary effort as the mainstay of youth organizations cannot be overstated. Every one of the groups in this Directory relies heavily on the service of volunteers and is rooted firmly in the national tradition of meeting needs through voluntary association.

The roles filled by volunteers vary from one organization to another. In most, however, it is a volunteer who actually brings the program to the young member. Volunteers are the leaders, coaches, advisers, and guides of the groups, clubs, troops, and teams.

The best-designed program of any national organization can only be as effective as the individuals who deliver it. As has often been said, "It all depends on the leaders." The recruitment, training, and continued support of volunteer leadership rank high among organizations' priorities. Failure to monitor individual unit activities can result in poor programs and even possible danger to or exploitation of young members. Fortunately, cases of the latter type are very rare.

The best insurance for good programs generally comes from the broad participation and support of parents and concerned adults. Many parents who have few other opportunities to observe their youngsters in group settings find that working as adult leaders gives them insights into the ways their children cope with new situations and get along with others. Until recently, most volunteers have been women. Now that a majority of women with children under age 18 have returned to the labor force, this traditional volunteer base is eroding. (Studies have indicated that working women have not stopped volunteering, but rather are entering fields related to their own personal and professional development.)

Some youth organizations have developed creative solutions to this problem. For example, leadership and unit-maintenance tasks are being shared by groups of employed adults. This reduces the load carried by any one person, provides all of the parents with a means of expressing concern and interest in their children's activities, enriches the variety of activities and role models available, and serves as an informal system for guiding program content and adhering to safety standards. It also requires considerable effort to coordinate.

Although parents still provide the bulk of youth group leadership, organizations are reaching out to students, unmarried men and women, childless couples, and retired persons. Various forms of peer leadership are being initiated or expanded. Many employers have been induced to provide release time with pay for volunteer service as an employee benefit; more would probably do so if properly approached.

The organizations are doing their part by trying to match tasks to volunteers' interests and skills. They are also providing such incentives as academic credit for training courses, and official records of services rendered that can be made part of a volunteer's career résumé.

Organization Administration and Staffing Patterns

All of the larger organizations and a good many of the smaller ones employ paid staffs of varying sizes to assist in administering the programs they sponsor. National offices may set the standards for and hire all agency-connected personnel. It is more common, however, for local units to hire their own staffs.

Regardless of structure, staffing patterns vary tremendously both between and within organizations. This is also true of the standards of professionalism demanded, opportunities provided for growth and advancement within the organization, levels of compensation, and retirement and other benefit plans.

Traditionally, many youth organizations have had pay scales well below the standards set for public school teachers. Local councils with over-stretched budgets can get caught in a downward spiral of low reward/low demand/low productivity from which it is difficult to extricate themselves. Upgrading the competence of and compensation for staff has become a priority for several organizations, and a number of national efforts continue.

Eleven of the largest youth-serving groups have recognized the program of American Humanics, Inc. (see page 142), which provides career-oriented undergraduate and graduate education programs in youth agency administration on 16 college and university campuses around the country. Several other universities have developed programs in the areas of youth studies, youth worker education, youth agency administration, and the like.

The findings of the Task Force on Youth Development of the Carnegie Council on Adolescent Development (see pages 167–168) has spurred increased interest in the field of youth work. Assessment of the needs of organizations engaged in positive youth development continues, as do efforts to enhance the professional development of youth workers. A number of private foundations are currently supporting staff development initiatives for youth organizations.

Efforts to improve administrative effectiveness have been accompanied in several organizations by revised corporate plans for board and staff composition, function, and operation. The introduction of change in youth organizations, as within other groups with longstanding traditions, has not always been received with equal enthusiasm throughout. The destructive rifts that developed between those who looked back and those who wished to move in new directions have largely been overcome by organizations that have faced, head-on, the realities of growing risks to the healthy development of our nation's youth.

Do Youth Organizations "Work"?

The mission statements of youth organizations are replete with expressions of lofty sentiments and hopes about what will be gained through participation. Goals shared by many organizations include:

- Providing a peer group in which friendships can develop and grow, and where there is opportunity for shared fun and cooperative work with others.

- Bringing youth and adults together in a setting where each may communicate with and learn from the other.

- Providing a forum for the discussion of youth concerns and problems; serving as advocates for youth in the formation of public policy.

- Strengthening family life by supporting values held to be important and providing activities that may be shared within the family.

- Fostering the highest possible physical, intellectual, social, emotional, and moral development.

- Developing self-confidence through the mastery of skills and situations.

- Developing self-awareness and increasing self-esteem.

- Expanding horizons through new experiences.

- Providing opportunities for career exploration and for the development of good work attitudes and habits.

- Developing a concern for the welfare of others and for the institutions of society.

- Providing channels of expression through which like-minded individuals may present and transmit their views.

- Providing experiences in democratic decision making, the basis of citizenship.

- Developing leadership skills and responsibilities; teaching the planning and management of time.

- Developing an interest in the natural environment and concern for its use and preservation.

- Providing opportunities for meaningful service to the community.

Do youth organizations really meet these goals? Unfortunately, information that might provide a definitive answer is scarce and often anecdotal in nature. There has been relatively little research aimed at assessing the outcomes of youth organization participation.

In part, this is related to the problems inherent in carrying out such research. For example, it is difficult to tell whether an organization helps young people to develop a particular belief, or whether it simply attracts those who already hold that belief. It is possible to draw false conclusions from the results of questionnaires because young members may respond along "party lines." When observing young people in a group setting, it is wise to remember that their behavior might be quite different outside the group.

And it may be that the true effects of participation are realized only much later in life. One rather discouraged staff member wondered aloud if "perhaps our touch is too light" to have any effect at all on the lives of young members.

On a more encouraging note, some evaluation studies have followed the introduction of specific programs within organizations. They show fairly consistently that such desired outcomes as gain in knowledge and attitude change do indeed take place. However, most of these studies have involved specific organizations and have used only members as respondents, so it is difficult to draw conclusions about how members differ from nonmembers or former members who have dropped out.

In contrast to this meager information, there is a growing body of data relating to extracurricular participation in high school. In studies conducted for the National Center for Education Statistics, participation was found to be associated with a more positive self-image and with a greater sense of control over life events. Participating students were more likely than nonparticipating students to engage in a variety of other forms of leisure activity (with the exception of television viewing). They had higher educational aspirations and turned more often to adult family members, school personnel, and friends for help in planning their school programs and later careers. They were more likely to consider community leadership and working to correct social and economic inequalities to be important life goals.

Several follow-up studies of adults have shown that those who participated in extracurricular activities during high school attained modestly higher levels of education, occupation, and income. They

were more often members of community organizations and more likely to take an active part in the political process.

Such studies have not produced much information about the causal processes that lead to such differences and outcomes. However, it seems safe to say that there are payoffs in later life for active young people who learn to handle themselves in a variety of situations and to interact with many different individuals. Organized activity facilitates such personal development.

Are Youth Organizations Still Relevant?

Youth organizations have come under fire in recent years for their failure to be relevant to the needs of today's young people. Although such criticism is not entirely without foundation, it tends to overlook the many changes that have taken place.

A number of the national organizations have developed program materials in such areas as substance abuse, self-awareness, eliminating racial and sex-role stereotypes, parenting education, consumerism, nutrition and health, preparedness for latchkey children, child-abuse prevention, building employability skills, career exploration, human sexuality, and restitution for victims of juvenile crime.

The newest class of organizations are meeting youth problems head-on. Several of these are dedicated to preventing or fighting substance abuse among their members and/or countering the effects of living in a chemically dependent family. Self-help groups for child victims of sexual and/or physical abuse, and support groups for children experiencing family problems such as divorce, death, and catastrophic illness, are also beginning to appear. Most of these are currently organized at the local level only.

No single organization has ever had the resources to develop equally strong programs of its own in all areas, and there is remarkably little sharing at the local level. Further, there have been problems of communication within organizations, both in introducing materials to local units and in follow-up to encourage their adoption. Many groups never discover just what programs are available. Finally, there have been instances where conservative local boards have rejected the use of innovative programs in their jurisdictions. This is symptomatic of some of the broader problems faced by youth organizations that seek to develop new courses of service.

By the middle of this century, many of the organized programs for youth, regardless of their origins, were viewed by parents as a means of segregating young people from the problems and contradictions of the adult world. This view of the "proper" role of adult-sponsored youth organizations persists in the minds of some of their leaders and supporters. Just as founders looked back nostalgically to the virtues presumably gained from life as lived on a long-dead frontier, a number of today's leaders now look back to a time of presumed youthful innocence and resist changes that might shatter their view of the "ideal" child or youth member.

It must also be remembered that youth organizations embody in their laws, promises, mottoes, and pledges an adult vision of the "ideal" future citizen and society. This vision did not arise in a vacuum, and its formation may have been subject to numerous stereotyping processes imposed on members by the wider society.

Youth organizations, as repositories of the group's heritage, cannot hope to remain immune to external pressure to change the definition of that group's rightful role in life and place in society. Attempts to translate changing definitions into organization policies and programs understandably have been another source of internal conflict.

Not all of the resistance comes from within the organizations, however. A number of times, with full member support, groups have launched innovative programs or extended programs to previously unserved groups to find themselves in deep trouble because they have violated the wider community's perceptions of their proper function. Because they may have repercussions on organization funding, such experiences have tended to make groups less bold in their approach to innovation.

Yet innovate they must, if they are to survive into the twenty-first century. Standing as a bridge between generations, and at the junction of home, school, and community, youth organizations have a unique potential to "re-connect" young people to the supports that they require for healthy development. They also have a unique educational mission. Back in 1907, Lord Baden-Powell created Boy Scouting to "fill the chinks" left in a boy's education by the schools: Character, Physical Fitness, Handicraft for Making a Living (today we would call this "practical skills"), and Service to Others. One or more of these themes continues to be prominent in the mission statements of most youth groups today. And certainly the needs remain, as well.

Current Trends and Future Directions in American Youth Organizations

Adult-sponsored youth organizations rarely have been at the forefront of movements for social change. It is more common to find them in a scramble to keep up with or adapt to new circumstances that govern the areas in which they operate. Some of the national trends and patterns currently affecting youth organization programs include:

- Demographic changes in the population of the United States, such as the decline of the child and adolescent population, the rise in the aging population, the increase in the number of childless couples, and the growth in the number of households headed by single parents (including many adolescents).

- Continued immigration and the increase in the proportion of young people of color in the U.S. population accompanied by growing knowledge of global interdependence and the need to become a truly multicultural society.

- Geographic shifts in the population, such as the movement away from the Northeast to the Sunbelt and the decline of families in the central cities.

- The increased influence of peers and the media on the values and behaviors of the young, and the concurrent decline in the influence of parents, teachers, clergy, and youth workers.

- Economic changes, such as the continued entry of women with children into the labor force; growing unemployment among youth, particularly minorities; unemployment and underemployment among adults; and increased numbers of children living below the poverty line.

- Changes in school structure, such as the growth of middle schools, the consolidation and closing of neighborhood schools, the increased costs of using school facilities, declining budgets for extracurricular activities, constant changes in busing patterns, and "mainstreaming" of students with special needs. It is too early to assess the impact of the growing "school choice" movement on both school and community-based organizations.

- Legal and moral obligations arising from the civil rights and women's movements in such areas as staffing and programs, increasing the admission of girls to athletic programs, correcting imbalances in public funding of boys' and girls' programs, making services available to disadvantaged youth, and addressing the special needs of abused children and adolescents.

- Financial strains, stemming from changes in federal policies for funding social programs, placing new or increased pressures on private-sector sources: changes in tax policies (e.g., deductibility of contributions); changes in United Way procedures from funding agencies to funding programs and the recent loss of support for United Way campaigns in many cities; rapidly rising costs of liability insurance for program participants.

- Increased demands for funds for programs designed to treat problems related to poverty, teen pregnancy, dropping out of school, drug and alcohol abuse, etc., that have diverted resources from programs designed to foster healthy youth development.

- Increased demands for accountability by funding agencies, and the lack of agency experience in building and using databases and in program evaluation.

Youth organizations have changed a great deal over the years and must continue to evolve within the communities where they operate. They must recognize their own potential as educational environments as well as providers of recreational activity to fill leisure hours. Young people of today have too many competing demands on their time to spend it in ways that are not meaningful for them.

Organizations must be aware of national trends affecting their membership and of the possibilities they create for new programs, as well as the problems they pose. For example, alarm at the rise in the numbers of teenagers becoming parents led to the development of some excellent parenting education materials. On the other hand, in spite of growing concern about problems created by increasing numbers of single-parent homes, few of the national organizations have yet developed comprehensive strategies to include noncustodial parents in their programs or made widespread efforts to seek them as volunteers. There are, however, encouraging approaches under development in local affiliates that may soon provide models that can be replicated nationally.

Numerous studies have confirmed that the need for affordable child care has reached crisis proportions. While initially concerns may have focused on issues of physical safety, they now include physical, social, and intellectual development as well. Many of the youth organizations are responding to this need. The YMCA, for example, has become the nation's largest provider of care for school-aged children. Nationally, Girls Incorporated and the Boys and Girls Clubs of America have also expanded and developed new programs and approaches for the after-school hours and summer vacation periods. Many YWCAs, local councils of Camp Fire, the Girl Scouts of the U.S.A. and the Boy Scouts of America, as well as county 4-H offices, are in various ways entering the after-school care field.

There are many other potential areas for program development. Some people feel that our society is becoming increasingly age-segregated to the disadvantage of all. Youth organization programs can cross age barriers. Not only are there well-designed materials and program models available for youth service to the elderly, but there are many programs that encourage older Americans to provide mentoring and guidance for youth. There are also oral history projects in which youth can interview or work with their elders to preserve their cultural heritage.

In other programs, youth work with younger children as tutors or aides in day camps, playgrounds, or church and synagogue schools. The same skills could be applied in other institutions for children such as school extended-day programs and daycare centers.

Recent research has also stimulated growing concern over poor dietary habits, declining physical fitness, and increasing obesity among our nation's young people. Promoting the development of healthy lifestyles has always been one of the cornerstones of most youth organization programs, and many are now increasing their emphasis on this area.

In good economic times, the schools added many enrichment activities, often encroaching on areas that out-of-school programs once held to be their own. With declining school budgets, many of these same activities are now defined as "frills" and are being dropped. Youth organizations could step in to fill the gaps. In educational areas such as literacy, English as a second language, health, and voter registration, the energies of young people have been put to effective use.

Not all of the future challenges and opportunities lie in the area of program development, however. In addition to creating new program options, the introduction of the computer has already made it possible for many groups to provide new and more rapid services to members.

Not the least among the possibilities for the future is presented by the expansion of the home video and cable television

industries. For example, these media offer new ways for delivering training courses to leaders and members. They also may provide new modes for communicating information about organization activities to the wider community. The applications of future technology will be limited mainly by the imaginations of organization personnel and their skills in raising the funds to pay for them.

It is tempting to continue at great length about what can be done through the programs of organizations for youth. What will be done, however, will always depend on creative and flexible leadership and on the continued commitment of time and community resources. Increasingly, it will also depend on collaborative efforts and interagency cooperation in program development and delivery at the national, regional, and local levels of operation.

RESOURCES FOR ADMINISTRATORS AND LEADERS

The following organizations offer a variety of services and materials of general interest to administrators, youth workers, and leaders of organizations for youth. Several of them maintain networks or serve as clearinghouses for information in areas such as volunteerism, educational and in-service training programs, and youth advocacy. Many of the youth service programs, although aimed at providing service opportunities for older teens and young adults, become sources of volunteers for agencies serving younger children.

Award Programs

Many organizations conduct contests and award programs. If you'd like to know more, write to the National Association of Secondary School Principals (see page 152) for a copy of the Advisory List of National Contests and Activities.

American Academy of Achievement (1961)

P.O. Box 4089
Malibu, CA 90265
Wayne R. Reynolds, Executive Director
310/457-8052
FAX: 310/457-1413

Seeks to "inspire youth with new dreams of achievement in a world of boundless opportunity." Holds annual three-day "Salute to Excellence" conference for about 400 of the nation's most outstanding high school honor students. Sponsors Achievement TV, a monthly series of live interpretive teleconferences that bring role models directly into the classroom; supporting curricular materials are available. There is no cost to schools who participate in the teleconference program.

The Civic Achievement Award Program (1987)

Close Up Foundation
44 Canal Center Plaza
Alexandria, VA 22314
800/356-5136

A classroom-based citizenship education program conducted in cooperation with the National Association of Elementary School Principals.

The Civic Achievement program aims to teach students in grades 5–8 their rights and responsibilities as citizens in a democracy. Three interactive components feature learning activities in U.S. history, government, geography, economics, culture, and current events. The program enables students to link civic knowledge and research skills with civic action. Students who complete the program receive award certificates.

Program descriptions available. See page 54 for more about the Close Up Foundation.

The Congressional Award (1979)

6520 Georgetown Pike
McLean, VA 22101
Kendall S. Hartman, National Director
703/761-6150

Through the combined efforts of Congress and the private sector, Congressional Awards may be earned by young people ages 14–23 who fulfill national requirements and accomplish high goals in voluntary community service, personal development, physical fitness, and expedition activities. Each award recipient is presented with a bronze, silver, or gold Congressional Award medal by a member of Congress. In addition, each receives a Certificate of Achievement from the Joint Congressional Leadership. Program description available.

See also:

The Giraffe Project, page 149; **The President's Council on Physical Fitness and Sports**, President's Challenge, page 30.

General Resources

American Association for Leisure and Recreation (1930)

1900 Association Drive
Reston, VA 22091
Christen G. Smith, Ph.D.
Executive Director
703/476-3472
703/476-3471
FAX: 703/476-9527

A professional association formed to promote school, community, and national leisure programs. Attempts to improve communication between theoretician and practitioner, professional and lay public, school and community members. Information is available on schools and universities offering curricula in the field, and on specific professions within the leisure and recreation field. Catalog available.

American Camping Association (1910)

5000 State Road 67N
Martinsville, IN 46151
John A. Miller, Executive Vice President
317/342-8456
FAX: 317/342-2065

Promotes organized camping programs; sets standards and accredits camps; provides information services in areas of administration, legal issues, education programs, and federal legislation; has certification programs in outdoor living skills, ecology, and camp directorship; holds annual conference. Publishes *Camping Magazine* and annual *Guide to Accredited Camps*.

The ACA Book Store carries ACA publications and distributes equipment and extensive materials related to youth development, camp management, youth sports, camp music, etc. Catalog available.

American Coaching Effectiveness Program (1982)

Human Kinetics Publishers (1974)
Box 5076
Champaign, IL 61825-5076
Rainer Martens, Ph.D., President
217/351-5076
FAX:217/351-2674

A leadership training program for preparing coaches (in and out of school) to lead young athletes more effectively. Consists of three levels of instruction: volunteer youth sport coaches, interscholastic coaches, and courses for undergraduate students and intersholastic coaches. Also publishes supplemental self-study courses with sport-specific content. ACEP Catalog available.

In 1994, Youth Sport Administrators Workshops will be introduced at regional sites throughout the U.S.; the SportParent program is designed to educate parents about the important roles and responsibilities that they have in guiding their children's sports experiences.

Human Kinetics Publishers produces an extensive line of books, journals, videotapes, and other educational resources in the fields of physical education, sport sciences and medicine, and physical fitness. Catalog available.

American Humanics, Inc.

4601 Madison Avenue
Kansas City, MO 64112
Dr. Kirk G. Alliman, President
Philip J. Jachowicz, Vice President
816/561-6415
FAX: 816/531-3527

Organized to provide career-oriented education for men and women who aspire to professional employment in youth agency leadership, administration, and delivery of programs. Has developed a core curriculum and co-curricular certified undergraduate and graduate level program used in 16 colleges and universities nationwide. Its specialized education is recognized by 11 of the nation's major youth-serving organizations. Publishes *Humanics: The Journal of Leadership for Youth and Human Services*. Program descriptions available.

Department of Adolescent Health (1986)

American Medical Association
515 N. State Street
Chicago, IL 60610
Director
312/464-5570
FAX: 312/464-5842

The Department was founded in response to the health problems of adolescents, and is dedicated to improving their health and psycho-social well-being through education, networking, coalition-building, and research. Work focuses on prevention and intervention. Works with the National Adolescent Health Coalition of over 30 national health and service organizations to review issues affecting youth. Conducts Healthier Youth by the Year 2000, a project dedicated to implementing national health objectives for adolescents. Publishes *AMA Policy Reports*, the AMA series *Profiles of Adolescent Health*, the *Public Health* series, research reports, and pamphlets. Publication list available.

American Youth Foundation (1924)

1315 Ann Avenue
St. Louis, MO 63104
Robert S. MacArthur, President
314/772-8626
FAX: 314/772-7542

A nonsectarian organization that welcomes youth of all races, religions, and nationalities to its programs. Seeks to develop adults who will achieve their best, lead balanced lives, and serve others. Pioneered camp conferences in youth leadership education; owns and operates summer camping facilities in Michigan and New Hampshire. Conducts year-round leadership programs in several U.S. cities.

Merged with STREAM, an adventure-based program; offers adventure and experience based leadership training programs in schools and youth agencies across the country. Financial aid makes programs accessible to youth from a broad range of economic backgrounds.

American Youth Work Center
1751 N Street, N.W., Suite 302
Washington, DC 20036
William W. Treanor, Executive Director
Alan Vanneman, Editor
202/785-0764
FAX: 202/728-0657

Works with community-based youth service agencies and other nongovernmental youth agencies to provide information, training, publications, advocacy, and exchange opportunities for youth workers and youth service leaders. Publishes *Youth Today*, the newspaper on youth work (bimonthly). Brochures available.

Associates for Youth Development (1976)
P.O. Box 36748
Tucson, AZ 85740
William A. Lofquist, Director
602/292-9767
FAX: 602/887-7242

Works nationally to provide technical assistance, training, and publications in the area of youth development with a special emphasis on positive prevention resources. "The Technology of Prevention" course offers two levels of training; undergraduate or graduate credit can be arranged. Other workshops include "How

to Initiate Effective Prevention Strategies," "How to Make the Juvenile Justice System Work Better," "Building the School Community," and "The Church and Youth Development." Publishes books and a practice-oriented magazine for youthworkers, *New Designs for Youth Development.*

Association for Experiential Education (1977)
2885 Aurora Avenue, Suite 28
Boulder, CO 80303-2252
303/440-8844
FAX: 303/440-9581

An international network of individuals, schools, and educational organizations that share a common interest in and commitment to experience-based teaching, learning, and training & development. Its mission includes empowering individuals by helping them assume responsibility for their own development, and promoting the definition, application, and evaluation of experiential learning. Maintains a consultant network; holds regional and international conferences; serves as clearinghouse for information about effective experiential education programs. Publishes *Journal of Experiential Education*, The *AEE Horizon newsletter*, a handbook, directories, and *Jobs Clearinghouse* (monthly).

Association for Volunteer Administration (1961)
P.O. Box 4584
Boulder, CO 80306
Executive Director
303/541-0238
FAX: 303/541-0277

A professional association for those in volunteer management who want to shape the future of volunteerism, develop professional skills, and further their careers. Provides skill-development and career-advancement programs for members on local, regional, and national levels. Sponsors International Conference on Volunteer Administration annually. Offers performance-based certification program. Publishes *The Journal of Volunteer Administration* (quarterly); members also receive *Update* (bimonthly) and other materials related to volunteer management. Student memberships are available.

Campus Compact: The Project for Public and Community Service (1985)

P.O. Box 1975
Brown University
Providence, RI 02912
Nancy Rhodes, Acting Director
401/863-1119
FAX: 401/863-3779

A coalition of more than 400 college and university presidents, Campus Compact was founded to create public service opportunities for college students and to develop an expectation of service as an integral part of student life and the college experience. It provides information and technical assistance to member campuses; helps to shape policy at the federal, state, and local levels; promotes a national awareness of the important resources college students offer in the public interest; and, offers the annual Howard R. Swearer Student Humanitarian Awards to recognize outstanding student community service efforts on member campuses. Campus Compact's project on integrating service and academic study focuses on the roles of faculty and institutional policy.

Publishes the *Campus Compact Newsletter* and several other resource materials and manuals. The Compact currently has 12 state offices, as well as offices for community colleges and historically African-American institutions.

Campus Outreach Opportunity League (COOL) (1984)

264 North Hall
2005 Lower Buford Avenue
University of Minnesota
St. Paul, MN 55108
Kristin Parrish, Executive Director
612/624-3018
FAX: 612/624-1296

COOL is a national non-profit organization which promotes, supports, and enhances student involvement in quality community service. COOL's mission is to educate and empower college students to strengthen our nation through community service. COOL is run by a highly creative and energetic staff of recent college graduates and students. Each year, COOL recruits dynamic student leaders from all over the nation to join the staff. Through the collective experience of the staff and network, COOL has developed and accumulated expertise and knowledge about organizing for effective community service.

Through training and consulting, conferences, programs, publications, networks, and other services, COOL helps campuses develop comprehensive community service programs that are student-run, diverse, of high quality, and effective in the impact that they have on important community and social issues. Contact national office for information on programs, publications, and services.

Center for Creative Leadership (1970)

P.O. Box 26300
Greensboro, NC 27438-6300
Linton Deck, Director for Education and Nonprofit Sector
910/288-7210
FAX: 910/288-3999

A nonprofit educational institution that seeks to improve the practice of management by providing practical, research-based tools for recognizing and developing creative leadership potential. Develops models of effective managerial practice and applies them in training courses as guides for assessment and development. Typical participants in programs are drawn from business and industry, educational institutions, government, and public service.

Publishes numerous books, technical reports, and audiotapes. Catalog of programs and products available.

Center for Early Adolescence (1978)

The University of North Carolina at Chapel Hill
D-2 Carr Mill Town Center
Carrboro, NC 27510
Frank A. Loda, M.D., Director
919/966-1148
FAX: 919/966-7657

Seeks to promote healthy early adolescent development and to improve the quality of services available to young people;

focuses on youth ages 10–15. Provides training, publications, technical assistance, and information services to a broad range of professionals; sponsors training institutes; provides consulting services; and maintains an information collection. Issues of expertise include school improvement, middle-grades teacher preparation, parent education, responsive community services, adolescent literacy achievement, leadership education, and adolescent health. Free catalog available on request.

Center for Human Resources (1970)

Florence Heller Graduate School
Brandeis University
60 Turner Street
Waltham, MA 02254-9110
Susan P. Curnan, Director
800/343-4705
617/736-3770

The Center for Human Resources conducts policy research, manages and evaluates demonstration programs, and provides technical assistance and management training in the fields of youth employment and education. Center interests include dropout prevention, school/business partnerships, teen parent programs, employability assessment, competency-based education and training, and programs linking work and remedial education. Recent projects include the design and management of a national, 24-city mentoring project for disadvantaged youth; operation of a year-long training institute for Jobs Training Partnership Act (JTPA) practitioners; development of a statewide work-education initiative; and publication of a guide to school/business partnerships.

The Center also publishes a newsletter, *Youth Programs*, and acts as a clearinghouse for information on youth employment through a toll-free number (800/343-4705).

Center for Youth Development and Policy Research (1990)
Academy for Educational Development
1255 23rd Street, N.W., Suite 400
Washington, DC 20037
Karen Pittman, Vice President
202/862-8820
202/862-1900
FAX: 202/862-8837

CYD is dedicated to contributing to better futures for disadvantaged children and youth in the U.S. CYD believes that available services are too few, too fragmented, too problem-focused, and too distant from family and neighborhood. Capitalizing on growing concern about youth problems and the growing willingness to search for new solutions, CYD has set as a goal, transformation of the concern about *youth problems* into public and private commitment to *youth development*. Center services include:

- conducting and synthesizing youth research and policy analysis;

- disseminating information about exemplary youth programs and policies;

- initiating and strengthening dialogue and coalition-building among researchers, practitioners and policymakers committed to the well-being of young people;

- designing and implementing program evaluations, community assessments, and demonstration projects, especially those that accomplish an understanding of how public and private efforts can be better coordinated to further the development of youth;

- providing technical assistance to national organizations, state and local governments, and public and private institutions interested in improving their youth development efforts.

Major Center projects include: Mobilization for Youth Development; Stronger Staff—Stronger Youth; Approaches to Enhancing Youth Development; and Youth Development Cities Consortium. Write or call for additional information.

The Center for Youth Studies (1985)
130 Essex Street
South Hamilton, MA 01982
Dean Borman, Director
Anne Montague, Coordinator
508/468-7111, Ext. 635
FAX: 508/468-6691

CYS publishes the innovative *Encyclopedia of Youth Studies*, a computerized information service focusing on the rapidly changing youth culture. Relevant data about young people—trends, attitudes, hopes, fears, sociocultural distinctives, etc.—are collected and put into a single database in a form convenient for youth workers. The database is available in a stand-alone version for IBM PC (or truly compatible) and MacIntosh equipment. The *Encyclopedia of Youth Studies* is available as a once a year purchase; annual publication of updates occurs in late summer or early fall.

The Chapin Hall Center for Children at the University of Chicago

1155 E. 60th Street
Chicago, IL 60637
Joan Wynn, Research Fellow
Renae Ogletree, Research Associate
312/753-5900
FAX: 312/753-5940

The Chapin Hall Center for Children is an independent, nonprofit center dedicated to research and development concerning the policies, programs, and practices that affect the lives of children. The Center's work analyzes both the needs of children and the societal response to those needs, and develops and tests alternative ways to support children's development.

One line of the Center's work is based on the view that services should promote the development of all children, rather than simply prevent or solve problems. In this view, primary services—the traditional resources such as organized sports, church groups, parks, libraries, and community centers—join the specialized services (e.g., child welfare, juvenile justice) as a single, citizen-planned infrastructure of services in communities. A $30 million initiative is testing this strategy in eight Chicago communities.

The Center publishes a *Discussion Paper* series including reports on the role of primary services in building communities that enhance youth development. Publication list available.

Child Welfare League of America (1920)

440 First Street, N.W., Suite 310
Washington, DC 20001-2085
David S. Liederman, Executive Director
202/638-2952
FAX: 202/638-4004

CWLA is the nation's oldest and largest organization devoted entirely to improving life for abused, neglected, and at-risk children, youth, and their families. Today CWLA has more than 700 members—public and voluntary agencies that provide assistance to more than two million children and families. Member agencies offer a wide range of services including kinship and family foster care, adoption, residential group care, child day care, family preservation, and programs for pregnant and parenting teens.

CWLA staff members provide expert leadership and guidance in 11 program areas; run the nation's largest child welfare consulting operation; provide training and conduct conferences and workshops covering a wide range of policy, program and practice issues; provide comprehensive support services for executives, senior staffs and boards of voluntary agencies; conduct research and disseminate information through a library/information service; work to pass national legislation to improve the quality of life for at-risk children and their families, and direct the Children's Campaign, a national network of thousands of individuals who are advocates for children.

In addition, CWLA is the world's largest publisher of child welfare materials and is widely known for its standards of excellence for agencies in these areas: residential group care, child day care, family foster care, independent living, services for abused and neglected children and their families, in-home aide services, health care services for children in out-of-home care, adoption, services for pregnant adolescents and young parents, and organization and administration for all child welfare services. Catalog available.

Children's Defense Fund (1973)

25 E Street, N.W.
Washington, DC 20001
Marian Wright Edelman, President
202/628-8787
FAX: 202/662-3510

Provides systematic, long-range advocacy for American children and youth. Carries out research, public education, and community organizing; monitors federal agencies and legislation; drafts legislation and testifies on behalf of children and youth; directs a public policy network. Publishes *The State of America's Children* (annually), as well as a newsletter, statistical and research reports, handbooks, and posters on issues affecting children and youth. Catalog available.

Community Partnerships with Youth (1990)

7025 Woodcroft Lane
Fort Wayne, IN 46804
Anne B. Hoover, Director
219/432-5819
FAX: 219/424-7533

CPY seeks to empower youth ages 12 and up in areas of trusteeship and governance, and to train adults who work with youth through organizations, churches or schools. *Youth as Trustees* curriculum

helps youth to understand the action and commitment needed to serve as trustees of an organization or community; they put belief into action through service. *Youth In Governance* curriculum focuses on the administrative functions and day-to-day workings of a board of directors. Program encourages youth to participate on boards and/or committees and provides the knowledge needed to be effective members.

Delta Education, Inc.

Box 915
Hudson, NH 03051
603/889-8899
FAX: 603/880-6520

A distributor for numerous educational publications including the *Delta Mathematics* and *Hands-On Science* catalogs, and the *OBIS* (Outdoor Biology Instructional Strategies) series of science educational materials developed for youth organizations. Catalogs available; specify area of interest.

Empowering People

7956 California Avenue
Fair Oaks, CA 95628
H. Stephen Glenn, President
800/879-0812
916/961-5556
FAX: 916/961-5570

Provides resources for the home, classroom, and corporate marketplace, including seminars, workshops, books, tapes, and videos relating to Developing Capable People, and Positive Discipline. Publishes a quarterly newsletter (call for a complimentary copy).

Father Flanagan's Boys' Home ("Boys Town")

Boys Town, NE 68010
Father Val J. Peter
Executive Director of Boys Town
402/498-3200
Boys Town National Hotline
(800/448-3000)

Publishes free and inexpensive materials relating to youth problems and issues, including parenting videotapes. Topics include adolescent abuse, divorce, family life, eating disorders, school problems, peer pressure, self-esteem, and learning disabilities. Catalog available.

The Boys Town National Hotline is a 24-hour crisis line for girls, boys, and parents.

The Giraffe Project (1982)

P.O. Box 759
Langley, WA 98260
Ann Medlock, President
206/221-7989
FAX: 206/221-7817

An organization that recognizes the courage of individuals of all ages who "stick their necks out" for the benefit of others; invites nominations of courageous individuals for recognition; offers lectures and training in community action; publishes *Giraffe News* (free to members). Is expanding into schools and colleges with teaching materials and after-school club ideas. K–2, 3–5, 6–9. and 10–12 guides are available from the Giraffe Project Education Office.

Group Publishing, Inc.

Box 481
Loveland, CO 80539
303/669-3836
FAX: 303/669-3269

A leader in Christian education publishing, Group's mission is to encourage Christian growth in children, youth, and adults. Events under their sponsorship include international and national Group Workcamps, Group's International Kidstitute and Children's Ministry Workshops. Publishes and distributes over 150 books; *Hands-on Bible Curriculum* for grades 1–2, 3–4, 5–6; *Active Bible Curriculum* for junior and senior high; *Apply-It-To-Life Adult Bible Series*; videotapes on subjects of interest to youth workers, parents, and teenagers; and magazines including *Group* (for all youth workers), *Jr. High Ministry*, and *Children's Ministry*. Catalog available.

The High/Scope Institute for IDEAS

High/Scope Educational Research Foundation (1963)

600 N. River Street
Ypsilanti, MI 48198
David P. Weikart, Ph.D., President
313/485-2000
FAX: 313/485-0704

Students ages 15–17 from the U.S., Europe, Far East, and South America participate in informal instruction in art, drama, music, and the sciences; small-group activities that sharpen problem-solving skills and enhance the ability to work in a team; sports that de-emphasize competition; overnight canoe trips; folk dancing; and lots of individual challenges to increase leadership skills and self-confidence. Catalogs available.

INDEPENDENT SECTOR (1980)

1828 L Street, N.W.
Washington, DC 20036
John H. Thomas
Vice President, Communications
202/223-8100
FAX: 202/416-0580

INDEPENDENT SECTOR is a national coalition of over 800 nonprofit organizations, foundations, and corporations with giving programs. It works through legislation, research, education, management training, and public information to preserve and enhance the nation's nonprofit sector and the giving and volunteering that support it. Publishes *Volunteering and Giving Among American Teenagers 12 to 17 Years of Age*, the results of a survey conducted for IS by the Gallup Organization, and *YOUTH SERVICE: A Guidebook for Developing and Operating Effective Programs*. Publishes and distributes books and other materials on giving and volunteering. Catalogs available.

Indiana Youth Institute (1988)

333 N. Alabama Street, Suite 200
Indianapolis, IN 46204-2151
Patricia Turner-Smith
Executive Director
317/634-4222
800/343-7060 (in Indiana only)
FAX: 317/685-2264

IYI is an independent, nonprofit center dedicated to the healthy development of Indiana's young people. IYI believes that Indiana can and should become a state that genuinely cares about is young people and that its national reputation should reflect that commitment and concern. To accomplish this, the Indiana Youth Institute works with adults who care about youth. IYI advocates for better services for Indiana's young people, both directly and in collaboration with others; develops strategies to increase youth-serving professionals' knowledge, caring, and competence; and cultivates and supports innovative projects that hold promise for improving the lives of Indiana's young people. IYI believes that the key to the success of young people is in the hands of the adults who care about them. Publishes *FYI* (quarterly newsletter), *Indiana Youth Poll* reports, issue-oriented pamphlets and papers. Publication list available.

KIDS COUNT (1989)

Annie E. Casey Foundation
111 Market Place, Suite 420N
Baltimore, MD 21202
William O'Hare, Director
410/234-2872
FAX: 410/234-2891

The Kids Count project fosters greater national commitment to improving outcomes for vulnerable children and their families by bringing together the best available data to measure the health, economic, educational, and social well-being of children in the United States. Since 1990, the annual *KIDS COUNT Data Book* has used a wide range of statistical indicators to document trends in the lives of our nation's children. This report covers each state as well as the nation as a whole. The Foundation supports Kids Count initiatives in nearly every state and the District of Columbia. State projects publish an annual Kids Count report using the same set of indicators to document the well-being of children in each of their states' counties.

The Links, Incorporated (1946)

1200 Massachusetts Avenue, N.W.
Washington, DC 20005
Marion S. Sutherland
National President
Jacqueline Finney Brown
Director, Services to Youth
Flavia R. Walton, Director,
Project LEAD: High Expectations!
202/842-8686
FAX: 202/842-4020

A membership group of more than 9,000 women in 250 chapters across the nation, Links, Inc. addresses community concerns in the areas of educational, cultural, and civic commitment. Links members seek opportunities for involvement and service that will have an impact in economic, political, and social arenas that affect the quality of life in their communities. They also seek to heighten community awareness of the problems faced by minorities and the underprivileged.

Services to Youth is one of four major program areas. Since 1987, the organization has developed, field-tested, and widely implemented Project LEAD: High Expectations! (Links Erase Alcohol and Drug Abuse). This program is an innovative, community-based educational outreach focused on preventing alcohol and other drug abuse, as well as premature sexual activity, unintended births and sexually-transmitted diseases among African-American youth living in circumstances that place them at high risk. Local Links chapters collaborate with other community-based organizations to strengthen and support the efforts of Project LEAD. A cadre of trained volunteers implements the program.

Melpomene Institute for Women's Health Research (1981)

1010 University Avenue
St. Paul, MN 55104
Judy Mahle Lutter, President
612/642-1951
FAX: 612/642-1871

A center for research and public education on health concerns and the impact of exercise on girls and women at all stages of life. Major research topics range from broad subjects (such as osteoporosis, PMS, and raising fit young people) to the more specific (such as body-image issues and fitness for high school girls). Melpomene Institute is a nonprofit, member-supported organization. Maintains a Resource Center with more than 3,000 books, articles, and journals (use free to members, available at a small fee to non-members). Publishes *Melpomene Journal* three times a year; produces educational brochures, information packets, and videos. Provides a Speaker's Bureau, research participation, brown-bag seminars, and special events.

National Association of Elementary School Principals (1921)

1615 Duke Street
Alexandria, VA 22314-3483
Samuel G. Sava, Executive Director, NAESP
703/684-3345
FAX: 703/549-5568

A professional membership organization committed to providing children with the best possible elementary and middle school education by helping school principals perform to the best of their abilities. It offers a host of periodicals, professional development programs, and meetings; holds a convention aimed at strengthening the principalship and the image of the principal, and promoting effective educational leadership. It is an advocate for elementary and middle school education with the U.S. Congress, state and federal government agencies, and the news media; maintains grassroots affiliations with principals in every state, Canada, and overseas. It offers a range of student services, including the American Student Council Association. Catalog available.

National Association of Secondary School Principals (1916)
Division of Student Activities
1904 Association Drive
Reston, VA 22091
Dale D. Hawley, Director
FAX: 703/476-5432

Promotes responsible student involvement in education and in the community; serves as a student advocate by providing responsible guidance; and operates as a resource center on student activities and school issues of interest to students. Offers leadership training programs, a resource information center, and consultation for member schools. Publishes *Leadership for Student Activities*, monographs and audiovisual materials, and the *Advisory List of National Contests and Activities*. Catalog available.

National Association of Service and Conservation Corps (1985)
666 11th Street, N.W., Suite 500
Washington, DC 20001
Kathleen Selz, Executive Director
202/737-6272
FAX: 202/737-6277

A nonprofit membership association made up of conservation and service corps programs and youth service advocates. NASCC serves as an advocate, central reference point and source of assistance for state and local youth corps around the country. It promotes quality practices in existing programs and assists in planning and development of new ones. NASCC sponsors an annual conference and regional seminars and workshops for youth corps practitioners and related youth service programs. Publications include: *Crew Supervisor Training Manual, Expanding the Definition of Diversity, Making JTPA Work for the Corps, Youth Corps Profiles*, and *Youth Can!* (quarterly newsletter). Publications list available.

National Association of Student Activity Advisers (1974)
1904 Association Drive
Reston, VA 22090
703/860-0200
FAX: 703/476-5432

An organization for advisers and other school personnel with responsibilities for student activities in middle, junior, and senior high schools. Provides workshops on legal aspects of advising, middle-level advising, recognition/staff appreciation, National Honor Society, motivation, leadership skills, self-esteem, service projects, fundraisers, and more.

National Black Child Development Institute (1970)
1023 15th Street, N.W., Suite 600
Washington, DC 20005
Evelyn K. Moore, Executive Director
202/387-1281
FAX: 202/234-1738

A national, nonprofit, charitable, and educational organization established to improve the quality of life of African-American children and youth. Seeks to educate communities about national, state, and local issues; focuses on four areas: education, child care/early childhood education, child welfare, and health. Monitors public policy issues and serves as a catalyst for change on national and local levels. Has trained thousands of people to work more effectively with African-American children. Distributes legislative and policy updates. Publishes *Black Child Advocate* and *Health Talk* (quarterly) and numerous other materials. Catalog available.

National Center for Learning Disabilities (1977)

381 Park Avenue S.
New York, NY 10016
Shirley Cramer, Executive Director
212/545-7510
FAX: 212/545-9665

Promotes public awareness about learning disabilities, neurological disorders, and deficits which can be a barrier to literacy. (An estimated one in ten families has a child or adult with a learning disability.) NCLD provides resources and referrals on a national level to a wide range of volunteers and professionals who touch the lives of people with this "hidden handicap," supporting their efforts to become self-sufficient. NCLD's innovative grantmaking, legislative advocacy, and publications assist youth leaders, employers, parents, educators, physicians, nurses, social workers, and psychologists in this country and abroad. Publishes *Their World* (annually).

National Center for Service Learning in Early Adolescence

CASE: The Graduate School
and University Center of CUNY
25 West 43rd Street, Suite 620
New York, NY 10036-8099
Joan Schine, Director
212/642-2946/2947
FAX: 212/642-4127

Provides a resource for educators, youth workers and policymakers seeking to meet the developmental needs of early adolescents. The Center offers training and technical assistance, and a variety of publications and materials, including program guides and videotapes. A publications list is available.

The Early Adolescent Helper Program is the National Center's action arm, a service-learning model that serves as a testing ground for innovative programming. Youth involved in the program work with elementary- and pre-school-aged children or the elderly in their communities on a weekly basis.

Through its central staff and Field Associate network, the National Center assists in program planning, curriculum development, training, and evaluation around the country. The Center's Clearinghouse collects and disseminates information on effective service-learning models, and welcomes suggestions of program models for its Field Associates to explore. The Clearinghouse may be contacted at 212/642-2306.

The National Center for Youth with Disabilities (1986)

University of Minnesota, Box 721
420 Delaware Street, S.E.
Minneapolis, MN 55455
Nancy Okinow, Executive Director
800/333-6293
612/626-2825
FAX: 612/626-2134
TTY: 612/624-3939

A project of the Society for Adolescent Medicine and the University of Minnesota's Adolescent Health Program, NCYD is an information and resource center focusing on adolescents with chronic illnesses and disabilities and their transition to adult life. The Center's mission is to raise awareness of the needs of youth with disabilities and to foster coordination and collaboration among agencies, professionals, parents, and youth in planning and providing services to address those needs.

NCYD maintains a National Resource Library that can be accessed by dialing 800/333-6293 and requesting that an information specialist search the files and mail the results. Fees are based on the amount of information provided.

The Center also organizes and coordinates national and regional seminars for parents, youth, and professionals from health, education, social services, and rehabilitation fields. These meetings provide opportunities to share new research and interventions; identify priority issues for further research, policy, and program development; and develop interdisciplinary and interagency collaborations to serve adolescents.

NCYD publications include *Connections*, a free quarterly newsletter. *FYI Bulletin* (fact sheets presenting statistical and demographic data on youth with disabilities), *CYDLINE* (bibliographies on selected topics), and selected policy monographs are available at low cost. Publication list available upon request.

National Collaboration for Youth (1973)

1319 F Street, N.W., Suite 601
Washington, DC 20004
Gordon Raley, Executive Director
The National Assembly
202/347-2080
FAX: 202/393-4517

The National Collaboration for Youth is 15 of the largest national youth-serving organizations in the U.S. working together on behalf of today's youth. Together, NCY members seek to provide a united voice for all youth, advocating for improved conditions and positive development opportunities. NCY is an affiliate of the National Assembly, an umbrella group of national health and human service organizations.

National Council of La Raza (1968)

810 First Street, N.E., Suite 300
Washington, DC 20002
202/289-1380

NCLR is a constituency-based Hispanic umbrella organization dedicated to securing civil rights and improving economic and social opportunities for Hispanic Americans. It provides policy analysis, public information, and education; assists community-based organizations with fundraising and institution building;

aids new and emerging organizations serving both rural and urban populations; and helps to start community-based organizations in areas in need of services and advocacy.

Among the youth-related issues of heightened concern to NCLR are school-to-work and apprenticeship proposals as well as current practices for educational testing of students with limited English proficiency that result in their being inappropriately labeled as having limited "ability-to-benefit" from educational opportunities—a label which makes them ineligible to access such opportunities.

NCLR holds an annual conference and publishes handbooks and manuals, special reports, statistical analyses, and several quarterlies including *NCLR Poverty Project Newsletter*.

National Crime Prevention Council (1982)

1700 K Street, N.W., 2nd Floor
Washington, DC 20006
Maria Nagorski, Deputy Director
202/466-6272, Ext. 155
FAX: 202/296-1356

A private, nonprofit organization dedicated to forging a nationwide commitment by people acting individually and together to prevent crime and build safer and more caring communities. A primary agency goal is to engage the nation's youth as a major resource in crime and drug abuse prevention.

NCPC reaches out to youth by providing training, information, materials, and other services, including demonstration programs that engage young people in crime prevention and community-building. Such programs include Youth as Resources, a youth-led community service initiative and Teens, Crime and the Community, a curriculum that couples classroom lessons with action projects designed to address specific crime problems. Both have been implemented in a variety of settings—from rural areas to inner-city public housing developments, to correctional facilities. Training and technical assistance on these and other youth-related programs and issues are available. Materials include information packets, hands-on program guides, videos, posters, and more. Catalog available.

National Peer Helpers Association

P.O. Box 2684
Greenville, NC 27858
Dr. Elizabeth Foster Harrison, President
919/522-3959
FAX: same

A professional organization dedicated to encouraging, promoting, and improving peer-helping programs as a way of improving individuals' abilities to solve problems, make decisions, and enrich their lives. NPHA is expanding a national network of leaders, educators, coordinators, and trainers, and promoting public awareness of peer helping as a powerful human service alternative. Serves as a clearinghouse for resources, training, research, and consultation. Publication list available.

The National PTA (1897)

330 N. Wabash, Suite 2100
Chicago, IL 60611-2571
Gene A. Honn, Executive Director
312/957-6782

An organization of 27,000 local groups of parents, teachers, students, and others concerned about children and youth. Areas of interest include public education, child/teen health and safety, and parent education. Maintains an office of governmental relations in Washington, D.C. Publishes *PTA Today* magazine for parents and educators, as well as many brochures on youth-related topics, some in Spanish. Publication list available.

National Resource Center for Youth Services

The University of Oklahoma College of Continuing Education
202 West 8th Street
Tulsa, OK 74114-1419
James M. Walker, Director
918/585-2986
FAX: 918/592-1841

Seeks to enhance the quality of life of the nation's youth at risk and their families by improving the effectiveness of human services. Acts as a national clearinghouse for information concerning child welfare and youth services; provides program models, curriculum materials, and training for child welfare and youth service professionals. Coordinates curriculum development with universities, agencies, and individual authors; provides on-site training and consultation. Annually sponsors "Working with America's Youth," a national training conference; also coordinates state independent living teen conferences and provides complete conference planning services. Publishes and markets materials and videotapes related to youth at risk and their care. Free catalog of materials and training courses available.

National Service Secretariat, Inc. (1966)

5140 Sherier Place, N.W.
Washington, DC 20016
Donald J. Eberly, Executive Director
202/244-5828
FAX: 202/363-6850

The National Service Secretariat is a clearinghouse of information about national youth service programs in the United States and overseas. The Secretariat publishes a semi-annual newsletter and conducts an annual survey of federal, state, and local youth service programs in the U.S. The Coalition for National Service, a project of the Secretariat, encourages the development of youth service programs and fosters the discussion of national service. The Secretariat provides speakers and technical assistance on national service. Write to the Secretariat for more information about its services and publications.

National Society for Experiential Education (1971)

3509 Haworth Drive, Suite 207
Raleigh, NC 27609-7229
Allen J. Wutzdorf, Executive Director
919/787-3263
FAX: 919/787-3381

A professional association that brings together the many types of people involved in providing the diverse array of experiential learning opportunities—internships, field experiences, service-learning, cooperative education, intercultural experiences, and others—for the exchange of ideas, professional support, training, research, state-of-the-art discussions, and help for institutions and programs.

NSEE members are concerned about students' intellectual and ethical development, their understanding of community responsibility, their career development, their cross-cultural awareness, and their personal growth. NSEE offers *NSEE Quarterly*, national and regional conferences, publications, information and consulting services, several interest groups, and a special set of services for employers and field sponsors.

National Urban League (1910)

Youth Services Department
500 E. 62nd Street
New York, NY 10021
Chandra Llewellyn
Director, Youth Services
212/310-9000

The National Urban League is a voluntary, nonpartisan community service agency that aims to eliminate racial segregation, institutional racism, and discrimination in the United States and to assist African-Americans in the achievement of social and economic equality. The Youth Services Department seeks to identify, support and create opportunities for the intentional involvement and empowerment of youth.

Program activities are focused on issues and concerns that youth themselves have identified: prevention of teenage pregnancy; the elimination of crime and violence, including the use of drugs and alcohol; the need for adequate education; the development of positive self-image and self-esteem; the affirmation of the African-American cultural heritage; promotion of community values and awareness; and the enhancement of young people's sense of responsibility to the global society.

The Youth Services Department conducts research and advocacy related to the concerns of urban youth, as well as sponsors an annual youth conference which convenes youth representing the National Urban League's 113 affiliate cities. In 1991, the NULITES (National Urban League Incentives to Excel and Succeed) organization was created; see page 112.

The Education, Health, and Social Welfare Departments of the National Urban League also conduct research, sponsor programs, and publish reports and other materials of interest to youth workers.

National Youth Leadership Council, Inc. (1983)

1910 W. County Road B
Roseville, MN 55113
James C. Kielsmeier, President
800/366-6952
612/631-3672
FAX: 612/631-2955

The National Youth Leadership Council is a Minnesota-based national nonprofit organization, affiliated with the University of Minnesota and dedicated to developing service-oriented youth leaders by supporting individuals, organizations, and communities that encourage youth service and leadership. The NYLC has pioneered innovative youth leadership training programs since 1983; in Minnesota, it has spearheaded a successful statewide public policy and training effort to develop service opportunities for young people from kindergarten through college. In part because of 1989 legislation supporting school and campus-based service, Minnesota is widely recognized to have the most comprehensive statewide youth service model in the nation.

The NYLC offers youth and adult training, consultation, and materials. Publications include *Learning by Giving: K–8 Service-Learning Curriculum Guide*, *The Generator: National Journal of Service Leadership*, and *Growing Hope: A Sourcebook on Integrating Youth Service into the Curriculum*. Contact the NYLC for a complete list of training opportunities and publications.

North American Youth Sports Institute (1979)

4895 Oak Garden Drive
Kernersville, NC 27284
Dr. Jack Hutslar, Director and Founder
910/784-4926

Conducts in-service educational activities (writing, editing, training, research, consulting) in all sports for youth leaders in community sports, recreation, physical education, fitness, and health including consultant services, leader training programs, coaches' clinics, teaching workshops, speaker's bureau, research center, and a clearinghouse for youth sports-related information. Publishes *Sport Scene* (quarterly), *Beyond X's and O's* (in English or Spanish), *NAYSI Compendium of Beech Games*, *Munchkin Tennis*, *NAYSI Resource List*, "How to Coach" correspondence courses in basketball, baseball, bowling, football, and softball, and other materials. NAYSI Technical Support line: 800/767-4916. Publication list available free.

Outward Bound USA (1962)

National Headquarters
Route 9D
R2 Box 280
Garrison, NY 10524-9757
Allen Grossman, President
800/243-8520
914/424-4000
FAX: 914/424-4280

Outward Bound is the largest and oldest adventure-based education organization in the U.S. The Outward Bound system in the U.S. consists of five independently controlled schools, one urban center, and the national office. Its purpose is to develop and enhance self-confidence and self-esteem, leadership skills, teamwork, and a sense of service to the community and environment in its participants. Courses include core components: skill training, physical conditioning, extended expedition, solo experience, service project, and a marathon-type event. Outward Bound is committed to making its courses available to all and seeks to provide scholarship funds on an adequate level. All courses emphasize personal growth through the vehicle of wilderness activity. Catalog available.

Points of Light Foundation

1737 H Street, N.W.
Washington, DC 20006
Cathy Quilty
Manager, Information Services
202/223-9186
FAX: 202/223-9256
TTY: 202/659-9229

The Foundations's Youth and Education Outreach division challenges young people ages 5–25 to engage in service to others and stimulates the creation of opportunities and support to make that service meaningful. Provides training and technical assistance through two programs. YES Ambassadors creates service and leadership opportunities for young people and engages them in service/service-learning undertakings. Communities as Places of Learning seeks to prepare community-based agencies to provide meaningful service opportunities for youth. Both programs work closely with schools and volunteer centers. also maintains Servlink database that catalogs exemplary youth service/service-learning programs. Publications include *Get Ready for Anything* and *Communities Creating Places of Learning.*

The Points of Light Foundation has incorporated programs of The National VOLUNTEER Center, a leadership organization for volunteers that serves as a national advocate for volunteer centers. Works with corporations that sponsor employee and retiree volunteer programs, and provides training and support to volunteers and managers. Sponsors National Volunteer Week and the annual VOLUNTEER conference; in conjunction with the White House, sponsors the President's Volunteer Action Awards. Publishes *Voluntary Action Leadership* (quarterly) and other periodicals and materials. Catalog available.

Project Adventure, Inc. (1971)
P.O. Box 100
Hamilton, MA 01936
508/468-7981
FAX: 508/468-7605

Project Adventure is an approach to education, counseling, recreation, and life that is engaging, active, challenging, and places a high level of expectation within

an atmosphere of support and caring. It helps others to use adventure education as a catalyst for personal growth and change; its training courses motivate clients to develop creative new applications in their own environments.

Project Adventure designs and installs Challenge Ropes Courses, publishes books and manuals, and distributes supporting materials and products related to adventure and experience-based education. Publishes *ZIP LINES: The Project Adventure Newsletter.* Catalog of materials and training course information available.

Project Service Leadership
12703 N.W. 20th Avenue
Vancouver, WA 98685
Kate McPherson, Director
206/576-5070
FAX: 206/576-5068

Assists schools and communities in implementing service learning in grades K–12. Conducts teacher institutes, outreach programs, and a yearly conference. Publications include *Enriching Learning through Service, Parenting for Caring, Infusing Service into Schools,* and *Service-Line,* a newsletter published three time a year.

Public/Private Ventures (1977)
399 Market Street
Philadelphia, PA 19106
Michael A. Bailin, President
215/592-9099
FAX: 215/592-0069

A national nonprofit corporation that designs, manages, and evaluates social policy initiatives aimed at helping youth to become productively employed and self-sufficient. To achieve its goal, P/PV works with schools, government, employment and training organizations, community-based agencies, foundations, and businesses to design new strategies to remedy pressing problems, evaluate program effectiveness, conduct demonstration projects, and assist the public and private sectors to replicate those initiatives that have proven effective. Publication list available.

Search Institute (1958)

Thresher Square West
700 South Third Street, Suite 210
Minneapolis, MN 55415
Dr. Peter L. Benson, President
612/376-8955
FAX: 612/376-8956

Search Institute is a nonprofit research and resource organization dedicated to exploring and addressing the needs of youth and those who work with them. The organization uses a positive youth development framework to examine healthy lifestyles, healthy relationships, prosocial values, and effective institutions and communities. Study topics have included factors influencing the effectiveness of youth-serving organizations and agencies, as well as the beliefs, values, concerns, and attitudes of specific youth population samples.

A major concern is building collaborative efforts among community leaders and empowering them with the skills they need to become change-agents and more effective "positive youth developers." The Institute offers evaluation and survey services to support community-based efforts.

Search Institute also develops research-based print and video resources for youth-serving organizations. Publishes *Values & Choices*, a course in human sexuality for 7th and 8th graders and their parents; *Search Institute Source* (quarterly); books and other materials. Catalog available.

Social Welfare History Archives (1964)

University of Minnesota
101 Walter Library
Minneapolis, MN 55455
David Klaassen, Archivist
612/624-6394
FAX: 612/625-5525

Supports research in the history of social services and social reform by collecting the records of national voluntary sector welfare associations and selected local agencies as well as the personal papers of individual leaders in late nineteenth and twentieth century America. Included are the records relating to settlement houses, child welfare and family service agencies, Big Brothers, the playground and recreation movement, and the YMCA and YWCA. Recent additions include the youth participation project records of the National Commission on Resources for Youth, and data from Project Girl and the National Youthworker Education Project. The collections must be used on the premises, but photocopying services are available and the staff will respond to telephone and correspondence inquiries. A published guide describing holdings is available.

Society for Research on Adolescence (1984)

c/o Search Institute
Thresher Square West
700 S. Third Street, Suite 210
Minneapolis, MN 55415
Dale A. Blyth, Ph.D.
Executive Secretary
612/376-8955
FAX: 612/376-8956

Seeks to promote quality research on adolescence and effective dissemination to all who are concerned about this age group. The Society's membership includes more than 900 psychologists, sociologists, educators, and other social science and health professionals. Sponsors a three and one-half day Spring meeting in even-numbered years, as well as a regular newsletter. The professional research journal under the sponsorship of the Society is the *Journal of Research on Adolescence*, published by Erlbaum.

Who's Who Among American High School Students

Educational Communications, Inc. (1967)
721 N. McKinley Road
Lake Forest, IL 60045
Paul C. Krouse, Publisher
312/295-6650

Honors outstanding students for their positive achievements in academics, athletics, school and community service; conducts on annual survey of high achievers; awards $125,000 in scholarships annually; organizes a network of youth who are available to media as spokespersons for youth viewpoints; provides small grants-in-aid to organizations that work with youth; conducts a reference and referral service for college-bound students listed in its publication. In addition to *Who's Who Among American High School Students* (annual), publishes *College Bound Digest, The National Dean's List*, which honors 125,000 outstanding college students, and *Who's Who Among America's Teachers*.

World Future Society (1966)

7910 Woodmont Avenue, Suite 450
Bethesda, MD 20814
Edward S. Cornish, President
301/656-8274

A nonpartisan, nonprofit scientific and educational organization devoted to promoting the study of the future, with membership drawn from the U.S. and 80 countries around the world. It strives to act as a neutral clearinghouse for information about the future. Hosts both large and medium-sized conferences that examine a wide range of future-oriented issues. Publishes *The Futurist*, a bimonthly general interest magazine about future trends, innovations, and activities. The Society's book service sells books, videotapes, games, and other future-oriented products. Catalog available.

YOUNG AMERICA CARES!

United Way of America (1918)
701 N. Fairfax Street
Alexandria, VA 22314-2045
Tonya M. Thomas, Manager
703/836-7100
FAX: 703/683-7899

United Way of America, the national training and service center for the United Way system, provides its 1,200 local United Way members a variety of support services including training, technical assistance and consultation, and product development in the areas of advertising and public relations, research, resource development, public policy, labor relations, human resources, marketing, volunteer development, and community partnerships and initiatives.

YOUNG AMERICA CARES!, the cornerstone of UWAs youth initiative, is designed to stimulate and support the efforts of more than 200 youth volunteer programs in United Ways and Volunteer Centers across the nation. The initiative employs a number of programmatic strategies to increase youth involvement in United Way, community service, and philanthropy; develop leadership skills among young people; and increase the understanding and awareness of the valuable contributions young people can make in addressing their communities' most pressing needs. The ultimate goal is to give young people from every socioeconomic, racial, religious, and ethnic background the opportunity and the means to begin a lifetime commitment of service to others.

Youth Communication (1977)

P.O. Box 65057
Washington, DC 20035-5057
Craig Trygstad, Executive Director
202/429-5292

A network of large-circulation, youth-written newspapers and news bureaus in cities across the country, and a national news service covering youth issues in Washington, D.C. Offers advice and technical assistance to individuals and groups who want to develop local Youth Communication newspapers. Youth Communication also publishes

Youth News Service, a computerized cooperative, covering issues of concern to young people and providing teen journalists with opportunities to share their writing and ideas while gaining realistic journalism experience. Subscribers include student and commercial newspapers and magazines. From its offices in Washington, DC, Youth Communication publishes *Young D.C.*, an independent citywide newspaper written and edited by teenagers from across the Washington metropolitan area.

Youth Development Information Center

National Agriculture Library
10301 Baltimore Boulevard
Beltsville, MD 20705
301/504-6400
FAX: 301/504-6409
Internet: jkane@nalusda.gov

The Youth Development Information Center was established as a joint project of the National Agriculture Library (NAL) and the Extension Service (ES) to support the professionalism of 4-H Youth Development. The Center provides information services to youth development professionals who plan, develop, implement, and evaluate programs designed to meet the changing needs of America.

New directions within ES and a virtual revolution in communications technology have allowed the Center to greatly expand its services. To utilize fully that technology, the Center is collaborating with the National Extension Service in CYFERNET (Child, Youth and Family Education and Research Network). Through technological and organizational collaborations, a greater variety and amount of information will be made available to a larger proportion of the child, youth, and family-serving community. CYFERNET is an on-line service on the Internet (currently available as a gopher server) that provides access to full-text documents and other information services through the user's own computer.

Youth Policy Institute (1978)

1221 Massachusetts Avenue, N.W.
Suite B
Washington, DC 20005
David L. Hackett, Executive Director
202/638-2144
FAX: 202/638-2325

A nonprofit, nonpartisan organization concerned with the future of America's children, youth, families, and communities. Monitors federal programs; tracks proposed legislation and congressional activity; follows the activities of non-governmental organizations as they relate to youth, families, and communities; and attempts to provide a framework for a comprehensive understanding of children's, youth, and family issues leading to responsible policy. Publishes *Youth Policy* (12 issues per year) and *Youth Record* (24 issues per year). Publications list available.

Youth Service America (1986)

1101 15th Street, N.W., Suite 200
Washington, DC 20005
Roger Landrum, President
202/296-2992
FAX: 202/296-4030

Seeks to help make service a universal experience among America's youth of all backgrounds. It serves as an advocate for the national promotion of youth service, provides technical assistance to existing and emerging youth service programs, promotes quality youth service, and provides an informational and policy guidance network for the various youth service streams. Sponsors National Youth Service Day, the Working Group on Youth Service Policy, the Youth Volunteer Corps of America Replication Project, the New Generation Training Program, the Youth Action Council, Superconference, and many other national initiatives. Offers the Professional Affiliate Program, a membership program for organizations interested in the field. Publishes *Streams*, a newsletter reporting on national news, trends, and information across the youth service field. Call for information about any projects sponsored by YSA.

Youth Specialties, Inc. (1969)

1224 Greenfield Drive
El Cajon, CA 92021
619/440-2333 (General)
800/776-8008 (To order books, products)
800/769-7624 (Periodicals)
FAX: 619/440-4939

A nondenominational organization that supplies quality resource materials to youth workers in some 75,000 churches in the U.S. and abroad. Sponsors annual National Youth Workers Convention (fall) and National Resource Seminars for Youth Workers (February through May). Publishes *Youthworker Journal* (quarterly); *Youthworker Update* (monthly newsletter); *Idea Library*; books; and tapes of convention sessions. Catalog available.

READINGS

The books, articles, and pamphlets listed below all relate to positive youth development or some aspect of the history, philosophy, or activities of formally organized programs for children and youth. Addresses for several of the publishers may be found in the Resources for Administrators and Leaders section (see pages 140–163). Books, journals, and government publications should be available through regular commercial outlets or libraries.

This list merely scratches the surface of what is available for leaders and members of youth groups to use. The selection is eclectic, and reflects personal choices made by the author.

Growing Up American

While it remains true that a majority of American children are doing well and are having their physical, social, emotional, spiritual, and educational needs met, it is also true that growing numbers are not. Many of these young people are "falling through the cracks." These publications offer statistics and descriptions of the nation's children and youth, pointing up the continuing need for programs that stress positive youth development.

Children's Defense Fund

A. Sherman, *Falling by the Wayside: Children in Rural America* (Washington, DC: CDF, 1992). Provides a portrait of the nation's rural children and families; covers the economic landscape, child poverty and assistance programs, housing, health, education, and child care and early childhood education needs.

The State of America's Children 1993 (Washington, DC: CDF, published annually). Annual analysis of the status of the nation's children; includes fact sheets for each state and the District of Columbia; includes information about systems and programs designed to serve children and families, federal and state-level developments and trends, funding streams, model programs, and more.

Children's Express

S. Goodwillie, (Ed.), *Voices from the Future: Our Children Tell Us About Violence in America* (New York: Crown Publishers, Inc., 1993). A no-nonsense examination of the lives of troubled American children and adolescents—based on interviews by young reporters with young people who have experienced violence first-hand.

KIDS COUNT

KIDS COUNT Data Book, 1994 (Baltimore, MD: Annie E. Casey Foundation, 1994).

Updated annually. National statistics and state-by-state profiles using a common set of indicators of child well-being; contains information about state KIDS COUNT projects. By the end of 1994, nearly every state will have produced a similar data book containing the same indicators for each of its counties. In 1994, Children's Express will publish a report based on interviews with young people from around the nation; this work will add faces and voices to the statistical report.

National Commission on Children

Beyond Rhetoric: A New American Agenda for Children and Families. Final Report of the National Commission on Children. (Washington, D.C.: U.S. Government Printing Office, 1991.) The findings of a two-year study by the bipartisan National Commission on Children created by Congress and the President to "serve as a forum on behalf of the children of the Nation." The report shows that although most American children are doing well, a distressing number of our youngest citizens are not. The Commission drew up principles for action and an agenda for the 1990s that, if adopted, could lead to a coherent national policy for children and families.

Speaking of Kids: A National Survey of Children and Parents. Report of the National Opinion Research Project (Washington, DC: National Commission on Children, 1991.) Presents the findings of two surveys of American children, parents, and adults not currently raising children that were undertaken by the Commission to help members better understand public attitudes and percep-

tions about children and contemporary family life.

National Council of La Raza

S. M. Perez and D. Martinez, *State of Hispanic America 1993: Toward a Latino Anti-Poverty Agenda* (Washington, DC: NCLR, 1993). Examines poverty among four groups within the Hispanic community: the working poor, female-headed households, Puerto Ricans, and children. Examines potential of public policy strategies to measurably and significantly reduce the number of Hispanic poor.

National Urban League

The State of Black America. (New York: NUL, published annually.) Each volume contains articles by leading researchers and a detailed chronology of events that took place during the year.

Office of Educational Research and Improvement
U.S. Department of Education

Youth Indicators 1993. (Washington, D.C.: U.S. Government Printing Office, 1993.) Presents longitudinal statistical data (since the 1950s) from both government and private sources related to the welfare of youth between ages 14–24; also examines external factors that influence the lives of youth.

Search Institute

P. Benson, *The Troubled Journey: A Portrait of 6th–12th Grade Youth* (Minneapolis: Search Institute, 1993). Responses from the first 111 communities in 25 states that conducted needs-assessment surveys as part of the RespecTeen program. Examines the impact of personal and community "assets" and "deficits" on the behavior and well-being of young people.

U.S. Bureau of the Census

Hispanic Americans Today. Current Population Reports, P23-183 (Washington, DC: U.S. Government Printing Office, 1993). Presents information in graphic form about the U.S. Hispanic population: distribution and composition, family, education, language, immigration patterns, labor force participation, income, poverty, health, housing, business ownership, and more.

The William T. Grant Foundation Commission on Work, Family and Citizenship

The Forgotten Half: Pathways to Success for America's Youth and Young Families. (Washington, D.C.: 1988). Summary of the findings of a two-year study of youth ages 16–24; concludes that non-college-bound young Americans (the "forgotten half") are badly shortchanged in the resources and community supports available to them; makes recommendations for achieving greater equity. The report and a series of working papers related to the study are available from The William T. Grant Foundation Commission on Work, Family and Citizenship, 1001 Connecticut Avenue, N.W., Suite 301, Washington, DC 10036-5541.

Related Readings

D.A. Ahlburg and C.J. DeVita, "New Realities of the American Family," *Population*

Bulletin, Vol. 47, No. 2 (Washington, DC: Population Reference Bureau, Inc., August 1992). A concise summary of changes in American family structure, patterns of marriage, divorce, child-bearing, labor-force participation, and more; looks at the challenges these changes create for American institutions.

G.L. Berry, and J.K. Asamen (Eds.), *Children & Television: Images in a Changing Sociocultural World* (Newberry Park, CA: SAGE Publications, Inc., 1993). A multidisciplinary perspective on the social-cultural issues of television and the development of children; examines the communication of social messages via television as a function of the personal attributes that children bring to the medium as well as program content.

F.A.J. Ianni, *The Search for Structure: A Report on American Youth Today* (New York: The Free Press, 1989). Descriptions of teen life in ten American communities gathered over a period of more than a decade. Concludes that when communities provide their youth with a firm, but sensitive set of expectations that avoid both outraged moralizing and benign neglect, they are a powerful supportive influence on the transition to adulthood.

J.U. McNeal, *Kids as Customers: A Handbook of Marketing to Children* (New York: Lexington Books, 1992). Children ages 4–12 represent a huge market for consumer goods—$9 billion of their own money to spend and $130 billion of their parents' spending to influence. Designed as a text for companies attempting to reach this market, this book provides insights for parents and youthworkers seeking to help young people become responsible consumers.

H.G. Unger, *But What If I Don't Want to Go to College? A Guide to Successful Careers through Alternative Education* (New York: Facts on File, 1992). We continue to encourage young people to go to college, yet college isn't for everyone. Looks at alternative routes to success in a variety of careers in trades, arts and crafts, the performing arts, etc.

The Emerging Profession of Youth Work

Carnegie Council on Adolescent Development

Carnegie Council on Adolescent Development, Task Force on Youth Development and Community Programs, *A Matter of Time: Risk and Opportunity in the Nonschool Hours* (New York: Carnegie Corporation of New York, 1992). Report of the Task Force that brings together what is currently known about the out-of-school community-based programs for youth; examines the roles of large national programs and grass-roots efforts in local communities. Includes recommendations and a call to action.

Commissioned Papers and Special Reports include:

L.A. Camino, *Racial, Ethnic, and Cultural Differences in Youth Development Programs*, 1992.

K.C. Dean, *A Synthesis of the Research on, and a Descriptive Overview of, Protestant, Catholic, and Jewish Religious Youth Programs in the United States*, 1992.

Evaluation of Youth Development Programs. Summary report of the January 1992 consultation.

A.K. Fitzgerald and A.M. Collins, *Adult Service Clubs and Their Programs for Youth*, 1991.

M. Freedman, C.A. Harvey, and C. Ventura-Merkel, *The Quiet Revolution: Elder Service and Youth Development in an Aging Society*, 1992.

E. Medrich, *Young Adolescents and Discretionary Time Use: The Nature of Life Outside School*, 1991.

S.W. Morris & Company, *What Young Adolescents Want and Need From Out-of-School Programs: A Focus Group Report*.

H.J. Nicholson, *Gender Issues in Youth Development Programs*, 1992.

R. O'Brien, K. Pittman, and M. Cahill, *Building Supportive Communities for Youth: Local Approaches to Enhancing Youth Development*, 1992.

K. Pittman and M. Wright, *A Rationale for Enhancing the Role of the Non-School Voluntary Sector in Youth Development*, 1991.

Professional Development of Youthworkers. Summary report of the May 1991 consultation.

V. Seefeldt, M. Ewing, and S. Walk, *An Overview of Youth Sports Programs in the United States*, 1992.

M. Sherraden, *Community-Based Youth Services in International Perspective* (Washington, DC: Carnegie Council on Adolescent Development and William T. Grant Foundation Commission on Work, Family and Citizenship, 1992).

C. Smith, *Overview of Youth Recreation Programs in the United States*, 1991.

L.W. Stern, *Funding Patterns of Nonprofit Organizations that Provide Youth Development Services: An Exploratory Study*, 1992.

N. Weber, *Independent Youth Development Organizations: An Exploratory Study*, 1992.

Center for Youth Development and Policy Research

K.J. Pittman, *A New Vision: Promoting Youth Development*. Testimony before The House Select Committee on Children, Youth and Families, September 30 1991 (Washington, DC: CYDPR, 1991). Examines the shortcomings of current policies and practices that aim to "fix" youth problems rather than promote the highest possible level of youth development; advocates developing national policy on "a clear vision of positive youth development and devoting adequate resources and energy to achieving it."

S. Zeldin and S. Tarlov, *Enhancing the Professional Development of Youth Workers: Recommendations from the Field* (Washington, DC: CYDPR, 1993). A report from the Stronger Staff—Stronger Youth project. Outlines issues related to legitimizing youth work as a distinct professional field and summarizes staff-development needs identified by youth workers and youth development organizations.

The Chapin Hall Center for Children

R. Halpern, *The Role of After-School Programs in the Lives of Inner-City Children: A Study of the Urban Youth Network After-School Programs* (Chicago: CHCC, 1991). Drawing on his study of nine Chicago after-school programs, the author examines the issues of appropriate and viable roles for such programs, staffing issues, and coping with various pressures from disintegrating communities.

J. Littell and J. Wynn, *The Availability and Use of Community Resources for Young Adolescents in an Inner-City and a Suburban Community* (Chicago: CHCC, 1989). Study examined the differences in access to organized program resources available to children in grades 6–8 in two very different communities in the Chicago area—a low-income, primarily African-American community on the city's west side and an affluent, primarily white suburb.

Girl Scouts of the U.S.A.

Girl Scouts: Who We Are, What We Think (New York: GSUSA, 1990). Results of a study of a representative sample of Junior, Cadette, and Senior Girl Scouts; examines their attitudes on issues related to personal values, their daily activities, and the role that Girl Scouting plays in their lives.

National Collaboration for Youth

Criminal History Record Checks: A Report for Nonprofits. Final Report to The National Assembly's National Collaboration for Youth by the ABA Center on Children and the Law (Washington, DC: The National Assembly, 1991). An examination of existing state policies, federal and state law, and possible models for state and national programs; offers guidance to nonprofit organizations considering the implementation of selection procedures aimed at protecting children and youth.

Search Institute

Working Together for Youth: A Practical Guide for Individuals and Groups (Minneapolis: Lutheran Brotherhood, 1993). A guidebook that helps translate individual and group concerns about youth into concrete, constructive action in the community.

Youth Specialties

L. Christie, *How to Recruit and Train Volunteer Youth Workers: Reaching More Kids With Less Stress* (Grand Rapids, MI: Zondervan Publishing House, 1992).

Related Readings

American Directory of Youth Work Educators & Trainers. Prepared by Institute for Youth Leaders at the University of Northern Iowa, The Academy for Educational Development, and the American Youth Work Center, 1993. A state-by-state listing of universities and organizations that provide pre-service and in-service training in the youth development field. Directory represents a first attempt to assemble such information and authors request information about additional programs for an expanded future addition.

P.B. Edelman and B.A. Radin, *Serving Children and Families Effectively: How the Past Can Help Chart the Future* (Washington, DC: Education and Human Services Consortium, 1991). Examines what experience since the 1960s has taught us about how to structure and improve human services, and what we should do differently in the 1990s.

J. Keith, *Building and Maintaining Community Coalitions on Behalf of Children, Youth and Families*. Research Report 529. (East Lansing, MI: Community Coalitions in Action, Institute for Children, Youth, and Families, Michigan State University, 1993). Although oriented to Michigan's needs and experiences, report contains information relevant to the formation of collaborative efforts anywhere. Reviews 13 collaborations; identifies common elements, challenges, and the unique features of coalitions formed on behalf of children, youth, and families.

R.F. Long and C.L. Martinez (Eds.), *Youth Leadership Professionals: Building Practice on Knowledge*, Monograph No. 3 (Cedar Falls, IA: Institute for Youth Leaders, University of Northern Iowa, 1992). Contains papers presented at the 1992 National Youth Leadership Symposium at the University of Northern Iowa. These annual meetings seek to foster formal connections between the developing base of youth development theory and professional practice.

P.W. Mattessich and B.R. Monsey, *Collaboration: What Makes It Work; A Review of Research Literature on Factors Influencing Successful Collaboration* (St. Paul, MN: Amherst H. Wilder Foundation, 1992). From an examination of existing literature, identifies 19 factors related to organization environment, membership, process/structure, communication, purpose, and resources that influence the success of collaborative effort; written for practitioners.

M. Smith, *Developing Youth Work: Informal Education, Mutual Aid and Popular Practice* (Philadelphia: Open University Press, 1988). Examines youth work in Great Britain as it emerged in the 19th century and as it is developing today.

Advocating for Youth

Children's Defense Fund

Advocate's Guides series:

An Advocate's Guide to the Media (1990).

An Advocate's Guide to Fund Raising (1990).

An Advocate's Guide to Using Data (1990).

An Advocate's Guide to Lobbying and Political Activity for Nonprofit Employees (1991).

L.S. Hoots (Ed.), *Prophetic Voices: Black Preachers Speak on Behalf of Children* (Washington, DC: CDF and The Black Community Crusade for Children, 1993). A collection of sermons by leading Black religious voices that "call on the Black church—and all Black adults—to act personally, socially, politically, and morally for our children."

Progress and Peril: Black Children in America, A Fact Book and Action Primer (Washington, DC: CDF and The Black Community Crusade for Children, 1993). This book provides an overview of the circumstances of African-American children in America and outlines a series of concrete action steps that individuals, businesses, schools, human service agencies, and communities can take to help.

Welcome the Child: A Child Advocacy Guide for Churches (Washington, DC: CDF, 1992). A revised edition of this useful guide describing how to involve congregations in child advocacy, include children and their concerns in the congregation's worship and programs, and more.

Related Readings

B. Armstrong, *Making Government Work For Your City's Kids; Getting Through the Intergovernmental Maze of Programs for Children and Families* (Washington, DC: National League of Cities, 1992). Written as a guide to help municipal officials understand and affect governmental processes that affect children and families to create "family-friendly" communities.

Children Now, *The Report Card Guide* (Sacramento, CA: Children Now, 1992). A practical, step-by-step guide designed to help organizations produce a Report Card to raise the level of awareness of child well-being in their own areas.

J.C. Westman (Ed.), *Who Speaks for the Children? The Handbook of Individual and Class Child Advocacy* (Sarasota, FL: Professional Resource Exchange, Inc., 1991). A series of chapters examine children's issues related to family, legal, educational, social service, and political systems. Concludes with a discussion of public policies for disadvantaged children and their families.

Youth Participation, Youth Service, and Civic Education

New publications related to citizenship education, service-learning, and youth service programs are appearing regularly; check with youth service networks and clearing-house organizations listed in the Resources for Administrators and Leaders section (pages 140–163) for the most current materials.

Commission on National and Community Service

What You Can Do For Your Country (Washington, DC: Commission on National and Community Service, 1993). Outlines what the bipartisan Commission, authorized by the National and Community Service Act of 1990, learned in its first year about the current state of community service in the U.S.; outlines what a well-developed network of community service opportunities might look like and how the nation might develop one.

Humphrey Institute

H.C. Boyte and K.S. Hogg, *Doing Politics: An Owner's Manual for Public Life* (Minneapolis: Humphrey Institute, 1991.)

P. Michels, S. Paul, and H.C. Boyte, *Making the Rules: A Guidebook for Young People Who Intend to Make a Difference* (Minneapolis, Humphrey Institute, 1991.)

INDEPENDENT SECTOR

D. Conrad and D. Hedin, *Youth Service: A Guidebook for Developing and Operating Effective Programs* (Washington, D.C.: IS, 1987.) A manual of practical information for school systems and organizations to help them increase the involvement of young people and foster long-term goals of active citizenship and personal community service.

National Center for Service Learning in Early Adolescence

Child Care Helper Program: A Guide for Program Leaders (New York: NCSLEA, 1991). A guide to developing a Helper Program that will make the service provided by young adolescents in after-school child care programs both meaningful and enjoyable.

The Partners Program: A Guide for Community Agencies (New York: NCSLEA, 1991), and *The Partners Program: A Guide for Teachers and Program Leaders* (New York: NCSLEA, 1991). The Partners Program strives to break down mutual stereotyping and make young people and elders equal participants in a venture. These guides provide information on implementing intergenerational programming.

Reflection: The Key to Service Learning; A Guide for Program Leaders (New York: NCSLEA, 1991). Offers practical guidelines for teachers and youth workers to help young people reflect on their service-learning experiences; shows how reflection "transforms an interesting and engaging experience into one which critically affects students' learning and development."

National Crime Prevention Council

Changing Our Course: Youth As Resources Program Guide (Washington, DC: NCPC, 1992). Includes videotape: *Youth As Resources: The Power Within.* Describes how to develop a Youth as Resources program; YAR is a locally-based grant program to support youth-led service projects that engage young people in addressing community needs.

National Indian Youth Leadership Project

"Something Shining, Like Gold—But Better" The National Indiana Youth Leadership Model: A Manual for Program Leaders (Zuni, NM: NIYLP, 1991). Manual developed for the successful Indiana Youth Leadership Project; explores ways that traditional models of Native American leadership can be used today to create "the best of both worlds" for young people.

National Society for Experiential Education

D. Giles, E.P. Honnet, and S. Migliors (Eds.) *Research Agenda for Combining Service and Learning in the 1990s* (Raleigh, NC: National Society for Internships and Experiential Education, 1991). Outlines questions, methodological issues, and strategies for encouraging and supporting research in the growing field of service-learning.

National Youth Leadership Council

R. Willits Cairn and S. Cairn (Eds.), *Collaborators: Schools and Communities Working Together for Youth Service* (Roseville, MN: NYLC, 1991). Offers help in building relationships between educators and community agencies; based on discussions with teachers and Minnesota agencies.

R. Willits Cairn and J. Kielsmeier, *Growing Hope: Sourcebook on Integrating Youth Service into the School Curriculum* (Roseville, MN: NYLC, 1991). A sourcebook for educators beginning or expanding curriculum-based youth service programs; includes background information, offers help for implementation, and describes programs and materials.

Points of Light Foundation

Get Ready for Anything! (Washington, DC: PLF, 1992). Provides a set of action principles to help guide the development of community-based youth service coalitions; includes examples of how young people in seven local communities have teamed up to address important needs.

Schools and Communities: Creating Places of Learning (Washington, DC: PLF, 1993). Defines service-learning as a "method of teaching and learning that combines academic work with service and social action." Discusses roles for service-learning, service-learning in action, and recommendations for creating a service-learning environment. Written for national and state policymakers, state education agencies, school boards, administrators, and teachers, students, parents, businesses and community members.

Related Readings

B. Checkoway and J. Finn, *Young People as Community Builders* (Ann Arbor: Center for the Study of Youth Policy, School of Social Work, The University of Michigan, 1992). Report describing several exemplary community-based youth initiatives that promote the well-being of youth by involving them in the process of building their communities.

W.S. Lesko, *No Kidding Around! America's Young Activists Are Changing Our World And You Can Too.* Activism 2000 Project (Kensington, MD: Information U.S.A., Inc., 1992). Describes remedies and reforms being pursued by American young people as they forge ahead with their own agendas for the environment, combatting racism, promoting animal rights, and so forth. Contains a practical "how to" section for launching an effective campaign.

B.A. Lewis, *The Kid's Guide to Social Action: How to Solve the Social Problems You Choose and Turn Creative Thinking into Positive Action* (Minneapolis: Free Spirit Publishing Inc., 1991). The title says it all! Areas covered include developing power skills (telephoning, surveying, speaking, reaching the media, etc.), initiating or changing laws, networking, and more. Provides a list of government contacts, resource groups providing opportunities for civic action, and awards and recognitions for young people.

S. Sagawa and S. Halperin (Eds.), *Visions of Service: The Future of the National and Community Service Act* (Washington, DC: National Women's Law Center and American Youth Policy Forum, 1993). Summarizes the major points of the National and Community Service Act of 1990 and background events that led to its passing; contains a collection of critical essays on the current state of youth service and relationships to citizenship, education reform, and youth development

M. Salzman and T. Reisgies, *150 Ways Teens Can Make a Difference: A Handbook for Action* (Princeton, NJ: Peterson's Guides, 1991). Designed for teens as a source of ideas and a guide to "volunteer employment." Includes personal accounts of teen volunteers; suggestions for matching volunteer activities with personal interests and personalities; and how to go about getting started. Provides a state-by-state sampling of organizations that encourage volunteering.

Model Programs and Activity Resources

American Camping Association

M. Westerman, *Easy Green: A Handbook of Earth-smart Activities and Operating Procedures for Youth Programs.* (Martinsville, IN: ACA, 1993). A guide to planning strategies for hazardous materials, toxics reduction, energy and water conservation, supply reduction, recycling, and composting at camps and program sites; includes ways to increase environmental awareness among youth and involve them in ecology programs.

Associates for Youth Development

The Prevention Dimension™: A Game to Promote Proficiency in The Technology of Prevention (Tucson, AZ: AYD, 1991). Another tool in the organization's Technology of Prevention materials, this game promotes exploration and discussion of innovative ways to meet the needs of youth and their communities. A successful training tool.

Boy Scouts of America

Recursos Scout en Espanol [Scouting Resources in Spanish] (Irving, TX: BSA, 1993). An annotated list of manuals, other print materials, and videotapes for families and adult leaders available in bilingual or Spanish-only formats.

Girls Incorporated

Girls Incorporated, *Truth, Trust and Technology* (New York and Indianapolis: Girls Incorporated, 1991). A summary of findings from the Preventing Adolescent Pregnancy project; program components included Growing Together, Will Power/Won't Power, Taking Care of Business, and Health Bridge.

The "Choices and Challenges" materials, developed by the Girls Clubs (now Girls Incorporated) of Santa Barbara, California, have been widely used in other youth programs and by individual young men and women. The series includes:

Choices: A Teen Woman's Journal for Self-Awareness and Personal Planning by M. Bingham, J. Edmondson, and S. Stryker. (Santa Barbara, CA: Advocacy Press, 1988.)

Challenges: A Young Man's Journal for Self-Awareness and Personal Planning by M. Bingham, J. Edmondson, and S. Stryker. (Santa Barbara, CA: Advocacy Press, 1988.)

Other books in the series, from the same publishers, include:

Instructor's Guide for Choices and Challenges: A Course in Personal Planning and Self-Awareness for Teen-Aged Women and Men by J. Edmondson et al.

Women Helping Girls With Choices: A Handbook for Community Service Organizations by M. Bingham and S. Stryker.

Human Kinetics

R. Martens, et al. *Successful Coaching* (Champaign, IL: Human Kinetics Books, 1990). Remains a definitive work for helping coaches learn a philosophy of working with young athletes as well as teaching sport skills.

G.S.D. Morris and J. Stiehl, *Changing Kids' Games* (Champaign, IL: Human Kinetics Books, 1989). Ways to change games to fit your own purposes, values, teaching styles, resources, and players (of all ages).

L.R. Morris and L. Schulz, *Creative Play Activities for Children With Disabilities: A Resource Book for Teachers and Parents*, 2nd ed. (Champaign, IL: Human Kinetics Books, 1989). Features games and activities that can promote growth through play for disabled young people. Describes adaptations for specific disabilities, equipment needed, etc.

Project Adventure

K. Rohnke, *Silver Bullets: A Guide to Initiative Problems, Adventure Games, Stunts, and Trust Activities* (Dubuque, IA: Kendall/Hunt Publishing Company, 1984. A classic in the field of "new games," initiative tasks, adventure education; games have been well-tested in a variety of settings; participants learn to deal with the process of risk-taking as the games become metaphors for life-experiences.

Related Readings

J.M. and C. Bergstrom, *All the Best Contests for Kids* (Berkeley, CA: Ten Speed Press, 1993). Updated regularly. Describes many contests and writing opportunities for young people ages 6–12 that can have payoffs both in fun and learning. Provides tips for choosing contests, preparing entries, as well as running your own. Several of the contests can be entered by groups.

Hallmark Corporate Foundation, Sponsor. *Talking With TJ About Teamwork.* (Available after July 1994 from: Talking With TJ, 1002 N. 42nd Street, Omaha, NE 68131-9834.) A complete curriculum for children in grades 2–4 designed to teach teamwork and cooperation skills. Includes broadcast-quality video stories to stimulate discussion and model pro-social skills, complete curriculum for six-session program, posters, and comics. Currently in use by several major American youth organizations.

S.L. Riehm, *Teenage Entrepreneur's Guide: 50 Money-Making Business Ideas,* 2nd ed. (Chicago, IL: Surrey Books, 1990). A discussion of what it takes to start a successful small business; looks at 50 different types of ventures in terms of the personal traits and experience required, materials needed, marketing possibilities, and expected wages; many ideas could be used by youth groups seeking ways to fund their activities.

L. Schwartz, *What Would You Do? A Kid's Guide to Tricky and Sticky Situations* (Santa Barbara, CA: The Learning Works, Inc., 1990). Describes more than 70 situations—from a forgotten lunch to an injured animal to an earthquake—that young people might encounter; suggests ways of advanced planning that will make coping easier.

INDEX

A

AAA. *See* American Automobile Association

AAAS. *See* American Association for the Advancement of Science

AAU/USA Youth Sports Program, 28

ABA. *See* American Bass Association

ACA. *See* American Camping Association

Academy for Educational Development, 146

Academy of Model Aeronautics, 21

ACF. *See* American Checker Federation

Acteens, 76–77

Acting. *See* Theater

ADL. *See* Anti-Defamation League of B'nai B'rith

Administration, of youth organizations, 133, 140–163

Adolescent health. *See* American Medical Association, Department of Adolescent Health

Adventure Corps, 76

Advocating for youth, readings, 170

AEE. *See* Association for Experiential Education

Aeronautics, 21

AFL-CIO, 50

AFLC. *See* Association of Free Lutheran Congregations

AFS International Intercultural Programs, 55

AFSC. *See* American Friends Service Committee Youth Programs

After-school programs, readings, 168

Agriculture and livestock associations, 6, 117–119

Agudath Israel of America, 84–85

AHEPA, Junior Order, 113

AIDS/HIV infection, 100

Air Force (U.S.), 16

Al-Anon Family Group Headquarters, Inc., 99

Alateen, 99

Alcohol abuse. *See* Self-help organizations; Substance abuse prevention and temperance organizations

All American Amateur Baseball Association, 31

Alliance Youth Fellowship, 75

AMA. *See* American Medical Association

Amaranth order, 116

Amateur Athletic Union Men's Senior Boxing Committee. *See* USA Boxing

Amateur Athletic Union of the U.S., Inc., 28

Amateur Press Association, 14

Amateur Skating Union of the United States. *See* Amateur Speedskating Union of the United States

Amateur Softball Association, 31

Amateur Speedskating Union of the United States, 39, 120

American Academy of Achievement, 140

American Amateur Baseball Congress, Inc., 31

American Angus Association, 119

American Association for Leisure and Recreation, 141

American Association for the Advancement of Science, 22, 25

American Automobile Association, 98–99

American Bass Association, 30

American Bicycle Association, 34

American Cadet Alliance, Inc., 16

American Camping Association, 141, 173

American Canoe Association, 35

American Carpatho-Russian Youth, 106–107

American Cavy Breeders Association, 117

American Checker Federation, 11

American Coaching Effectiveness Program, 141–142

American culture, readings, 164–167

American Double Dutch League. *See* National Double Dutch League

American Friends Service Committee Youth Programs, 55

American Hearing Impaired Hockey Association, 38

American Horse Shows Association, 36

American Humane Education Society, 91

American Humanics, Inc., 133, 142

American Hungarian Catholic Society, 117

American Indian Science and Engineering Society, 25

American Industrial Arts Student Association. *See* Technology Student Association

American-International Junior Charolais Association, 117

American Junior Academy of Science, 21–22

American Junior Golf Association, 38

American Junior Hereford Association, 117

American Junior Paint Horse Association, 117

American Junior Quarterhorse Association, 118

American Junior Rodeo Association, 122

American Junior Shorthorn Association, 118

American Junior Simmental Association, 118

American Legion, 32, 52, 104

American Legion Auxiliary, 52–53, 104

American Legion Baseball, 32

American Medical Association, Department of Adolescent Health, 120, 142

American Milking Shorthorn Junior Society, 118

More Free Spirit Books

Books on the Move: A Read-About-It, Go-There Guide to America's Best Family Destinations

by Susan M. Knorr and Margaret Knorr

This one-of-a-kind travel guide describes hundreds of great destinations across the United States—and hundreds of related children's books to read before, during, and after. All ages.

368 pp; illus; s/c; 6"x9"; ISBN 0-915793-53-9; $13.95

Doing the Days: A Year's Worth of Creative Journaling, Drawing, Listening, Reading, Thinking, Arts & Crafts Activities for Children Ages 8–12

by Lorraine Dahlstrom

A total of 1,464 fun learning activities linked to the calendar year. Spans all areas of the curriculum and stresses whole language, cooperative learning, and critical thinking skills. Grades 3–6.

240 pp; illus; s/c; 8 1/2"x11"; ISBN 0-915793-62-8; $21.95

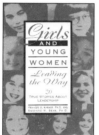

Girls and Young Women Leading the Way: 20 True Stories About Leadership

by Frances A. Karnes, Ph.D., and Suzanne M. Bean, Ph.D.

These inspiring stories from girls and young women ages 8 to 21 prove that leadership is for everyone, that leadership opportunities are everywhere, and that leadership has many faces and takes many forms. Ages 11 and up.

168 pp; B&W photos; s/c; 6"x9"; ISBN 0-915793-52-0; $11.95

The Kid's Guide to Social Action: How to Solve the Social Problems You Choose—and Turn Creative Thinking into Positive Action

by Barbara A. Lewis

A comprehensive guide to making a difference in the world. Teaches letter-writing, interviewing, speechmaking, fundraising, lobbying, getting media coverage and more. Ages 10 and up.

208 pp; illus; B&W photos; s/c; 8 1/2"x11"; ISBN: 0-915793-29-6; $14.95

School Power: Strategies for Succeeding in School

by Jeanne Shay Schumm, Ph.D.
and Marguerite Radencich, Ph.D.

Covers getting organized, taking notes, studying smarter, writing better, following directions, handling homework, managing long-term assignments, and more. Ages 11 and up.

132 pp; illus; B&W photos; s/c; 8 1/2"x11"; ISBN: 0-915793-42-3; $11.95

To place your order, or to receive a free copy of our catalog, write or call:

Free Spirit Publishing, 400 First Avenue North, Suite 616, Minneapolis, MN 55401-1730

TOLL-FREE: (800) 735-7323, LOCAL: (612) 338-2068